Lean Leadership for Healthcare

Approaches
to Lean
Transformation

Lean Leadership for Healthcare

Approaches to Lean Transformation

Ronald G. Bercaw

Foreword by
John P. Poole, SVP, ThedaCare Improvement System

CRC Press
Taylor & Francis Group
Boca Raton   London   New York

CRC Press is an imprint of the
Taylor & Francis Group, an **informa** business

A PRODUCTIVITY PRESS BOOK

CRC Press
Taylor & Francis Group
6000 Broken Sound Parkway NW, Suite 300
Boca Raton, FL 33487-2742

© 2013 by Taylor & Francis Group, LLC
CRC Press is an imprint of Taylor & Francis Group, an Informa business

No claim to original U.S. Government works

Printed on acid-free paper
Version Date: 20130321

International Standard Book Number-13: 978-1-4665-1554-3 (Paperback)

Visit the Taylor & Francis Web site at
http://www.taylorandfrancis.com

and the CRC Press Web site at
http://www.crcpress.com

Contents

Foreword

Leadership and management competencies are necessary to ensure organizational vitality. These two competencies should be specified for each assignment with responsibilities to serve the members who directly create value for the customer. The competencies must include the curriculum for *knowledge*, direct observation of *skill*, repetitive practice of *behavior*, and *judgment*. Specifically, these assignments must bring clarity to the development and improvement of both people and processes for the purpose of delivering products and services to the customer.

The organization's purpose (the products and services) must be clearly defined. The strategy of what will be the organization's point of differentiation from its competitors and strategy deployment and the creation of those new competencies to support strategy also must be clearly defined.

In a Lean organization, every member should have the competencies for their assignment specified. All assignments have clear processes from recruitment to succession. The supervisors must ensure that their reports on development match the requirements of the processes to which they are assigned.

A system of highly organized work, divided by value stream, process, and steps to deliver products and services to the customer, must be defined. Clear challenges are issued to promote improvement by the maintenance and innovation to this structure of highly organized work. Through this improvement work, the leaders and management develop their competencies and those they serve.

Leaders/managers must acquire the competencies necessary to focus the organization on the purpose, create and deploy strategy, and develop and improve people and processes. When done properly, an organization can deliver performance previously thought unattainable, and with far fewer resources.

Lean leadership is needed in healthcare to solve some of the chronic issues facing the industry today. Declining reimbursement rates, an aging population, a shortage of clinical resources, and less than acceptable clinical quality have taken our industry to a point where dramatic transformation is necessary. *Lean Leadership for Healthcare* is a book that can lead the way toward transforming healthcare as we know it. The challenge within the industry is in having the right vision on how to achieve this elusive transformation. A leadership vision needs to be created to set the right direction, in an appropriate timeline to create the sense of urgency required to overcome the resistance to change.

Fortunately, there are a handful of healthcare organizations and a host of industrial organizations that have successfully transformed using Lean thinking. Using the transformed organizations presented in this book as a model, we can now understand how these transformational efforts were led, and we can leverage their lessons learned to take our industry to a better place.

John Poole
Senior Vice President
ThedaCare Improvement System
Appleton, Wisconsin

Preface

In late March 2011, I completed the manuscript for my first book titled *Taking Improvement from the Assembly Line to Healthcare* (CRC Press). This book was my translation of the application of Lean within the healthcare industry. While not everyone was able to figure out what the assembly line had to do with improving healthcare, the book's title was an homage to the greatest management system in operation across the world today, the Toyota Production System.

Before the book was published, I had a chance to reflect on the message I intended to convey to the many dedicated healthcare professionals working hard to deliver worldclass care to the patients, families, and communities they serve. The book was a comprehensive approach to Lean improvement. Topics included understanding of the fundamentals of Lean improvement, understanding the tools and the applications of these tools to help us "see and eliminate" waste in the healthcare setting, and a review of several case studies that demonstrated the change that can occur in terms of both performance and culture when a focused team of individuals applies the Toyota Production System in the healthcare setting. I included the necessary steps an organization must take prior to applying the Lean model, and closed with a chapter on leadership behaviors essential for success.

Throughout the development of *Taking Improvement from the Assembly Line to Healthcare,* I simultaneously operated my consulting business. My company services a wide range of clients in creating a culture of improvement through the application of the Toyota Production System. The majority of this client base consists of healthcare organizations servicing patients and clients with the continuum of care. Although it was critical that our consulting practice dedicate a large amount of time to teaching organizations the tools and techniques of Lean improvement, I found that I was spending the majority of my time teaching organizations to lead change and my efforts were largely focused on leadership development. Perhaps the most important part of creating a culture of continuous improvement is "leading" the change. Despite this fact, there are few resources available that help to develop these skills at the various management levels. This book, which you are about to read, *Lean Leadership for Healthcare*, was created to provide healthcare leaders a resource on how to *lead* transformational improvement within the healthcare industry.

Why leadership? Why not management? I frequently hear in my work that "our organization needs to better the job of managing improvement." Rarely do I hear, "We need to do a better job leading improvement." Organizations certainly spend a lot of time on management development, and universities and colleges teach myriad management courses. Fewer university courses and public workshops are dedicated to leadership, and organizations spend significantly less time on leadership development. What's the difference?

Management is the set of work processes that keep a complex organization—one filled with departments, people, and technology—operating effectively and efficiently. There are many aspects of management, including planning, budgeting, staffing/scheduling, and controlling. Organizations spend a lot of time and resources optimizing these management systems. *Leadership* is the set of processes that creates organizations and then helps these organizations change to meet ever-evolving business conditions. The key aspects of leadership include creating a future vision (the direction of the organization), aligning the resources, and then inspiring people to realize this new future.

In creating a culture of improvement, are we trying to create a management system to plan, budget, organize, control, and staff our way to improvement? Or, are we trying to create a new direction for the organization, aligning the resources and then inspiring our people to realize this vision in spite of the obstacles we are sure to encounter along the way?

In reality, we do need some management systems to be successful. I will discuss several of the management systems, tools, ideas, and behaviors necessary to foster a culture of continuous improvement. However, we also need plenty of leadership. This book will provide you with many Lean leadership approaches, thoughts, visual tools, and applications to put your healthcare organization on its way toward world-class performance and culture.

This is a place your organization has likely never been, and any transformation process will require great leadership. Done well, you can create an environment where worldclass healthcare quality, patient safety, and customer service are the norm. The workplace can be transformed to one where medical staff are engaged in their work and inspired to do better and be better every day. You can help shape a healthcare system that delivers more "value." Value from a healthcare system perspective is broadly defined as outcomes divided by cost. My goal is to help you create a healthcare system that, through your people, continually improves outcomes at lower and lower costs.

There will be plenty of skeptics along the way, and perhaps some of you who are reading this book are already skeptical. "Lean" is not common sense; rather, it is counterintuitive. It takes a long time to learn and a lifetime to master. But, those organizations that have applied Lean thinking to their processes, with the diligence of effective management and strong leadership support, are already realizing the benefits of their efforts. And, many of the benefits far exceed what was thought possible just a few years ago. If you speak with a "Lean" hospital, "Lean" clinic, or "Lean" healthcare service provider, they will tell you the reward far exceeds the efforts. To be successful, these organizations had to provide the leadership to create their future state. I hope to leverage many of their leadership stories, successes and failures, plus a few of my own, to help you transform your organization using Lean leadership.

Acknowledgments

The final product you will be reading has been enhanced by review and contains valuable Lean input from Scott Brubaker. He spent many hours critiquing and editing the manuscript, and he has my gratitude. Heather Wood policed my grammar and made my attempt at writing "readable" by the rest of the world. The writing of the manuscript took about ten months and went back and forth between Heather and me several times. Thanks, Heather, for all your help.

Taylor & Francis Group senior editor, Kristine Mednansky, and project coordinator, Kathryn Everett, made my job much easier than it could have been and provided countless valuable insights on the process of writing and publishing. I am thankful to have them and their valuable guidance.

I am grateful to Rouge Valley Health System in Toronto, Ontario; Mackenzie Health in Richmond Hill, Ontario; and Spectrum Health in Grand Rapids, Michigan, for providing photographic and illustration copy for the book. These three organizations are doing some fantastic Lean work and their patients, medical staff, and management are all better off because of these efforts.

For the many organizations that are using Lean management systems, you have my respect. Lean enterprise transformation is very difficult. I know, having gone through three different transformations as a leader, and having helped dozens of organizations over the past twelve years. I can promise you that if you stay true to the Lean principles and avoid taking any shortcuts, your organization, your patients, and your staff will be rewarded for your efforts. I know it doesn't always feel that way throughout the process, but doing things the right way and for the right reasons will always be rewarded.

To John Poole and Kurt Knoth, two friends and great Lean leaders, thank you for your words of wisdom about the book.

Finally, to my wife, Tami, and family (Heather, Ashley, Michael, and Ryan), thank you for allowing me to sequester myself in my office for days on end and letting me write this work. I love you all.

About the Author

Ronald Bercaw is the president of Breakthrough Horizons, LTD, a management consulting company specializing in worldclass improvement through the application of the Toyota Production System, more commonly known as "Lean." With over twenty years of experience in operations, his Lean management experience was gained through multiple enterprise transformations in different industries including custom packaging, power reliability electronic assembly, and test and measurement products.

Educated at Purdue University, Bercaw learned the details and disciplined applications of Lean principles, habits, and tools from both the Shingijutsu Sensei and their first generation disciples. Working in both shop floor and above-the-shop-floor areas, he has vigorously strived to remove waste from businesses through the involvement and ideas of the people doing the work.

Bercaw has consulting experience in the healthcare sector (U.S. and Canadian health systems including primary care, acute care, and community applications of both clinical and back shop improvement), the commercial sector (administrations, manufacturing, distribution, supply chain, and engineering), and the public sector (U.S. Army, U.S. Navy, U.S. Air Force including maintenance, repair, and overhaul (MRO) assignments, Pentagon, and Surgeon General assignments). He is also the author of *Taking Improvement from the Assembly Line to Healthcare: The Application of Lean within the Healthcare Industry*, published by CRC Press (2012), which is the recipient of the Shingo Research & Professional Publication Award and has been recognized for advancing improvement knowledge.

Chapter 1

Lean at a Glance

Leadership and learning are indispensible to each other.

John F. Kennedy

What Is Lean Healthcare?

Lean is a management system, predicated on the Toyota Production System, which is used to deliver world-class quality and customer service to patients, care-givers, and their surrounding communities. The Toyota Production System (yes, the same Toyota that makes personal transportation in the form of cars, trucks, and sport utility vehicles) is the comprehensive business approach and correspond-ing culture Toyota embraces toward continuous process improvement to deliver compelling value to their customers. The words *Lean* and the *Toyota Production System (TPS)* are used synonymously. Technically, these two terms are not identi-cal, but both words are recognized as being one in the same, so I will use the term Lean going forward. Before I describe what is meant by continuous improvement, it will be helpful to better understand a few essential Lean terms. After we under-stand these Lean concepts, we can more easily define Lean healthcare.

Value-Added

Lean improvement is based on two themes; Continuous Improvement (a differ-ent way to state elimination of waste), and Respect for All People (Figure 1.1).

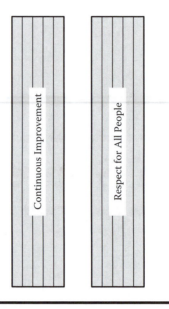

Figure 1.1 Themes of Lean improvement.

To understand the first theme, continuous improvement, it is necessary to understand the value-added/nonvalue-added principle. Every activity that occurs in any organization falls into one of two categories; value-added or nonvalue-added. A value-added activity when producing a physical product is easy to grasp. Activities that change the form, fit, or function of the product would be considered value-added. Another definition of value-added activity is any action (either product or service related) for which a customer is willing to pay. An industrial example of value-added activity might include drilling, painting, heat treating, or assembly of a product. For a service, a value-added activity might include help desk services offered on the telephone. Within healthcare, a value-added activity is any activity that directly meets the needs of a customer. An example of healthcare value-add would be the action of a surgeon completing a surgery. The need to have a problem resolved through surgery is directly meet.

Nonvalue-Added

Nonvalue-added is by default, the opposite of value-added, or any activity that takes time, space, or resources, but does not change the form, fit, or function of the product. Another definition would be any activity taking time, space, or resources for which the customer is not willing to pay. Examples of nonvalue-added activity would include conveying a part from one machine to the next or counting inventory items to ensure accuracy of on-hand quantities. Within healthcare, an excellent example of nonvalue-added activity would be filling out insurance forms. No patient would "pay" to complete this activity. Filling out insurance paperwork doesn't directly meet a patient's need to receive assessment, diagnosis, and treatment for a medical condition.

A third category of activities that organizations perform are activities required by law or by business obligations (accreditation or third-party certification). These might include following Occupational Safety and Health Act standards (OSHA), or ISO standards, or Generally Accepted Accounting Principles (GAAP). While it can be tempting to classify these differently, at the end of the day, many of these activities are usually nonvalue-added to the end customer. Changing the classification of the activity doesn't change the value-adding/nonvalue-adding principle.

In healthcare, the definition of value is slightly different. A value-added activity is any activity that *directly* meets the needs of the customer. In order to determine if a step is value-added, you need to be clear on two things: (1) who is the customer and (2) what are their needs? Many times, in healthcare the dialog jumps from the customer being the patient and/or the caregiver to the customer being the provider or the administration, etc. It is helpful to remember value is always specified by the *customer*. And, there can be only one.

One must determine who is creating the *pull* for the services needed in order to understand who the true, single customer is. So, if we are trying to figure who the customer is in a surgical procedure, we try to understand where the pull (need) for the service comes from. Because we would not need a surgical center, sterile processing, materials and supplies, equipment, surgical staff, a surgeon, a billing department, etc., without a patient needing surgery, the patient is the customer. In this surgical procedure, value will be specified by the patient, so value-added and nonvalue-added activity is from the eyes of the patient.

The second decision we need to make is to define what the customer *needs*. Healthcare professionals often have expertise and knowledge that can be very helpful in determining customer needs. However, it is not exclusively the role of the staff and provider to specify the customer's needs; nor is it the insurance company's role. With information available at a click of a mouse, many customers (patients) are quite capable of specifying their needs. As I tell healthcare professionals, when I work with highly skilled engineers designing new products, they are quick to articulate that the consumers do not know what they want/need. The engineers have to make those decisions for the consumers because they have the technical expertise. I think every consumer can determine the features and benefits he/she is looking for in a new product or service. It would be quite expensive, and impractical to drag an engineer around with us every time we shop for a product. As a consumer, we have no problem specifying value-added and nonvalue-added activity within our purchases. This same theory holds true with patients when they seek medical services. Even though you may be the healthcare "engineer," the patient is generally quite capable of determining his/her needs. Your job as the service provider is to identify the activities that directly meet those needs, as those are the value-added activities. To further illustrate the differences between value-added and nonvalue-added activities, let's discuss a clinic visit to see your doctor. Being an outdoor enthusiast, you fell while skiing a black diamond trail during a recent snow skiing trip, and your knee is hurting. The physician provides an examination and gives a diagnosis of an ACL (anterior cruciate ligament) injury. To further refine this diagnosis, he or she orders you to get a CT (computed tomography) scan. When one gets a CT scan, one will likely need to schedule the exam date and time, register with someone when on arrival, and complete some paperwork. While all of these activities are common during a typical CT exam experience, none of them will directly meet your needs. So, the collection of all of the activities, as described, would be considered nonvalue-added activity.

To summarize, in order to determine the value-added activity, we need to identify the customer, specify his/her needs, and determine which activities directly meet those needs. The customer in this process is you, the patient needing the exam. Your "needs" include the examination and the corresponding results. The value-added activities would be the actual exam (which takes minutes) and the actual reading of the exam (which also takes minutes). But, what about the cleaning of the table, the preparing for the exam, the transcribing of the results, the charting of the activities, the sending of an invoice, etc. These are all classified as nonvalue-added activities. The understanding of value-added (VA) and nonvalue-added activity (NVA) is the first lesson that must be learned in improvement, and it is not always an easy lesson to understand. When we can understand both VA and NVA activity, we can start to look at the ratio between the two activities. A typical process is 95% NVA to 5% VA. World-class organizations understand this and take advantage of the insight this ratio provides (Figure 1.2).

Improvement using Lean fundamentals involves the identification and elimination of nonvalue-added activity. Another term for nonvalue-added activity is *Waste*. When 95% of the activity is nonvalue-added that leaves a *lot* of room for improvement. Focusing on nonvalue-added activity provides two benefits. First, the improvement potential is much larger. Would you rather pay attention to the 95% opportunity or the 5% opportunity? This is why Lean organizations can and do routinely show 25 to 50+% improvements. They understand the value-added/nonvalued-added principle and they choose to play in the 95% space. Secondly, the cost of the improvement is significantly less. When we focus on eliminating nonvalue-added activity, we are in essence "stopping" some

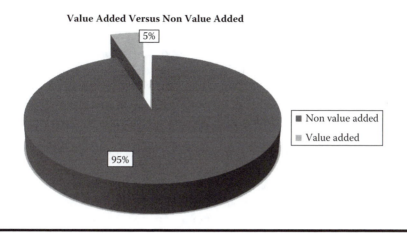

Figure 1.2 Value-added/nonvalue-added principle.

kind of work. How much does it cost to stop doing something? The definition of nonvalue-added activity is an activity taking time, space, and resources, but not directly meeting a patient's needs. So, if we eliminate nonvalue-added activity, then we free up time, space, and resources. These newfound resources can be used to add even more value to our customers.

First Theme of Lean Improvement: Continuous Improvement

Earlier I discussed that Lean improvement is based on two themes, continuous improvement (the elimination of nonvalue-added activity) and respect for all people. We just spent a fair amount of time discussing value-added and nonvalue-added activity. Understanding this concept is the foundation of continuous improvement. In the simplest terms, improvement consists of seeing nonvalue-added activity and eliminating it. Lean organizations frequently shorten this phrase to "seeing and eliminating waste."

The theme of continuous improvement, however, has two other tenets. Culturally, we want to create a work environment where we strive to meet targets using *courage* and *creativity*. Courage implies making individual and team decisions in the best interest of serving the customer. For example, clinic hours of operation may best serve their customers from 1 to 9 p.m. However, many clinics have been comfortable working from 8 a.m. to 4 p.m. A courageous decision would include altering work hours in the best interest of the customer. How many times have you given up your lunch break to get something accomplished, only to find out the organization is closed during traditional lunch hours?

Creativity entails using new approaches and techniques in lieu of adding resources and capital cost. A phrase used by Lean practitioners is use "creativity before capitol." This implies generating solutions that take minimal resources to implement before making a significant capital investment in equipment, IT (information technology), space, and facilities or hiring additional staff. Remember, if the solutions implemented involve eliminating nonvalue-added activity, then by design, additional time, space, and resources have been freed up. Even after becoming a giant amongst electronic companies, Hewlett-Packard used a phrase "let's go back to the garage," which elicited the process that the company started with: no money, few materials, just a garage to work in. This phrase was a battle cry to take another look at the problem without immediately going to the "just add more resources" to the inefficient process or identified need. This is the essence of the concept of "creativity before capital."

Another tenet of continuous improvement is the concept of *genchi genbutsu*, loosely translated from Japanese as "go to the source to find facts." When problems arise in the workplace, how would a manager traditionally respond? Many organizations would schedule a meeting, get a small group of knowledgeable experts together, and try and solve these problems. To illustrate my point, if you are a manager/leader in healthcare, I would be willing to bet the majority of time you spend each day is either attending a meeting or travelling from one meeting to the next. A Lean company views problems as treasures of information, telling a story of where the current process is not adequate. A Lean manager will always go to the area where the problem occurred and observe the process to see if the source of the problem can be identified. This is tremendously different than the traditional approach. Not going to the area where the problem occurred is the equivalent of a police investigator not going to the scene of the crime to uncover forensic evidence. How effective would investigations be if the standard approach to crime solving involved scheduling a meeting at police headquarters and bringing in some experts to try and solve the crime? The healthcare example I like to use is that of assuming an instance where a dose of medicine was missed. This resulted in an adverse event, that while not catastrophic, warranted further investigation. The question I'd like you to ponder is how many missed doses occurred in the conference room? We need to go to the source to find the facts.

Second Theme of Lean Improvement: Respect for All People

From a global perspective, respect for all people means having a purpose for improvement. How can improvement in healthcare benefit patients, staff, physicians, community agencies, and service providers? How can we improve our local community, country, and the world as a whole? From an individual and organizational perspective, showing respect for people comes in the form of understanding each other. What work do I do and what work do you do? Together, how do we build a foundation of mutual trust? Respect also is demonstrated in taking individual and team responsibility. Are we doing the right thing—every time? Are we following the best known method? Are we putting forth our best effort? As an organization, we want to optimize both team and individual performance. Additionally, we must also ask ourselves if we are sharing opportunities for personal and team development.

A Lean organization is not excited by benchmark performance and peer comparisons, rather, a Lean organization gets excited about knowing it is making a difference in the world. Maybe it is not directly affecting the entire world, but most certainly its community and customers (patients). This organization's staff knows that they are continually providing better and safer care, reducing lead times for services, thus increasing access, and continuously lowering the cost of services, which increases the value of the healthcare that is delivered. This relentless pursuit of perfection is how respect for all people is realized.

Seven Wastes

As we discussed earlier, nonvalue-added activity and waste mean the same thing. The early founders of the Toyota Production System spent a lot of time observing waste. Because of the repetition of certain forms of waste, it proved helpful to put the wastes into several different categories. The major forms of wastes found in operations became known as the seven operational wastes. I will provide a brief discussion of each below (Figure 1.3).

Overproduction

Overproduction is producing too much stuff, or producing stuff too early. Let's say we were unable to use a premix IV (intravenous) and had to mix IV solution in the pharmacy. Subsequently, we delivered two days' worth of this mixture to the unit where the patient was being treated. At the end of the first day, following the delivery of this solution, the patient was discharged and sent home. The remaining solution would need to be returned to the pharmacy and likely disposed of properly. We overproduced. When overproduction occurs, we have expended labor to mix IV solutions that can never be recovered. Additionally, the corresponding solution now has to be disposed of—another unnecessary and unrecoverable expense.

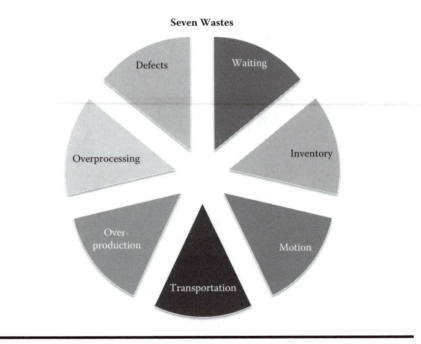

Figure 1.3   Seven wastes.

Waiting

Waiting causes a disruption of workflow. This disruption can result in idle resources, stopping and starting, and time delays to our customers (patients or staff). Within healthcare, we can experience waiting for service providers, diagnostics, information, equipment, and materials. I typically find waiting as the largest single waste within healthcare. For service providers that work in the emergency department or a clinic, I'm sure you can recall an occasion where a patient or family member verbally expressed disappointment with the time they were spending in the waiting room. Staff members do not always see waiting as a waste. If a therapist walks to a patient's room to provide some therapy and the patient is not present, then the therapist likely would not wait. The therapist would simply go to their next patient. So, since the therapist is not idle and is now adding-value (providing therapy) to a different patient, the waiting was not considered wasteful.

I would like to point out that this argument is flawed on two fronts. First, waste was created when the therapist walked to the patient's room only to find out the patient was not present. This walking to a missed appointment would be the waste of motion. However, more importantly, remember that waste is always viewed from the customer's perspective. For the therapist to not see the missed therapy session as wasteful is looking at the waste from the wrong pair of eyes. The patient is the customer and it is that customer that is *waiting* for his/her therapy. Even though 95% of the activities going on around us are nonvalue-added, it still takes time and practice to be able to see waste. Understanding the seven key wastes is a good start to being able to identify waste in your organization. I do find it humorous that oftentimes in healthcare, the waste of waiting is easy to spot. Do any of your organizations have a *waiting* room?

Overprocessing

Overprocessing is a waste generated by performing work in excess of value. While this may be hard to believe, it is possible to do *more* work than the customer values. For example, many of us use spreadsheet solutions on a daily basis. Software solutions are invaluable; they enable us to sort numerical data, determine averages, sum column totals, and quickly build charts ands graphs. Have any of you ever considered the work that went into the engineering process of these solutions? You have the ability to do conditional formatting, data validation, pivot tables, and logical formulas in a matter of moments. It is my belief that you could spend years trying to learn all the functionality of this type of software, but 99.9% of us will never use greater than 10% of this capability. For many customers, the product is overengineered; the use of this product can easily create overprocessing. It is important to note, however, that other people may find these many features beneficial. Thus, from their perspective, the product does not appear to be overprocessed.

As an example of overprocessing within healthcare, we might consider interprofessional assessment. A complex patient might get assessed by multiple nurses, multiple physicians, and several members of the allied health team. While each team member is looking for different pieces of information to provide the best possible care, a patient might be asked the same question by two or more people. Many of you, in the course of your work, have heard from patients, "I've been asked this five times already. Do you people not talk to one another?" Again, from the patient's perspective, as an organization, you have overprocessed. The redundancy in questioning creates work in excess of value.

Another example of the waste of overprocessing within healthcare: Are all tests ordered really necessary?

Inventory

When we think of inventory, we think of supplies. It is my belief that everyone, whether in a production environment or a service environment, can relate to the disruption in work when we run out of materials and supplies. The opposite is also true; when we have too many supplies. Excess supplies can lead to damaged product, obsolescence, and time wasted on inventory management. We all also have to ensure supplies and light them and heat/cool them in our facility. None of these activities meet the need of the customer.

In healthcare, however, there are other forms of inventory present. One inventory that we do not frequently think about is patients waiting for services. Patients could be waiting for an admission, waiting for an inpatient bed, waiting for test results, etc., but the collection of these patients is inventory as they are queuing up and occupying space. A simple definition of inventory is "things" (people, items, information) waiting to be worked on. Another form of inventory is things waiting in your inbox. Within administration, there are lots of places where work queues up. Bills waiting to be paid, charts waiting to be coded, invoices waiting to be processed and mailed, e-mails waiting to be answered, performance appraisals waiting to be completed, payroll waiting to be processed, supplies waiting to be ordered, financial reports waiting to be generated. The backlog of these items is inventory.

Motion

When we speak of the waste of motion, we are talking about movement in excess of that required to create value; this movement is from the staff and providers. One form of motion is present when we walk from one area to the next looking for supplies and equipment. A simple example of wasted motion occurs when we have to walk an extra ten steps to get to the sanitizer because the dispenser is not located at the point of use. I often hear the argument that it is "healthy" for the staff to be active. I agree that it is healthy to have an active lifestyle, but unnecessary movement in the workplace is wasteful. The following example demonstrates how easily wasted motion accumulates in the workplace.

One organization (I'll call it St. Gerard) did an extensive study of the waste of motion for their inpatient nursing staff. They used a stopwatch to record the percentage of time that nurses spent walking during their 12-hour shift. The results of the study revealed that 53% of the time a nurse was simply walking from one place to the next. More than half of their time working was spent walking. This organization had over 800 full-time nurses on their staff across the hospital. After some simple mathematical calculations, it was deduced that over 400 nurses were being paid throughout the week to walk from one point to the next. If this organization could reduce the nurse walking time across the organization by 25%, that would be the equivalent of getting an additional 100 nurses (25% of 400 nurses = 100 nurses). Could any of your organizations use 100 nurses? For free?

Defects

Defects create waste because they result in work needing to be completely redone or corrected. Before we get too far into the waste of defects, we need to differentiate between a defect and an error. Work that is completed by humans is subject to errors; an error is a mistake in the execution of a task. An example of an error is a physician order for a medication that was inadvertently not signed. Regardless of how well trained people are, how often they complete a given task, or how diligent/conscientious they are, errors will be made. However, an error need not turn into a defect. A defect is an error that makes its way to the customer and results in work needing to be redone, corrected, or clarified. In healthcare, defects frequently appear in the form of missing information, incorrect information, or information received in the wrong format. However, defects also can be clinical in nature and appear in the following ways:

■ The wrong test could be ordered
■ The wrong diagnosis could be made
■ Patients can be harmed through infections acquired at the hospital
■ Recovery can be lengthened by not following evidence-based best practices.

Regardless of whether the defect is related to the outcome of the service, the quality of the service provided, or the back office work required to run the business, a defect is wasteful because it leads to activities of rework, checking, and clarification. None of these activities support directly meeting a customer's need.

Transportation

Transportation is the conveyance of materials, equipment, information, and patients through an organization. From the patient's perspective, the movement of items or information doesn't create value, thus transportation is considered a waste. Transportation consumes staff resources and also takes time, while failing to directly meeting the needs of the customer. Motion is different from transportation in that motion involves the movement of staff, while transportation is the movement of items. Consider a patient that shows up for a surgical preadmission visit. This patient must first be registered. Next, the patient has to go to the lab for a blood test, followed by walking to diagnostic imaging for a chest x-ray. Finally, the patient returns to the clinic for a nursing screen and pre- and post-surgical education, followed by a trip to a different office for a meeting with the anesthesiologist. While we have optimized the utilization of the staff and leveraged the footprint of the facility, we have created a lot of transportation for the patient. Consequently, the customer perceives the visit as a nuisance rather than as an efficient process engineered to benefit the customer.

Type of Waste	Inventory	Motion	Transportation	Over-production	Over-processing	Defects	Waiting
Instance 1							
Instance 2							
Instance 3							
Instance 4							
Instance 5							
Instance 6							
Instance 7							

Figure 1.4   Seven by seven waste chart.

While this transportation example focuses on the movement of a patient, wasted movement also applies to conveying cotton swabs, Band-Aids®, and tensors as well. Conveyance of an item does not deliver value to a customer.

In summary, great organizations work relentlessly to identify and eliminate waste. Operational waste presents itself in seven common forms. The seven common wastes include overproduction, waiting, overprocessing, inventory, motion, defects, and transportation. As a practical exercise, pick any area in your organization. Find thirty minutes in your work day and walk to a place where work is being done. Stand in a single spot and observe. Look for waste. In this time period, you should be able to complete a large portion of the waste chart shown in Figure 1.4.

You should be able to identify seven different instances of the seven common types of waste. If you can find forty-nine forms of waste in thirty minutes, how many forms of waste do you think the people that actually do that work can identify?

Two Additional Wastes

There are two other types of waste that show up within organizations that are not operational in nature: the waste of unused human capital (creativity) and the waste of organizational design. From an improvement perspective, the focus is generally on process and the seven wastes will show up when we study the process in detail through either direct observation or time observation. The waste of unused human capital and the waste of organizational design do not generally present themselves when studying a process, but they can be present and do generate some of the seven common wastes we just discussed.

Unused Human Capital

This waste presents itself when we fail to take into consideration and utilize all the talents that people have. I believe that every staff person, administrator, and physician want to do great work; the challenge is in creating the structure to enable this great work to happen. Many organizations are top-down in their approach with a command and control management structure. With heavy amounts of firefighting that occur each day, it is difficult to even find the time to empower and engage support staff and medical staff. Without daily formal and informal mechanisms to engage and empower, opportunities for process improvement and personal growth are missed. These missed opportunities are the unused human capital. Sometimes in healthcare we believe that when we underutilize a clinician's scope, we are wasting human capital. An example of this would be paying a nurse to perform stocking or housekeeping tasks. While this might be frustrating to the clinician, this is *not* an example of unused human talent. Without getting too technical, sometimes given the frequency of the task and the cycle time to complete the task, this clinician is the appropriate resource to complete the activity. For those of you who are Lean technicians, there are instances where in order to balance the work to the takt time, nonclinical tasks need to be loaded on the clinician. The loading diagram or cycle time/takt time bar chart would be the tool you would choose to help make this decision (Figure 1.5).

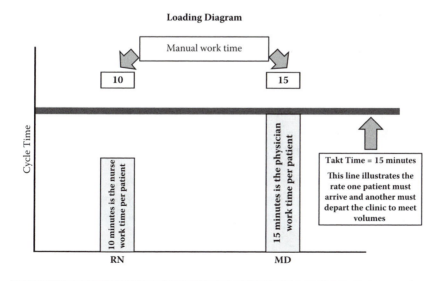

Figure 1.5   The loading diagram and the waste of unused capital.

The loading diagram is used to show the relationship between the workload of each team member (known as manual cycle time in Lean circles) and the frequency with which a process must be completed (loosely known as takt time). In this simple example, a nurse needs to see a patient every fifteen minutes. The physician also needs to see a patient every fifteen minutes to maintain a steady "flow" within the clinic. The nurse work content consists of ten minutes of work per patient, meaning that the nurse has five minutes of idle time between patients. While we would prefer this work to be professional in nature, this specific clinic is not providing that opportunity. To be efficient, we could have the nurse perform additional tasks; these tasks could include restocking the rooms or cleaning the rooms between visits. Is this unused human capital? I believe it would be even more wasteful to have a different resource provide these services when idle capacity exists.

Waste of Organizational Design

Can the management structure and design of your organization create waste? One of the common problems we find in healthcare is that many of the departments operate in silos. Each department has its own budget, management, staff, patients/services, and measurement targets. Is this bad? Let me provide an example of silos outside of healthcare. One of things that people in the manufacturing sector learned long ago is that optimizing a department can have negative effects on a system. For example, if a machining department is operating without concern for the downstream welding department, then many wastes can be created. The machining company could outperform the welding department, creating **inventory** between the departments. The inventory would need to be transported. When the inventory is **transported,** it can become damaged, creating **defects** that necessitate rework. Because the machining department will try to optimize its department targets, the typical day consists of long runs of parts. This ensures good productivity. However, this can have negative effects on the downstream welding department that might need two different parts to make their subassembly. This can lead to downtime in the welding department **waiting** on pieces from machining, while machining is meeting their budget and operating targets. Actually, the Toyota Production System evolved by solving these exact types of problems.

But what about healthcare? Patients frequently encounter more than one department during a visit. Let's take a simple visit to the emergency department for an ankle sprain. During this visit, the patient would likely encounter the following departments:

- Registration
- Emergency services (triage, primary care nurse, and physician)
- Diagnostic imaging (x-ray technologist, radiologist)

- Support services (portering)
- Billing

There is also a host of other departments that are indirectly involved with the patient. Minimally, this includes environmental services, infection prevention and control, and materials management. Do you think that all of these departments have aligned goals? Or perhaps I should ask a different question, such as: Do all your departments have aligned goals? What waste is present when the goals of the departments are not aligned? Can we find rework transportation, overprocessing, and inventory?

When waste is present within the organizational design, you see extra hand offs of patients and information, lots of reporting requirements and data collection that doesn't add value to the customer, and layers of management with politics between departments that makes it tough to provide high quality, patient-centered care. Now that we have a working definition of the common forms of waste (with the addition of two others), we will discuss some tools to help us identify and then eliminate this waste.

Principles of Improvement

The value-added/nonvalue-added principle holds that 95 to 99% of the work we observe is nonvalue-added to the patient. After you practice identifying waste over a short period of time and get comfortable with the concepts of value-added and nonvalue-added, waste will start to become obvious and abundant. The harder of the two tasks is eliminating the waste. Before we discuss how to eliminate waste, we must first understand some improvement principles to help guide our thinking. Every time we want to eliminate waste, we should use these principles as the foundation: flow, pull, defect-free, visual management, and kaizen. Let's review each of these in further detail (Figure 1.6).

Flow

The place we almost always want to begin when making improvement is by creating flow. People often think of flow as a means of lining up the activities to be completed one after another in a continuous manner. In healthcare, we want to "flow" patients though our healthcare system. Lining up all of the activities to occur one after another would be a great improvement, albeit very difficult, to accomplish. However, the concept of flow is more than just continuous processing of tasks. The Lean definition of flow is completing *value-added* tasks in continuous flow, at the rate of customer demand in a standardized way.

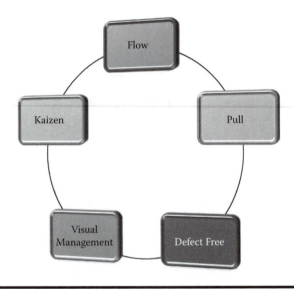

Figure 1.6 Lean principles.

By linking only the value-added steps together, this implies that we have eliminated the nonvalue-added activity between the steps. This is important because we want to avoid expending resources completing nonvalue-added work.

Let's imagine that we have eliminated some waste and now we have linked the value-added tasks together. For an x-ray procedure, assume that the x-ray technologist can perform the exam and, immediately following, have the exam read by a radiologist. The result is now available for review by the ordering physician. The physician can now complete the diagnosis and discuss the treatment plan with the patient. The patient can then leave with a full understanding of what the next steps would be. This would be flow in practice. Now we need to ensure that this new process is capable of meeting customer demand. If this process can be repeated twenty-eight times in an eight-hour shift, but we have patient demand of thirty-six per shift, we still have not satisfied the principle of flow. A process meeting the spirit of flow has to be paced to the rate of the customer demand into the process. Finally, let's assume we have now lined up the value-added steps and have a process capable of meeting customer demand. However, due to variation in the process, we get varying outcomes. If we fail to perform the activities in a standard way and continue to get consistent outcomes, we have not met the spirit of flow. A process is flowing when the value-added activities are lined up one after another with no waiting or inventory between each step. The process will be capable of meeting the customer demand, and the work is being done in a standardized way with consistent outcomes.

Pull

Sometimes it is not possible to create continuous flow across all of the steps. Constrained resources, used very infrequently, can make continuous flow very difficult. An example of this would be a patient arriving in the emergency room (ER) with considerable trauma after being hit in the mouth by a hockey puck. The patient is in need of a dental plastic surgeon. How many ERs have one of these on staff? Thus, the work will come to a halt while the referral is made and a response is received. The principle of pull enables areas of continuous flow to be linked together.

The concept of pull comes from the supermarket, the same supermarket where you buy your groceries. How does the grocer know when to stock the shelf? The answer is when there is an empty space. How did the empty space get there? A consumer put something in their grocery cart to take to the register for purchase. The signal to restock the shelf comes from the consumer removing an item. The item has been pulled from the shelf creating a signal to replenish. This simple concept is the basis for pull. Without a signal to replenish, what could happen? We could run out of product, causing a loss of sales, or we could overstock the area leading to spoilage or obsolescence (think about meats, dairy, and produce). Overstocking the area causes us to lose time, space, and resources while failing to meet the customers need. This is the waste of overproduction, and pull was designed to prevent overproduction. Conversely, understocking creates wasted motion and unnecessary waiting or worse—a total failure to deliver the product to the customer.

Pull in its simplest form is a signal to do work. In the case of the grocery store example, consumption is the signal to replenish. In Lean terms, the principle of pull implies that we would only perform work when we have a true need from the customer. To satisfy the principle of pull, the signal should contain certain attributes in its design. First, we would like to standardize the signal to one type. Although there are multiple ways to trigger any form of work, we would like to have a single trigger. Other attributes for a good pull system include words, such as seamless, no gaps, no overproduction, no asking, no searching, no clarifying, and synchronized.

We will first discuss the standardization of a trigger signal. As an example, let's talk about referral workflow in healthcare. On an inpatient medical floor, let's assume we need to trigger a respiratory therapist (RT) to perform an assessment. To trigger the assessment, we could page the RT, call the RT, write a written referral, send an e-mail, do a face-to-face request, trigger the referral in medical rounds, etc. A great Lean organization has a *single*, authoritative way to trigger the referral. Pick the best one for your organization.

Once you have standardized the signal to perform work (trigger), then we want to find one single way to respond to the signal. How do you acknowledge the referral? Again we could acknowledge by calling, e-mailing, etc., but a great pull system employs a single method in response to a trigger.

In healthcare, an example of a good pull signal is placing a physician order in an "orders to be entered" basket for order entry into the system. There is one way to trigger the work—placing the order in the basket. There is one way to respond—pulling the order from the basket. Assuming the order entry resource has other responsibilities besides just order entry, the response time to get orders entered can be standardized to get us near continuous, but not full, continuous flow. Additional examples of where pull signals have been utilized in healthcare include

1. Using the supermarket concept to trigger supply replenishment of medicine, supplies, and equipment
2. Triggering of a physician to see the next patient in a clinic
3. Triggering that results are available so reassessment can occur
4. Triggering a consult for a specialty service not always in-house
5. Triggering a service referral for home care
6. Using a visual queue to know when to porter the next patient for a procedure
7. Triggering a room clean following a discharge
8. Triggering the build of the next two hours of operating room (OR) case carts

There are literally thousands of examples, and a great Lean organization utilizes the principle of pull to link steps together every single time that work cannot flow continuously.

Defect-Free

Let's assume now that we have begun to design our work process and we have been able to implement pockets of continuous flow, and where we couldn't create continuous flow, we have been able to implement pull systems that link our areas of continuous flow together. So far, so good. Work completed that meets the principle and spirit of continuous flow and pull will still be unacceptable if the outcomes are bad. And bad outcomes in healthcare can be very serious. In fact, our first mission in healthcare is to do no harm.

To prevent bad outcomes, we utilize the principle of defect-free. In Lean terms, defect-free means doing the work in a way that meets customer-specified quality requirements the first time. This implies that as the work moves from step to step, quality inspection is designed into the process along with immediate feedback when problems do arise so the outcomes are consistent, meet customer requirements, and can be completed without rework and inspection. Some of the attributes of defect-free work would include no errors, no rework, standardized, quality at the source, nonpersonality based, and no overprocessing or redundancy.

Expanding on the defect-free principle, there are several design approaches to allowing value to be delivered defect-free. Review a few of the more common tools and concepts in Table 1.1.

Some of these tools might look familiar to you. These tools are the same as the ones used for total quality management approaches and certification and accreditation standards. Once a process has been designed using the principles of flow, pull, and defect-free, we need a system to manage the process.

Visual Management

A Lean system is one that is designed to be managed visually. Visual management allows everyone to "see normal from abnormal conditions." What kinds of things are we interested in managing visually? Anything you can imagine. Are we ahead or behind in the schedule? Is everyone following the standard work? Are all of the necessary equipment, materials, and supplies available? Do we have a home for everything? What are the top three problems we are working on? Who is responsible for the corrective actions? When will they be completed? What have the results been for the last month? Are we on budget? All of these types of scenarios can be managed visually.

There are a few attributes we like to see in a Lean visual management system. First, we need absolute transparency. This means that everyone has the ability to see normal from abnormal in five seconds or less. We shouldn't need to run a report or open a drawer to see the status of normal from abnormal. An important point to remember in creating a Lean culture is that finding issues is a good thing. Every effort must be put in place to have the organizational culture accept both good and bad information with a respect for both accuracy and appreciation. Let's discuss a very simple example of transparency.

Figure 1.7 is a picture of an appointment card used to create transparency for an inpatient diagnostic imaging test. The card has two sides: a red side (dark shading) and a green side (light shading). The red side shows that an exam has been scheduled. It also shows the patient room and bed, patient name, and appointment time. When an exam is scheduled, the card is filled out and placed on the appointment board. Thirty minutes before the exam, the nurse will prepare the patient for the exam and when complete, turn the card over showing the green side. The green side highlights the steps for preparing the patient to eliminate portering delays and time waiting in diagnostic imaging. The porter will arrive fifteen minutes before the exam and transport the patient to the appropriate test location, properly prepared, and on time, allowing for a seamless transition into

Table 1.1 Defect-Free Concepts

Concept	Description
Successive Staff Checks	Each staff member checks the previous work before adding his/her own value. This ensures that work is not completed in addition to previous work that may have a defect.
5S	A management system for creating a high performing work area that designs the work space, tools, supplies, equipment, and information in a way that enables the work to be done defect-free.
Operational Methods Sheets	A visual tool that explains the work to be done at the task level, defines the quality specifications of the work, and shows the checks the staff member must take to ensure the work is defect-free. This approach ties closely with Successive Staff Checks. The operational methods sheet is sometimes also known as a Key Points Sheet.
Andon	Andon loosely translates to stopping the line. This is a management principle where the staff stops performing work when a defect is found and will not begin performing work again until a countermeasure is in place to prevent further defects. This creates time to identify the root cause of the problem, allowing for a permanent solution to be found.
Poka Yoke	Poka Yoke loosely translates to mistake proofing. This concept is in action when work is designed to make it impossible to do the work improperly. A simple example would be designing a coffee pot warmer that shuts off automatically after 30 minutes. This shut-off system prevents (mistake-proofs) the device from being left on inadvertently.
7 Quality Tools	The seven tools include the cause and effect diagram, the check sheet, the control chart, the histogram, the Pareto diagram, the scatter diagram, and the flow chart. These tools are used to explain what is happening in a system and are used because they do not require a lot of statistical training for the user. They are used frequently in healthcare to explain and interpret data.

Table 1.1 (*Continued*)   Defect-Free Concepts

Concept	Description
Cause and Effect Diagram	Expanding on one of the seven quality tools, the cause and effect diagram, or Ishakawa diagram, or fishbone diagram, is used to determine causes of problems and helps sort the problems into useful categories.
5 Whys	This is a technique used to determine the root cause of a problem. By asking Why five different times, it is possible to get to the underlying source of the problem so a solution can be identified that permanently solves the problem. Beyond impacting the principle of defect-free, 5 Whys is also a technique used to develop people.

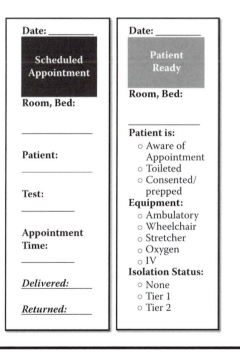

Figure 1.7 Diagnostic imaging appointment scheduled/patient ready. (Courtesy of Craig Wickens, Rouge Valley Health System.)

the testing process. Prior to this visual management system, patients would be delayed upwards of an hour for their exams, and, in some cases, the exam would be canceled, leading to delays in diagnosis, treatment, and discharge.

Another attribute of visual management is that it must trigger action. Part of the system is to see normal from abnormal; the other part is doing something about it. If we are behind, what is the intervention to catch up? If something is not in the correct place, who is going to find the missing item and return it to its home? Many Lean visual management systems operate exactly as designed, but the staff and management fail to take action. In concept, visual management systems should deliver visualization of issues at a stage in the process that allows "abnormal" to be seen at the earliest possible point. This allows corrective action to occur sooner minimizing risk of harm to patients.

It doesn't matter how great the Lean design was, how great the flow and pull worked, and how many defects were eliminated if the system *cannot* be managed visually. The culture of your organization will always pull the new system back to the previous status quo without a robust visual management system. A sound visual management is the first key step to sustaining improvement.

Great organizations can see normal from abnormal conditions at a glance, and take immediate action when abnormal conditions arise.

Kaizen

The fifth principle of improvement is known as kaizen. Kaizen is actually two words: The first work "kai" means "change" and the second word "zen" means "for the better." In order to create a culture of improvement, we must build a system that is continuously improving. Great organizations get better every day; employees leave the workplace in better shape than when they arrived. Imagine what that could look like.

To practice kaizen, we want to make small, incremental, continuous changes to our work in order to deliver more value to the customer. This usually shows up in eliminating small amounts of nonvalue-added activity by creating better standard work, relocating items to eliminate wasted movement, or mistake proofing something to avoid a defect being made.

In the spirit of practicing kaizen, Lean organizations frequently benchmark their performance against their peers or within their industry, but not in the areas you might think. Actually, two types of benchmarking occur simultaneously. The first is benchmarking against perfection—deliver all value-added activity in continuous flow with no defects. When you compare your current performance against perfection, you will see that you have much to improve upon. This comparison of current performance against perfection can create a state of tension spurring further improvement.

The second benchmark is to compare their performance against the best in the world. Great organizations compare their processes against industries with world-class performance. How does your performance in infection prevention compare with safe drinking water? How does your quality in medicine administration compare with the safe practices of a nuclear power plant? You can compare your organization to other healthcare organizations, but I am not aware of anywhere the world quotes healthcare performance for benchmarks as the best in the world. To achieve dramatic results, you to match later pronoun need to do things dramatically different so stop comparing yourself with your peers and look outside of healthcare.

Industry has many examples that healthcare should aspire to. This is not meant to put healthcare beneath other industries, but rather give you a different vision for what is possible. Practice kaizen. Improve every day. You never get to a state of being "Lean." *Never* be satisfied with your current performance. Challenge the management, staff, and the medical staff to do better. When you create a mindset of continuous improvement, you are meeting the spirit of kaizen.

Lean Healthcare Defined

Let's return to the discussion at the beginning of the chapter. What is Lean healthcare? Envision a system where work is constantly scrutinized to eliminate waste and deliver more value to your patients. Envision a system where the entire workforce is engaged and inspired to improve. A workforce continuously improving the quality and safety of care approaching a defect-free system, reducing wasted time, an activity freeing up capacity for other work, decreasing lead times for services, and lowering the cost of the delivery of these services. Envision the delivery of healthcare with accurate and timely information shared seamlessly amongst the care team. A system where the medical staff and support staff collaborate to provide patient-focused, evidenced-based care with seamless transitions between specialties and subspecialties. Where the staff constantly strive to ensure the majority of work content is value-added. Resources that are freed up when redundancy and nonvalue-added activity are eliminated are redeployed so all talent can be maximized. Envision a system where the patients, families, and communities participate in the design of the services leading to healthier communities with preventative strategies driving lower and lower costs. I'm not sure there is enough ink to describe all the attributes of Lean healthcare. Table 1.2 provides a brief glimpse into what Lean healthcare is and what it is not.

Lean healthcare is a management system of continuous improvement. This healthcare system was constructed based the two Lean themes: elimination of

Table 1.2 Lean Healthcare

What Lean Healthcare Is	What Lean Healthcare Is Not
Patient focused	• Provider focused • Staff focused • College focused • Organization focused • Insurance focused
Seamless care	• Care provided in silos
Collaborative and integrated care	• Profession centric care
Transparent information	• Hidden and difficult to access information
Quality and safety first	• Access and cost first
Inspired and engaged support staff and medical staff	• Leadership and management make all the decisions
Continuously improving	• Spot improvement or firefighting
Creativity before capital	• Technology, equipment, and adding resources lead the solution set
Systems thinking	• Program focus
Problems solved in the workplace (Gemba)	• Problems solved in the conference room
Focus on the process	• Focus on blaming individuals
A team of interprofessionals	• Individual contributors and heroes

waste and respect for all people. Work is designed for the patient in systems and subsystems that reflect continuous flow processes. Work is pulled through the system, not pushed. Activities are designed and delivered in a defect-free manner. The status of work, results, and process are monitored visually; any abnormalities to the work are identified and fixed in real time. Every system is continuously being improved by an inspired and engaged support staff and medical staff, working side by side with one focus: servicing the patient.

The results of these efforts are reflected in improvement of key measures tied to the strategic desires of the organization, the board, the support staff, the medical staff, and the community. These key measures show world-class rates of improvement in quality and patient safety, access, cost, staff morale, and growth. With this vision in mind, we will explore how to provide the leadership to make this healthcare system a reality using Lean.

Summary: Key Points from Chapter 1

- Lean improvement is based on the fundamental concept of value-added and nonvalue-added. A value-added (5% of a typical process) activity directly meets the needs of the customer. A nonvalue-added activity (95% of a typical process) takes up time, space, and/or resources, but does not directly contribute to meeting the needs of the customer.
- The two themes of Lean improvement include continuous improvement and respect for all people.
- Nonvalue-added activity is also known as waste; there are seven common forms of operational waste. These include overproduction, waiting, over-processing, inventory, motion, defects, and transportation. Two additional wastes present within organizations include the waste of unused human capital and the waste of organizational design.
- Waste is eliminated using the five principles of improvement: flow, pull, defect-free, visual management, and kaizen.
- Lean healthcare can be defined as a business system of continuous improvement. This system is operated by an inspired and engaged team to deliver more and more value to patients. A well-run Lean healthcare system will deliver year over improvement in performance and culture.

Chapter 2

Creating and Deploying a Lean Strategy

Great leaders are almost always great simplifiers, who can cut through argument, debate, and doubt to offer a solution everybody can understand.

General Colin Powell

Creating a Culture of Improvement

Two activities are key in creating a culture of improvement necessary to achieve your organizational vision. These would include tightly linking the improvements in your organization to your strategy and utilizing operational excellence to realize the strategy. Synergies are provided by focusing the organization on your strategic goals, linking your improvement focus toward these strategies, and utilizing Lean tools and techniques to become operationally excellent.

Why is creating alignment in your organization important? It takes resources to improve. I'm not talking about information systems, capital equipment, staff, and bricks and mortar resources, rather, the hearts, talents, and minds of the support staff and providers are the resources utilized by a Lean organization. You might have heard the saying "people are our most precious commodity." While this statement is true, you also need an improvement system to unleash these precious resources and help you to identify an area of focus. Improvement in this "area of focus" should link directly to accomplishing your strategy. Table 2.1 discusses the importance of linking strategy to improvement.

There is an additional consideration when linking strategy to improvement: Financial obligations tied to implementing the improvement in a specific area of focus. In order to illustrate the importance of correctly identifying the area of focus, let's walk through some "fuzzy" math. Assume there are eight staff members and one physician on a newly formed improvement team. Assume this team is together for forty hours. If we take the hourly pay of the staff and add in the physician expense (whether in salary or loss of salary or loss of revenue), we are already at a sizeable investment. Factor in the replacement costs for the staff covering the team while working on improvement. Factor in the investment in training when the new design is complete and the project expense will be even larger. I estimate a typical team will cost anywhere between $10,000 and $30,000 for any improvement. With an expense this large, you will want to ensure that you have picked an area that directly aligns with your strategy.

Sometimes, I have to field the argument that having a "Lean" program is too expensive. How can we afford to invest $10,000 to $30,000 per team? Actually, you are likely already making this investment. I find countless teams, committees, and projects across most any healthcare organization. Your investment is buried in these teams. The broader question is what is the return for these efforts?

Table 2.1 The Importance of Linking Improvement to Strategy

It is very difficult to impossible to improve all areas of an organization simultaneously. Begin improvement in the areas that best enable you to meet your key outcome measures.
Each team requires time from your support staff and medical staff. Focus on the high leverage areas to maximize your return on your investment.
The effort to change a process with minimal return is the same as the effort to change a process with a large return. Allow your middle and line management and medical leadership to focus on the areas of highest return.
Change takes time. Do not lose precious days, weeks, and months on areas not directly aligned to your strategy.
All support staff and medical staff should be able to immediately see the correlation between improvement and attaining your strategy. This gives the team a sense of purpose and shows them how they fit into the big picture.

If the focus is on access or patient satisfaction or support staff and medical staff satisfaction or quality and safety, the results can be quite difficult to measure.

If you can reflect a minute, the reason for improvement using Lean management might become obvious. Count how many hours are spent in meetings during the course of a week, a month, and then a year trying to make improvement. Truly assess the success of this "meeting after meeting" approach to *change* your organization. This meeting approach cannot coordinate the tidal wave of performance and culture change that a Lean approach does.

So, why is linking the improvement to the strategy of your organization so important? Ask yourself this: If you were incommunicado for two weeks with no cell phone, computer, or "connection" with your work, what would be the **first** metric you look at upon your return? Would you know? I have been amazed at how many senior healthcare leaders cannot answer this question effectively. If the senior leaders cannot answer this questions, how can the workforce possibly know what is important to the organization? Hoshin kanri answers this question for the organization.

> Create and deploy your strategy using hoshin kanri (strategy deployment).

The word *hoshin* is composed of two Chinese characters: *ho* meaning method or form and *shin* meaning shiny needle or compass. Taken together, the word hoshin means "methodology for strategic direction setting."[*] Kanri, in Japanese, means "management."

No matter how great your strategy, if you can't execute the strategy, you will not deliver the results you are expecting. Hoshin kanri provides a step-by-step planning, implementation, and review process for managed change.[†] In a Lean organization, hoshin kanri is the system used to manage system change of the core business objectives. Hoshin kanri operates at two levels: first, at the strategic planning level, and, second, at the daily management level on the more routine or fundamental aspects of the business operation.[‡] When translated to English, hoshin kanri is also known as policy deployment or strategy deployment.

There are seven steps to the hoshin kanri process broken into the three phases of planning, implementing, and review.

---

[*] Pascal, D. 2007. *Lean production simplified*. New York: Productivity Press, p. 123.
[†] Watson, G. 1991. *Hoshin kanri, policy deployment for successful TQM*. Portland, OR: Productivity Press, p. xxi.
[‡] Ibid, p. xxii.

Seven-Phase Policy Deployment Process

Step 1: Establish the Organizational Vision

The first step in the policy deployment process is to establish the organizational vision. Organizations should first obtain a thorough understanding of the customer's needs (known as establishing the voice of the customer in Lean circles) before establishing their vision (Figure 2.1). Understanding the voice of the customer helps us with three key activities:

1. Measuring performance as aligned with how the customer measures performance
2. Hitting targets as set by the customer
3. Developing and deploying objectives that deliver value to the customer

Recall that in healthcare, the customer is the patient/caregiver the majority of the time. When possible, we should use the same measures that our customers would use. Some examples of this would include wait times for services, quality and safety outcomes, and cost for services.

From the voice of the customer, we can develop our strategic plan, which should answer the questions: Where are we going and how do we get there? Strategic planning is used to develop a shared vision of the future. This planning

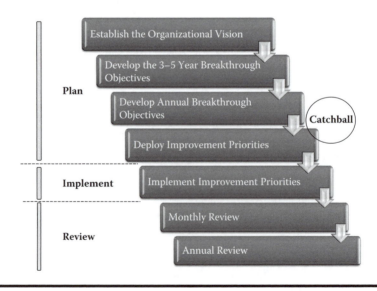

Figure 2.1 Seven-phase policy deployment process.

should be a pull system, with a vision so compelling that it pulls us into the future.* A great example of this type of vision is President John F. Kennedy's famous May 25, 1961 statement, **"I believe that this nation should commit itself to achieving the goal, before this decade is out, of landing a man on the moon and returning him safely to the Earth."** This statement created the vision for change that NASA followed for nearly a decade.

Planning should also follow the scientific method, the method used most frequently in improvement sciences. Planning should include an assessment of the current situation, identify a target condition, and countermeasure the gaps between current and target.

Step 2: Develop Three- to Five-Year Breakthrough Objectives

It is breakthrough thinking that drives us to achieve a world-class performance. A "breakthrough" represents a significant change in performance and culture as seen through the eyes of the customer. This breakthrough will always be a stretch target for the organization, and to be realized, will likely require a cross-functional approach. In most cases, there will be no standard system or process in existence; the system will need to be created to realize the breakthrough. To understand what a breakthrough objective looks like, a forecast of customer expectations should be made (Figure 2.2).

Great Lean organizations create benchmark goals targeted against a level of perfection, not based on measures of others in the industry. To see what world class looks like, view benchmarks of organizations *outside* of your industry. How does the nuclear power industry or airline industry approach safety? You must first understand how their customers measure performance, determine an appropriate breakthrough for your organization, and then aim high. Aiming high is essential because your customers are constantly raising their expectations, your competition is not standing still, and aiming high will require your organization to constantly change their paradigm about what is possible. The high jumper does not aim for the bar, he instead aims above the bar. Similarly, your breakthrough needs to aim above the bar.

True North Measures

A Lean organization defines their breakthrough objectives as true north measures. True north, like a compass, implies direction; this direction is the singular focus of the efforts of an organization. The true north measures of an

---

* Pascal, *Lean production*, p. 123.

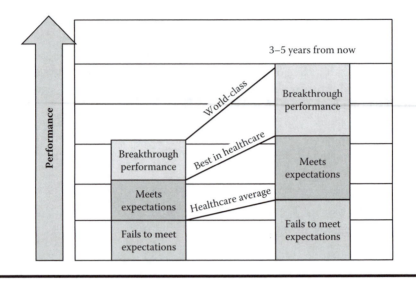

Figure 2.2 Meeting customer expectations.

organization consist of a small suite of operational measures (not to exceed five in number) tied directly to your organizational vision. If we could look at all the measures that exist for an organization and then put them into categories, what would we find? The common categories for true north measures include

1. People/human development
2. Quality
3. Delivery
4. Cost/productivity
5. Growth

The history of true north measurement comes from an analysis of the pursuit of perfection. As discussed in Chapter 1, in a perfect process, all activities are considered value-creating activities, where these activities are lined up for continuous flow. In this environment, the lead time for products and services equals the cycle times for the value-creating activities. The process, products, and services are created without any defects. Without any waste, the products and services can be generated at the lowest possible cost. A common question at this point is very simple: Perfection can never be achieved, so why would we allow an impossible goal to be selected? In Lean, we pursue perfection with every goal. An example is hospital-acquired infections. Say, we start with an average of twelve cases per month. After completing the proper Lean activities, we are able to reduce this number to six per month over a twelve-month period. We have not eliminated this issue, but we have reduced our hospital acquired infections by 50%. This is worthy of a celebration. Then we get busy with eliminating the remaining opportunities. We may never get to zero, but the pursuit of perfection is the goal.

True North Measures are based on delivery of goods and services that can be created with perfect quality, at the shortest lead time, and at the lowest cost. Because improvement is not possible without the engagement of people, a measure of staff engagement or staff morale is often added to the true north measures. Table 2.2 describes the True North Measures in more detail.

To be more specific, we can show an illustration of the true north measures for a hospital known as Pleasant Valley Health. Pleasant Valley is an urban, teaching hospital with acute care services. This organization supports a little over 800 inpatient beds (Table 2.3).

The requirements for measurements to make "True North" status are few (Figure 2.3). The first requirement is that a True North Measure must show a minimum of a double digit improvement, namely, greater than 10%. When we

Table 2.2 True North Measures

True North Category	True North Measure Definition	True North Measure in Healthcare
People	Staff morale or staff engagement	Support staff and medical staff morale or engagement
Quality	Defects per unit of service or process outcomes related to meeting the customer's requirements	Service Quality: Patient and family satisfaction Outcome Quality: Measures of clinical outcomes and patient safety Process Quality: Measures of defects per unit of service
Delivery	Lead time for goods and services	Measures of *access* including lead times for services and wait times between services
Cost	Hours or $ consumed per unit of service; typically a measure of productivity	Hours or dollars consumed per unit of service
Growth	Increases in revenues or volumes	Increases in revenues or volumes

Table 2.3 Pleasant Valley Health True North Measures

True North Category	Strategic Direction	True North Measure
People	Create a working environment that inspires our support staff and medical staff	Have 100% of our support staff and medical staff engaged in verifiable improvement by the end of fiscal year 2015
Quality	• Eliminate unnecessary mortality and morbidity • Provide patient/family centered care	• Reduce hospital-acquired infections by 80% by December 2014 • Improve patient satisfaction scores by 15% by December 2014
Delivery	Reduce needless patient waiting	Reduce wait times for our five major service lines by 50% by June 2014
Cost	Become a benchmark, low-cost service provider	Operate in the 98th percentile as a low-cost service provider in all five of our major service lines by the end of the fiscal year in 2015
Growth	Increase access to all of our service lines	Grow each service line in visits/cases by 10% per year ending December 31, 2015

eliminate waste, we will be focused on eliminating or reducing the nonvalue-added activity. Recall that nonvalue-added activity comprises 95% of the work in most organizations. With this 95% opportunity, a great Lean organization expects 10% plus improvement at a minimum. If we choose a small number, like say 2%, we really do not need to eliminate waste. We can put this process under the microscope, measure it frequently, make it a priority, work extra hard, and will likely get a 2% improvement. How many times do you think we can work extra hard? That card can be played occasionally, but continually working harder is not a sustainable improvement strategy. On the other hand, methods to eliminate waste can be repeated for decades.

Figure 2.3   True north.

Now comes the mental challenge. Lean organizations do not go for double digit improvement (improvement greater than 10%) in one true north category. The second requirement for true north measures is that *all* of the categories of true north require double digit improvement. We set all of the targets at 10% plus for a couple of reasons. First, we want to balance risk. It may be possible to improve cost by 10% if we sacrifice quality or access. It might be possible to grow volumes by 10% if we sacrifice customer service or staff morale. A Lean organization wants to have its cake *and* eat it too. We do not expect to achieve one measure at the expense of another. Secondly, when wasted time and activity is eliminated, all five categories of true north should improve simultaneously. We want the focus of our support staff and medical staff to be on the continuous elimination of nonvalue-added activity. When this focus occurs, en masse, all of the measures should improve simultaneously.

Our first requirement in providing Lean leadership is to be clear on the strategic direction and the true north measures. This alignment must be supported by all of the senior leadership team, including the medical leadership, and also should be supported by the hospital board. Any chink in the "support armor" by the senior levels of the organization will have negative downstream impact on the management, support staff, and medical staff. Do not underestimate the effort it will take to create consensus between the senior leadership team. You might say, "We are already aligned." If that statement is true then the following conditions should exist:

1. The number of measures on your highest level organizational scorecard should be between 4 and 7. How many measures does your board scorecard contain? The most I have seen is over 54, and most all are over 20.

Keep in mind that as the measures cascade, 4 to 7 measures at the top of the organization could easily lead to 20 or 30 submeasures at the unit or department level. When there are many measures, the unit/department starts assuming what the priorities are. Make this decision simple; we want the focus on eliminating wasted time and activity.

2. The measures should be able to tie *directly* back to each of the five operational dimensions of "true north," namely staff morale/human development, quality, delivery, cost/productivity, and growth.

3. The measures should represent double digit improvement.

Everyone in the organization should be able to tell how their improvement effort ties back to the true north measures. This is a real challenge. Very often the most senior leaders of the organization have a view of true north that is not fully understood by those who will actually make change happen. Time and effort needs to be spent carefully communicating what was selected for true north measures and why those particular measures were chosen. Care must be taken when cascading these measures down throughout the organization.

You might have realized that these breakthrough objectives are identical to the true north measures for Pleasant Valley Health. One thing that might not be apparent is the fact that there are only a handful of breakthrough objectives. One of the most important activities within hoshin kanri is the process of deselection. Focusing on the ***critical few*** breakthroughs related to quality, delivery, cost, and growth is a key to achieving success. Organizations need to focus to increase throughput of critical projects. Deselecting breakthrough objectives helps immensely with this focus.

Step 3: Develop the Annual Breakthrough Objectives and Improvement Priorities

Once the three- to five-year breakthrough objectives have been identified, they must next be broken down into annual objectives. The annual objective will determine how far toward our three- to five-year breakthrough objective you will travel in the next fiscal year. Assuming that you have selected a three-year breakthrough objective, it would seem logical to travel one-third of the way toward that target each year, although organizations that follow that recipe tend to fall short of the goal. I encourage organizations to think about a 50% improvement in the first year. This will accomplish two things: (1) a stretch goal will break any paradigms about status immediately, and (2) you will want to aim *above* the bar if you want to get *over* the bar. Shooting for a 50% target and coming up short will most likely keep you on track to meet the three-year

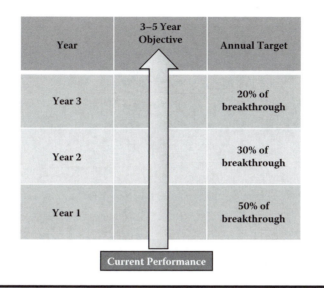

Figure 2.4 Annual breakthrough objectives.

objective. It is important to note that your organization will not achieve this level of improvement without using Lean thinking to "see and eliminate" waste.

To identify the annual breakthrough (Figure 2.4), three steps are necessary. First, you must obtain a fact-based understanding of the current situation. Fact-based means that the understanding is based on current, and accurate, data. Many healthcare organizations use data that are a quarter behind, or a month behind at best, which makes selecting targets more troublesome. Second, identify how much you improve in the first year in order to meet your three- to five-year breakthrough objective, as an improvement of 50% was merely a suggested guideline. Finally, quantify the gap between the current state and the target area for the first year. When the time comes to cascade the improvements down throughout the organization, it must be clear and obvious what the gap is and what targets need to be meet (Figure 2.5).

Identify Top-Level Improvement Priorities

Once the annual breakthrough objectives are identified and the gap between current and target is identified, a second part of step three is to identify the top-level improvement priorities. Selecting the top-level improvement objectives answers the question: How will we accomplish our annual breakthrough objective? The top-level improvement priorities are the corporate-wide objectives that will be executed in order to meet the annual objective. Great top-level improvement

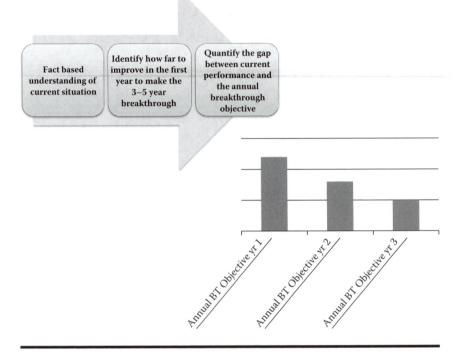

Figure 2.5   Three steps to defining annual breakthrough objectives.

priorities should be process-oriented, meaning that the improvement priority should lead to the creation of a sustainable results-oriented business process. The improvement priority should not be a short-term task. Top-level improvement priorities also should be very focused on new or emerging customer needs, and also on a critical few. Always separate the "critical few" from the "many good."

Selecting the Top-Level Improvement Priorities

Perhaps one of the most difficult challenges in hoshin kanri is selecting the correct top-level improvement priorities. The art in selecting the correct top-level improvement priority is understanding the driver process of the breakthrough objective. The driver process is identified using problem-solving techniques. Using a cause and effect diagram, in combination with the technique of 5 Whys, is a very effective approach to identifying the driver process.

There are three steps to identifying the driver process. First, determine the gap between the current situation and desired condition and apply 5 Whys to the current situation to identify the root causes of the gap. This step can take some time and requires data. Don't jump to conclusions on the root cause of the gap, and don't avoid the white elephants if they indeed are the root cause. Next, use problem-solving approaches to find ways to bridge the gap toward your annual breakthrough objective. Finally, identify the driver process with the greatest influence on closing the gap and correctly identifying the top-level improvement priority (Figure 2.6).

Once you have selected the improvement priorities, target measures will need to be identified. A target is used to measure the effectiveness of a process and should be used in conjunction with the improvement priorities. The improvement priorities tell "how" and the targets explain "how much." Targets are best expressed in the following format: "from **x** to **y** by **when**." For example, reduce the cost per case of surgery from $1,190 per case to $1,050 per case by June of 2013.

Finally, the key resources with accountability for the annual breakthrough objective need to be identified. These resources should be the individuals with the greatest influence on the improvement priority or the resources with the greatest opportunity to impact the priority. Be careful not to select the most

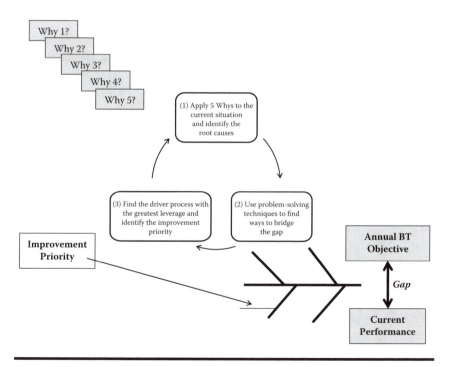

Figure 2.6   Three steps to identifying the improvement priority.

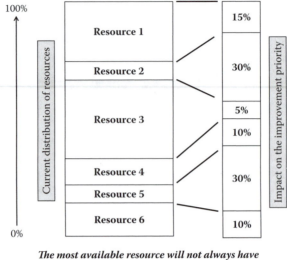

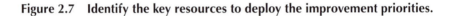

*The most available resource will not always have
the greatest impact on the improvement priority*

Figure 2.7 Identify the key resources to deploy the improvement priorities.

readily available or the largest resource, as they may not always have the greatest impact on the results. Because most all of the breakthrough objectives will span more than one department, expect to find that resources across different functions will be necessary to improve (Figure 2.7).

There is a considerable amount of activity in developing the annual breakthrough objectives and determining the top-level improvement priorities. The annual breakthrough objectives are selected using careful analysis of the current situation, quantifying how far to go in the next year, and quantifying the gap. Once the gap is quantified, problem-solving approaches can be utilized to determine the root cause of the gap, and additional Lean tools can be used to determine the potential solutions that will bridge the gap; these solutions become the top-level improvement priorities. Once the priorities are established, then the targets for improvement can be created using a "from x to y by when" statement. The cross-functional resources with the greatest opportunity to impact the target are then identified.

Step 4: Deploy the Improvement Priorities

Now that the annual breakthrough objectives and top-level improvement priorities have been defined, the next step involves deploying the improvement priorities through a process known as *catchball*. As the name describes, the deployment of objectives and priorities requires give and take. This back and forth occurs between peers, horizontally across the organization, and between managers and subordinates vertically through the management levels. While the priority, along with the target, is defined from the top down, the process to meet the target is not. The purpose of catchball is to link the vision of the company officers and the daily activities of the staff.*

Here is an example of catchball in practice. Meadowvale, a 250-bed rehabilitation hospital, has a three- to five-year breakthrough objective to reduce patient safety-related incidence by 90% within a three-year period. The leadership team, upon a thorough analysis of the voice of the customer and analysis of data selected, identified fall reduction as the top-level improvement priority. It was decided that the annual target for the upcoming year is to reduce the number of falls from 216 annually to 108 by December 31, 2014. Note that this number was determined by looking at the number of falls across the organization. While I recognize that healthcare would normally report falls as a percentage of patient days, it was my intent to measure it differently to keep the example simple (Figure 2.8).

The target is now deployed to the next management layer of the organization. In the case of Meadowvale, the executive sponsor will be the vice president of patient services. The program that is most influential is the stroke and neurology rehabilitation program. Catchball will occur between the senior team conduit

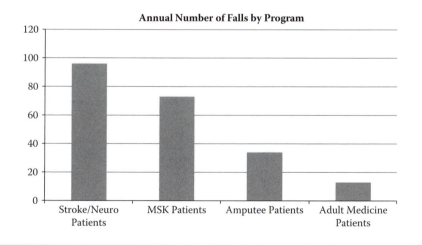

Figure 2.8   Annual fall rates at Meadowvale.

---

* Ibid., p. 130.

(the vice president of patient services) and the program. The stroke/neuro program will take the top-level improvement "vision" and translate that objective into specific activities that will meet their target. These activities (or hoshins) will be "tossed" back to the leadership, in essence, to ensure that the approach is correct and will achieve the vision. Leadership will then provide feedback to the program. The hoshins might be tossed back and forth several times. In our example, the program will deploy a collaborative care model using "next" practice fall prevention strategies to reduce falls in the stroke/neuro program by 75% in the next year.

In the early days of practicing strategy deployment, a common rework occurrence for catchball happens because the receiving area doesn't agree with the target, or perhaps the year 1 target is perceived to be too high. The catchball will happen several times, trying to negotiate an easier target; just keep in mind that a lower target in year 1 means a higher target for the upcoming years. As a simple gauge for your target setting, if the receiving department leadership is not uncomfortable with the new target, the goal is likely set too low.

The next layer of catchball occurs between the program level and the department or unit level. Again the cascaded improvement priority, now called the second-level improvement priority, is "tossed" to the unit level where the more specific hoshins are generated. This process of catchball can occur between different levels of the organization, all the way down to the staff level. When action plans can be created in great detail, the cascading can stop. Action plans can be created at any level, but ideally, should be as close to the place where the customer is serviced as possible. Real customer breakthroughs will be seen/realized at this level. Action plans are used to flush out the true root causes of the gaps between current and target.

When starting out, I would encourage your organization to start as follows for the first year:

- Begin with the level 0 planning: Developing the three- to five-year vision.
- Create the level 1 plan: The annual breakthrough objectives and top-level improvement priorities.
- Deploy the level 2 plans: Develop and deploy the second-level improvement priorities across the senior team.

It takes a solid year to get good at these three levels. Many organizations suffer greatly because of the desire to push strategy deployment down to the business unit, program level, and department/unit level before the senior team has a thorough understanding of the policy deployment process. You will see in the next few steps how hoshin kanri differs from traditional planning processes. You also will need some time to get your data collection systems in alignment with the timely capture your hoshin kanri system.

Step 5: Implement the Improvement Priorities

Once the priorities, the means, and the targets are deployed, improvement can begin. Before improving, it is best to have detailed action plans from which to work. An example of an action plan is shown in Figure 2.9.

An action plan should contain the specific action (the "**what**"), **who** is responsible, and **when** the action will be started and completed (I call this part the WWW, or the what, who, and when). Without this minimum amount of information, you have not yet created an action plan, but merely a dream.

Use a Value Stream Approach to Improvement

Improvement is best when completed not in isolation, but rather as part of a bigger plan. The Lean approach to improvement projects that "see the whole" involves utilizing value mapping and analysis. W. Edwards Deming, a famous management quality consultant, once said, "It is not enough to do your best; you must know what to do, and then do your best."* There are countless opportunities to improve. Where do we begin? Value stream mapping and analysis

Improvement Priority: Reduce Falls		Process Owner: Jill Wilson	Current Performance: *1 Fall per Week*	Target Performance: *75% Reduction*
What	**Who**	**When**	**Expected Impact**	**Status**
Complete value stream analysis	J. Wilson	5–7 May 2012	Detailed plans for improvement	Scheduled
Post daily falls data and deliver updates in a daily huddle	B. Smith	4 April 2012	Gather three new ideas for fall prevention per incident	**Complete**
Complete first kaizen event following value stream analysis	J. Wilson	8 June week	Reduce falls 30%	Scheduled

Figure 2.9   Action plans for deploying priorities.

* Quotations, 1999–2010. Online at: http://thinkexist.com/quotes/w._edwards_deming/ ThinkExist.com

provides the process and structure to identify knowing what to do. From here, you can begin to improve and do your best.

A value stream consists of all of the process activities required to deliver value to a customer. Beginning with the customer's definition of value (as defined in Chapter 1), the value stream is all of the tasks done to deliver this value. A value stream typically begins with a customer's need and ends when the customer's need is met. Likely, the work will span many different departments, so a value stream is *not* a department.

For example, if a patient arrives for a preadmission surgical consult, this patient will meet with registration, a nurse, and an anesthesiologist. In addition, there may be a lab test required and perhaps a chest x-ray if the patient has been recommended for surgery by a surgeon. At the end of the visit, the area is cleaned by environmental services, and supplies are restocked by materials management. This work spans at least six departments, demonstrating that the value stream is broader than a single department.

Think of a value stream as a chain. If each link is not equally strong, the "weak" link will destine the improvement process to failure. To make an improvement in isolation, like by only the operating room (OR) department, would only create marginal improvement. Improvement needs to be made across the entire value stream engaging all departments in delivering value to the patient. In improving the value stream, waste is eliminated from the system, and not simply moved from one department to another. Spot improvements, while holding some promise, rarely add up to revolutionary change.

To complete a value stream mapping and analysis activity, you must first accomplish the following high-level activities:

1. Assemble a team with the cross-functional representation across the value stream.
2. Determine measureable outcomes from the improvement (aligned to your true north measures and top level improvement priorities).
3. Determine the beginning and ending points of the value stream.
4. Specify value from the customer's perspective.
5. Process map the current process (the real "as is" process) (Figure 2.10).
6. Capture data on the current process, then add a data box to each process step (Table 2.4).
7. Identify the waste in the current process (Figure 2.11).
8. Analyze the current state and summarize performance (Table 2.5).
   Can you identify the waste from this data summary example? Why are there so many nonvalue-added steps? Why does the process have more than twenty handoffs of information? Why is there so much waiting

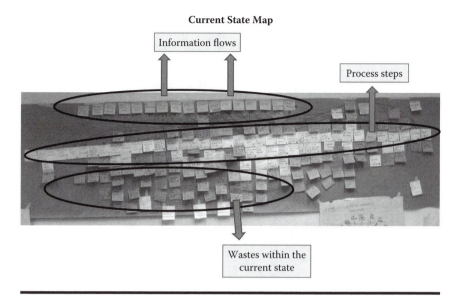

Figure 2.10 Sample current state map.

Table 2.4 Data Captured for Tasks

Measurement	Definition
Step name	Document the name of the task
Begins with	Document what specifically initiates the activity
Ends with	Document what specifically ends the activity
Task lead time	The calendar (clock) time from the beginning of the task to the end of the task
Manual touch time	The actual hands-on time for completing this task (includes walking, writing, talking on the phone, and doing the task)
Items in queue	Document how many identical tasks are sitting in the in-box for this task at this specific time
Process quality (%)	Document the percentage of the time you can complete this task without having to check, clarify, or repeat the activity

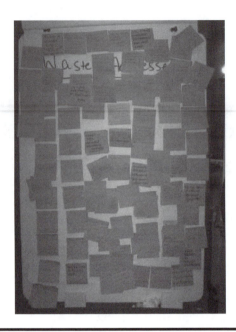

Figure 2.11 Example of wastes identified in the current state.

Table 2.5 Data Summary

Measure	Value
Number of steps	174
Value-added steps	11
Nonvalue-added steps	163
Value-added percentage	6.3%
Lead time	845 min
Manual touch time	72 min
Number of handoffs	46
Items in queue	385
Process quality percentage	.000494%
Demand/volume	21,239

between steps? Why is the reliability of the process so low? Remember, however you see your process, the summary of the current state is what your customer actually experiences.

9. Develop a future state process using the Lean improvement principles of Flow, Pull, Defect Free, and Visual Management (Figure 2.12).

10. Perform a gap analysis between the current state and future state to identify the specific projects needed to realize the future state.

11. Prioritize the projects identified in the gap analysis based on an assessment of their impact to goals and effort to implement (Figure 2.13).

12. Sequence the improvements on a timeline (Figure 2.14).

13. Document the improvement plan in detail by completing the reason for improvement, the current conditions, the target conditions, the measures you are trying to move, and the appropriate team to resolve the problem. Normally this activity is accomplished using an A-3 form that will be discussed a bit later in this chapter.

The key deliverables from the value stream mapping and analysis activity are the future state vision and the detailed improvement plan as well as the measures of success.

The future state map creates the vision for the team that reveals what the new process will look like across the entire value stream. The detailed action plan lists the specific projects that will be completed in order to transform the value stream. By transform, I mean move from the current state to the future state. These projects include "kaizen activity," "projects," and "quick wins" that will create flow and pull, eliminate defects, and enable visual management of

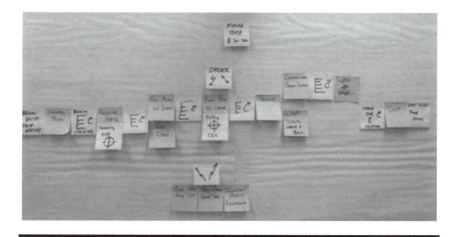

Figure 2.12 Sample of future state map.

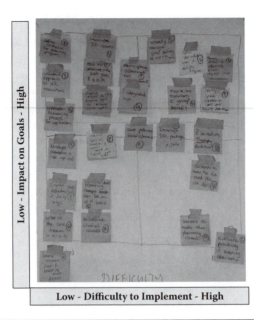

Figure 2.13   Prioritizing the projects.

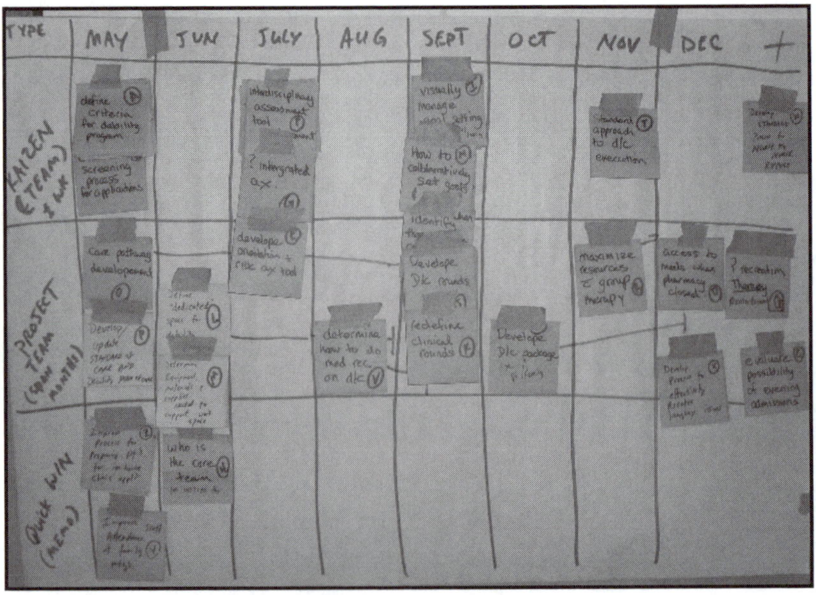

Figure 2.14   Sequence of improvement.

the entire value stream. It is important to note that nothing is changed as a result of the value stream analysis. However, let's refer back to W. Edwards Deming's words of wisdom from the beginning of the chapter. Now that you know what to do, you can do your best.

A value stream mapping and analysis event typically requires a cross-functional team of twelve to fifteen members. It is important that both line staff and management participate in the session. If the focus is clinical, it is mandatory to have physician input as well. The activity can take between two to five full days, depending on the scope of the value stream; in healthcare, two and a half to three days is typically what is required. I recommend that you run the session in consecutive days. When the session runs consecutively, the team maintains continuity, which in turn delivers a better end product. Additionally, the activities build on one another, so running the days consecutively improves linkage from one activity to the next, making the process easier for the team. One important lesson learned is that your improvement team must go through the process of creating their own "current state." Efforts to complete a value stream analysis with a previously completed current state map results in low team buy-in and limits the success of the activity.

Lean Tools

Deploying your improvement activities will require Lean tools. There are well over 200 discrete Lean tools. Some are designed to identify waste and others to eliminate waste. A small sample of some of the more common tools is shown in Table 2.6.

The definitions of these tools are listed in the glossary of terms in the back of the book. Over time, it is expected that the Lean leader has a working knowledge of many of these tools. If you are just getting started, I would recommend that the Lean leader focus on the common tools for seeing and eliminating waste, then the tools for visual management, followed by the tools for developing people, and finally the tools for quality improvement.

To excel in the deployment of Lean and to meet your targets identified as the true north measures, there are two other approaches worthy of further discussion. The first tool is A-3 thinking. Almost all improvement approaches follow what's called the "scientific method"; something you are probably familiar with from ninth grade biology. In healthcare, clinical trials and evidence-based practice are based on the scientific method, which involves developing a hypothesis, testing the hypothesis, and drawing conclusions. Improvement thus becomes an experiment in which new approaches are tested to determine if a measureable impact can be made as a result of the new approach.

Table 2.6   Lean Tools

Common Tools to See and Eliminate Waste	Supply Chain Tools	Project Management Tools	New Product/ Process Introduction Tools	Visual Management Tools	Quality Tools	Tools for Developing People
Takt Time	Takt Time	A-3 Thinking	Obeya (The big room)	5S	FMEA	5 Whys
Direct (time) Observation	Kanban	Vertical Gantt Chart	Production Preparation Process (3P)	Performance Boards	Fishbone Diagram	Leadership Standard Work
Loading Diagram	Supermarkets	Freeze Points	Production Preparation (2P)	Production (Process) Control Boards	5 Whys	Gemba Walking
Spaghetti Mapping	ABC Analysis	Toll Gate Reviews	Vertical Gantt Chart	Pull Signals	7 Quality Tools	Skills/ Competency Matrix

Circle Diagram	Standard Work	Standard Work	Voice of the Customer	Skills/ Competency Matrix	PDCA – Shewart Cycle	Kaizen Training (Kaizen event)
Flow Diagram	Order/Due In Board	X	Quality Function Deployment	Heijunka Box (Leveling system)	Poke Yoke	X
Value-added/ Nonvalue-added Analysis	Inventory Reduction Kaizen	X	Design of Experiments	Andon	Andon	X
Standard Work	X	X	Process at a Glance (7 Flows)	X	Variation Reduction Kaizen	X
Production (process) control	X	X	X	X	A4 Problem Solving	X

Lean organizations use A-3 thinking as a tool used to implement the scientific method. Using A-3 thinking ensures consistency in the problem-solving approach. Consistency not only leads to more repeatable and better outcomes, but also will shorten the learning curve for your organization.

The scientific method can be used at the strategic planning level and at the tactical problem-solving level. The A-3 reader should be able to understand the content very quickly. Great care should be taken to distill the essential elements of the thinking and activities. In the modern era, digital photographs and charts can be easily inserted to paint the picture graphically. The A-3 was designed to tell the entire story on a single sheet of paper. The common paper size for this story is using 11 × 17-inch paper, which is commonly known (as you might have guessed) as A-3 paper. As mentioned above, the A-3 can be used for several different purposes, but the key uses include the following:

■ Documentation of strategy
■ Problem solving/Improvement in the course of work
■ Communication of problem solving/improvement activities (status)
■ Approval/justification of resources (business case)

Try not to get hung up on the form. I *hated* the form when it was first introduced. I thought it was nothing more than another bureaucratic exercise for management. Over time, I came to value the thinking and the clarity the A-3 form provided. I now view it as an indispensible tool in developing strategic plans and in making improvement. The A-3 form for strategic planning is shown in Figure 2.15. The key features of this A-3 include

■ Ensuring an understanding of the previous year before planning the next year.
■ All of the thinking is contained to a single page.
■ Actions plans are built into the strategy helping with execution.
■ Gaps in strategy are quantifiable and measured so success can be evaluated.

The A-3 form and corresponding thinking used for problem solving looks a bit different. An example of the problem-solving A-3 form is depicted in Figure 2.16. The problem-solving A-3 walks the user through each of the steps in the scientific method. Following A-3 thinking, steps ensure problems and their root cause(s) are identified before developing solutions.

Kaizen

The second tool of mention is one designed to deliver some real results while simultaneously changing the culture of your organization, and is an approach known as the kaizen event. The kaizen event also can be known as practical

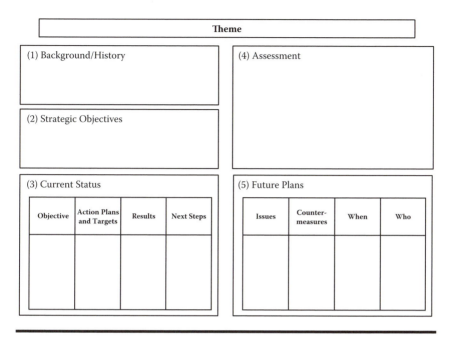

Figure 2.15 Strategic planning A-3.

kaizen training, kaizen blitz, rapid improvement event, rapid cycle improvement, or kaizen workshop. All of these are based on the same principles.

A kaizen event follows A-3 thinking to improve part of a value stream, and typically involves six to ten team members. A typical kaizen event takes between two and five days to complete, depending on the scope of the problem you are trying to solve. It doesn't matter how much time it takes; what matters is that **all** of the A-3 thinking must be completed with the correct level of detail, discipline, and integrity. The standard agenda for a kaizen event is listed in Table 2.7.

The kaizen event actually begins several weeks prior to the actual improvement week. First, measures and targets are selected, and then baseline data are collected on these measures. Next, appropriate team members are selected to participate on the improvement team. Finally, support logistics and supplies are prepared to ensure that the team can operate with minimal barriers. Preparation meetings should be held prior to the event to ensure accuracy, and clarity, of the event requirements.

Following the week of the actual kaizen event, there is an intense "sustaining period." During this time period, all of the affected team members are trained to the new standard work. Visual management systems are monitored on an hourly basis to ensure that the new standard is being followed, the correct results are

A-3 Theme:	Date:		Revision #:
Team Members:			
Reason For Improvement: •			

Current Performance and Reflections on Current Performance: •	Target Performance: •

Dimension	Measure	Current	Target
Morale/HD			
Quality			
Delivery/Access			
Cost/Productivity			

Anticipated Hard Savings:

Anticipated Soft Savings:

Gap Analysis:

Waste Theme	Root Cause

Figure 2.16   Problem solving A-3.

delivered, and that no unintended consequences are uncovered. New problems that arise are solved immediately and communicated to the team. The first week following a kaizen event is a bit like starting a diet. It is hard at first and the results don't come quickly enough. There is a strong urge to "go back to the way we were doing it before." This must not be allowed. After thirty days of

Countermeasures and Action Plans:

Waste Theme	Root Cause	Countermeasure	Expected Result

Follow Up Plans:

What	Who	When

Measurement Tracking:

Dimension	Measure	Current	Target	Week 1	Week 2	Week 3	Week 4	Week 5	Week 6	Week 7	Week 8
Morale/HD											
Quality											
Delivery/Access											
Cost/Productivity											

Verified Hard Savings:

Verified Soft Savings:

Reflections:

Figure 2.16 (*Continued*)

sustainment of a properly designed kaizen effort, the results will speak for themselves and you will not be able to, nor choose to go back to the old way.

The key benefits of kaizen include the following:

1. Identification of the correct team members to solve a problem
2. Selection of focused key improvement measures

Table 2.7   Kaizen Event Daily Agenda

Day 1 Define Current Conditions (See Waste)	Day 2 Develop Solutions (Eliminate Waste)	Day 3 Implement/Test Solutions	Day 4 Document New Standard Work
• Team training • Review measures and targets • Use appropriate tools to see waste • Gather time observation data and observe waste • Generate 50 to 100 forms of waste	• Affinitize and prioritize wastes • Develop countermeasures and action plans to eliminate waste • Use Lean principles to design a new work flow • Begin testing of countermeasures	• Implement countermeasures • Train team members on new process • Verify effectiveness of solutions by measuring • Problem solve in real time	• Finalize standard work • Finalize visual management systems • Document standard work • Document event results • Deliver presentation • Recognize team

3. Removal of organizational barriers to enable the team to make rapid change
4. Ability of the team to move quickly through the team cycles of forming, storming, norming, and performing as a result of the kaizen event structure
5. Compression of the timeline to see results
6. Transfer of improvement knowledge as team members learn to see and eliminate waste by doing
7. Improvement based on the more strategic value stream plan, thus eliminating the spot improvement phenomenon

As we conclude this section, I'd like to emphasize the importance of kaizen activity. In all my years of studying Lean improvement, I have never seen an organization transform without doing kaizen activity. Of course, there are many approaches to improvement, and project-based approaches can and do generate amazing results as well. But if you want to change your culture to become one where everyone has the ability to see and eliminate waste, you must routinely practice kaizen. I have never seen organizations succeed (successfully transform their culture) otherwise.

Step 6: Monthly Review

If your organization is like most organizations, you will not always be hitting your improvement targets. This is particularly true if you are going through your first cycle of hoshin kanri. The step within hoshin kanri that manages the process of hitting the targets, as well as the results, is the monthly review. This monthly review is a formal process where each hoshin is reviewed. The difference between a monthly review and an operational review is that the process is viewed as even more important than the result. During the monthly review, each improvement priority is discussed along with the trended measures. The purpose of the review is to determine the degree to which the targets are being met, to verify that the results are sustainable, to understand the sources of bad results, to review the process of achieving the results, and defining if the improvement is adequate.

The level 1 policy deployment review is typically an eight-hour meeting. A typical agenda for this meeting would include the topics seen in Figure 2.17.

This review will happen at each of the layers of the improvement priorities. The reviews begin at the department/unit levels, and then cascade up to the program level, concluding with the review of the top-level improvement priorities at the senior team level. (Note: The lower level policy deployment reviews do not usually take the full eight hours.)

One of the great features of the policy deployment review process is the accountability inherent in the review. For *each* target that is missed,

**Monthly Policy Deployment
Review Agenda (8 Hour Meeting)**

Agenda Item	Percentage of Agenda Time
Review Budget Performance	10%
Review Policy Deployment Actions, Results, and Countermeasures	65%
New Product/Service/Construction/ Development	10%
People/Organizational Issues	10%
Other	5%

Figure 2.17   Monthly policy deployment review agenda.

a countermeasure must be developed. A countermeasure is a data-based corrective action to get your plan back on track to meet the target. The countermeasure will follow one of two paths. The first path will involve some quantitative analysis and the critical few corrective actions to get you to the target. Alternatively, the countermeasure will involve changing your action plan because it is not working. **Never** is the target changed due to missing the number. Missing one year's target will require a makeup effort in the outlying years to achieve your strategic plan.

A countermeasure form is prepared for the monthly review meeting whenever a target has not been met. The countermeasure form has four sources of information: historical data showing the trended performance, a frequency chart showing why the target is being missed, a root cause analysis explaining the missed target, and the countermeasures (Figure 2.18).

When first starting the policy deployment process, many organizations frequently miss their targets. Personally, I gained a lot of experience in completing the countermeasure sheet in the first and second year. A helpful hint is that if you wait for electronic data to complete your countermeasure sheet, you will be in serious trouble at the review meeting. Your measurement systems must be capable of capturing relevant process and results data on a daily basis. Otherwise, you cannot implement any countermeasures in the time frame required to show improvement.

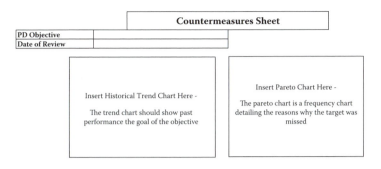

Figure 2.18   Countermeasure sheet.

Another common problem that many organizations have is that, a large portion of leaders simply fail to execute their action plans. In fact, this will be the biggest issue you will encounter when you first launch hoshin kanri. To avoid this, make sure everyone is accountable for their plans, the process of improving, and the results.

Having walked this road a few times before, I can offer a few helpful hints when conducting your policy deployment review. First, hold at least a monthly meeting for each policy deployment matrix. Second, validate that each countermeasure is fact-based; the countermeasure **must** be supported with data. I worked for a CEO in a previous job and she used to say that everyone is entitled to their own opinion, but not their own set of facts. Later in my career, when working with Danaher Corporation, I frequently heard: "In God we trust, everyone else bring data." Continuing with the countermeasure process, ensure that the countermeasures are specific with clear accountability and due dates (what, who, and when). Follow up in the next review meeting that the due dates were met. Problem-solving tools should be used to develop the root cause of the problem prior to developing a countermeasure; avoid jumping to a solution.

Finally, measure the targets frequently enough to provide adequate data for analysis. Monthly snapshots of data, including month end reporting, do **not** meet this requirement.

Step 7: Annual Review

As your complete your monthly reviews and work toward obtaining your target for the current year, at some point, the year will near completion. The final step in the hoshin kanri process is the annual review. The annual review consists of hansei (deep personal reflection). How did we do? For your areas of focus, document your performance and your team's performance in achieving the targets. This activity is commonly documented as shown in Figure 2.19.

In the annual review process, you also will want to evaluate the process of hoshin kanri. Most of this evaluation has nothing to do with results, but rather with the process. As a starting point, the areas seen in Table 2.8 can be reviewed.

Along with your annual review, you will be repeating steps 3 through 5 to prepare for the next year on your path to meeting your strategic objectives. Steps 3 to 5 encompass developing the next year's breakthrough objectives and top-level improvement priorities, deploying the improvement priorities using catchball, and implementing the improvement priorities using A-3 thinking and value stream management.

Annual Policy Deployment Review

Policy Deployment Objective	Review/Assessment
PD Objective 1	
PD Objective 2	
PD Objective 3	
PD Objective 4	
PD Objective 5	

= objective met

= objective not met, but performance improved
(shade in relative performance)

= performance was worse than baseline

Figure 2.19 Policy deployment objective review.

Table 2.8   Policy Deployment Process Review

Did I Follow the Policy Deployment (PD) Process?	Was the PD Process Effective?
Are the results sustainable or were they short term?	Did the results become incorporated into daily standard work?
Did the deployment of the targets get cascaded to the appropriate level?	Did the targets get deployed to the action plan level?
Did we appropriately use Lean tools to deliver results?	Were the monthly reviews effective?
Did we make the PD process a living and breathing tool or did we glance at it occasionally throughout the year?	Did the customer goal change during the year and did our PD targets change as a result?

Organizations new to hoshin kanri frequently want to change the targets when they realize that the targets are going to be very difficult to reach. As a guideline, you will *not* change your policy deployment targets during the year. However, there are some circumstances in which you might be well served to change your improvement activities and their corresponding targets. Circumstances might include completing your top-level improvement initiative(s) or a significant shift in the market caused by regulation, competition, or market conditions. If your top-level improvement priorities are completely ineffective, you also might change the priority midyear, but not the target.

Enablers of Hoshin Kanri

In order to meet your strategic objective, improvement must be made. The cornerstone to Lean improvement is standard work, daily management, and visual management. Masaki Imai, in his book *Kaizen*, describes in great detail the benefits and necessity of workplace standards.*

These include

1. Represent the best, easiest, and safest way to do a job
2. Offer the best way to preserve know-how and expertise
3. Provide a way to measure performance
4. Show the relationship between cause and effect

---

* Imai, M. 1997. *Gemba kaizen*. New York: McGraw-Hill, pp. 54–56.

5. Provide a basis for both maintenance and improvement
6. Provide objectives and indicate training goals
7. Provide a basis for training
8. Create a basis for preventing recurrence of errors and minimizing variability

Standard work is like a recipe. If we follow the recipe, then we create the ability to provide a consistent outcome. Let's use baking pies as an example. If we mix the right ingredients in the right order and in the right amounts and then bake at the correct temperature for the correct amount of time, we end up with pies that consistently look and taste great. In healthcare, the recipe is different, but the expectations are the same. If we follow the correct recipe for administering medication—following the correct order, for the correct dosage, for the right medicine, at the right time, delivered to the right patient—then we end up with favorable outcomes. The first favorable outcome is that the patient is safe, and the second is that the treatment will do what it is intended to do. The organization benefits as well because standard work provides an excellent training tool for new support staff and medical staff.

Now consider an alternative method for delivering medicine. Assume we do not have a consistent recipe for medicine administration. Different physicians and different nurses use different approaches to ensure that they are following the most current order. The safety systems in place to ensure that the right medicine is delivered to the right patient at the right time vary slightly. Some people may double check their steps, while others may take information at face value. Is it unrealistic to think that we will get different outcomes? Perhaps a dose is missed, or the dose is wrong since the orders were updated, but have not yet cycled through the system. In severe cases, we may even see an adverse drug event. Standard work ensures a consistent and repeatable outcome. This is the first step in creating improvement. Another marvelous advantage is that standard work is completed using the knowledge of those who will use it. This allows building of the treasure trove of developing a best practice and being able to share it with all performing the work.

In any work environment, we can define our recipe as the easiest, safest, and best known method of performing a task. In healthcare, many sources of evidence-based care are documented. There are many research organizations whose existence is based on developing standards for care. Some of the recipes are well known, such as how to administer CPR for example, or how to perform proper hand hygiene. However, thousands of standards do not exist in many organizations. What is the standard method for cleaning a patient's room? What is the standard work for OR turnover? And most importantly, if there is a standard, is it consistently followed? We need only to look at hand hygiene compliance to illustrate this point. Healthcare professionals are generally aware of the industry statistics on hand hygiene compliance. Clearly this is one area that can benefit from everyone consistently following the standard.

Standard work enables daily management systems to flourish. Effective daily management systems need to be in place as a prerequisite for strategy deployment. An effective daily management system governs routine, day-to-day activities. These activities have known and followed standards in place. Daily management systems usually, but not always, have limited cross-functional activity. Improvement within the daily management systems is typically incremental, and process and outcome measures are monitored; these measures are called key process indicators (KPI). Key process indicators are monitored and managed by exception. Small levels of improvement may be obtained, but action is typically taken against these measures only when an abnormal condition arises.

The major improvement work resulting from the top-level improvement priority deployment must be moved to daily management, thus ensuring the results are sustained (Figure 2.20).

The process used to monitor the daily management systems is known as visual management. This visual management system is the same one discussed in Chapter 1. There are many "things" a Lean organization will manage visually,

Daily Management Systems Are Needed to Sustain the Gains

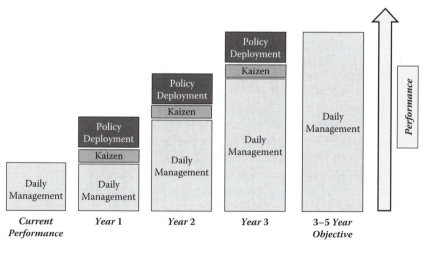

Figure 2.20 Moving the breakthroughs to daily management.

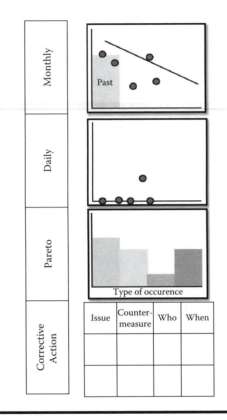

Figure 2.21   Four-chart visual management system for performance.

but at this point I want to discuss two key elements of visual management: management of process and results. An example of visual management used to monitor results is shown in Figure 2.21. These four charts are an example of a closed-loop system that allows "seeing normal from abnormal," in this case, x-ray production. The first chart illustrates the monthly targets for productivity. The second chart breaks the monthly target down into daily targets. The third chart captures sources of variation. When the targets are missed, the reason is documented in real time. The fourth chart shows the corrective action to be taken to allow the team to meet the target.

The visual management tool that feeds the data for the performance system is the process control board. Process control is used to manage process. This activity is much different than results. The Lean term for process control is *production control*. This board shows the plan versus actual performance for

X-Ray Process Control Board			Date: January 26, 2011
Hour	Plan	Actual	Comments
0700-0800	5	5	no issues
0800-0900	5	4	outpatient failed to show
0900-1000	5	5	no issues
1000-1100	5	3	couldn't find O/P req, and isolation clean held up room
1100-1200	5		
1200-1300	5		
1300-1400	5		
1400-1500	5		
1500-1600	5		
1600-1700	5		
1700-1800	5		
1800-1900	5		
1900-2000	5		
2000-2100	5		
2100-2200	5		
2200-2300	5		

Figure 2.22   Process control board for x-ray.

the daily schedule captured on an hour-by-hour or patient-by-patient basis. Sources of variation are documented in the comments section (Figure 2.22).

When the documented comments are placed into a histogram, or even better, a Pareto diagram, a great source of information is now provided. Because our goal is to create a culture of improvement, these data provide the prioritized information necessary for the next layer improvement. In the example shown in Figure 2.23, the largest source of variation is patients failing to show up to their appointment. This opportunity can now be studied to develop the root cause of this problem and then to develop countermeasures to resolve the cause(s). Verifying the effectiveness of the solutions should be easy to determine as well.

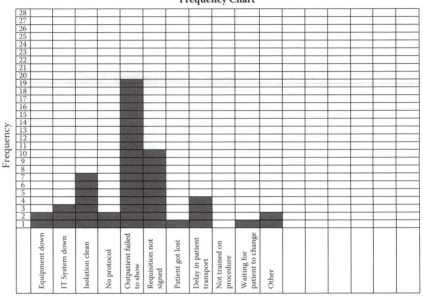

Figure 2.23   Pareto of sources of variation.

The data from the Pareto chart provides the baseline, and the future performance will show the impact of the solutions.

An organization that has developed a Lean strategy and then deployed this strategy through the organization using hoshin kanri will see results when the improvements have made their way into daily management. Results will be managed visually through the performance board, and the process will be managed visually through the process control board.

World-Class Targets for Improvement

When I first was introduced to Lean, there were no fancy PowerPoint® presentations. Training was delivered through handouts or, if you were lucky, through slides viewed on an overhead projector. In my very first indoctrination to Lean, I was shown a slide about what world-class performance looked like, as depicted in Table 2.9.

I learned two things from this slide. First, benchmarking against competitors or your industry is not a useful activity. You are performing how you are performing. Said differently, your jump off point is where you are right now,

Table 2.9   World-Class Rates of Improvement

• 1–2% per month productivity improvement
• 2–4% per month improvement in inventory turns
• 25–50% year over year reduction in cost of quality
• 99%+ fill rate to true customer demand
• Lead time in hours/days versus weeks and months

Source: J. D. McCormick Associates, Inc.

regardless of how everyone else is performing. Secondly, what I needed to be interested in is the world-class rates of improvement. I was told by my sensei that if you try and improve faster than the world-class rates of improvement, then you will have a hard time sustaining your improvements. This was clearly great news. No need to worry about a stretch target that couldn't be obtained. The journey on cloud nine lasted about fifteen seconds, as I was exposed to the world-class rates of improvement shown in Table 2.9.

I was used to getting a 2–3% productivity improvement a year. World-class organizations improve productivity by 25% year over year. Imagine your cash flow if you can get improved inventory turns from your pharmaceutical, therapeutic, and operating supplies. Envision your organization with wait times and access to services slashed in half or better. Imagine the high quality of care provided when adverse events are reduced by 50 to 60%.

Now is the point where you might be thinking, I can't get my organization, program, or unit to that level of performance. There are too many barriers, both internal and external, to my area of responsibility. And you might be right. I admit, I thought I was a pretty decent Lean leader, and I never got to world-class levels of performance within my organization(s). But, you might be missing the point. What if you could get to 25% of the rate of improvement of a world-class organization? What if you could get to 10% of that place? I can ensure you, that even at the 10% year over year improvement rate, you would be thrilled with the quality, access, and cost performance of your organization. Table 2.10 is a sample of the results delivered by some Lean organizations.

The bar to get to being world class is very high. Even the examples above, with their double-digit gain in performance, did not get to world-class rates of improvement. Not everyone achieves world-class status, but every organization that gets the focus and attention from senior management has seen dramatic increases in performance and culture.

Table 2.10 Sample of Results from Lean Improvement

Medicine Patient Flow	• Reduced acute length of stay by 15% across all programs • Reduced discharge-planning resources by 17% by creating a new patient navigator role which combined discharge planning, clinical coordination, and resource utilization functions (reduction of 5 FTE)
Emergency Services Patient Flow	• Reduced average emergency department length-of-stay from 3.1 hours to 2.1 hours per patient for lower acuity patients with 9% higher patient volumes (32% reduction) • Reduced average emergency department length-of-stay from 5.1 hours to 3.3 hours for nonadmitted medium acuity patients (35% reduction) • Reduced the left-without-being-seen percentage from 6.1% to 0.78% (allowing ~2,000 more patients to be seen each year)
Outpatient Rehabilitation Services	• Increase in number of clients seen per clinician per day from 8 to 12 (50% increase) • Increase in patient satisfaction (overall rating of care) from 90 to 96 (7% improvement) • Reduction in time from approval to initial visit from 12.3 days to 4 (67% reduction)
Physician Lead Clinic Flow	• Lead time reduced for medical record preparation from 2 weeks to 2–3 days (75% reduction) • Patient total visit time reduced from 80–90 minutes to 40 minutes (50% reduction) • Provider capacity increased by 3 patients per day • Provider work day decreased from an 11-hour day to an 8-hour day with transcription, e-mail, and voice mails completed by the end of each day (27% reduction)

Table 2.10 (*Continued*)   Sample of Results from Lean Improvement

Diagnostic Imaging	• Reduced MRI Pt LOS by 24% while reducing staff MCT by 42%
	• Increased a 2 x-ray unit capacity by over 100% negating the need for 2 techs and an additional machine
	• Value stream improvement in MRI resulted in a 18% increase in daily throughput with 25% less technologist manpower yielding annualized savings of $100K
	• Optimized imaging schedule utilization with a net result of additional 15% capacity
Mental Health Services Outpatient Referral Processing	• Rejected referrals received per month reduced from 47 per month to 23 per month (50% reduction)
	• Reduced the referral processing time from 30 days to 6 days (80% reduction)
	• Reduced the cost of travel in support of referral process by $800/month (20% reduction)
Peri-Operative Services	• Reduced the cost per case from $1,290 to $1,150 over 9 months during value stream improvement (10.8% reduction)
	• Reduced overall budget variance by a favorable 14%
	• Increased same day surgical volume by 10%

Summary: Key Points from Chapter 2

■ To make improvement meaningful, it must be linked to your organizational strategy.

■ Creating a culture of improvement involves developing and deploying a Lean strategy. This process consists of two main steps:
- Effectively using a "strategy" deployment process
- Sustaining the improvements with effective daily management systems managed visually

■ Hoshin kanri is a system used to manage enterprise change of the core business objectives. This approach provides a roadmap for planning, implementing, and reviewing managed change.

■ There are seven steps to hoshin kanri:
- Establish the organizational vision
- Develop the three- to five-year breakthrough objectives

- Develop the annual breakthrough objectives and top-level improvement priorities
- Deploy the improvement priorities
- Implement the improvement priorities
- Conduct a monthly review of the results and process to get the results
- Conduct an annual review of the process

■ Implement your strategy using value stream improvement plans, Lean techniques, and A-3 thinking.

■ Effective daily management systems are a prerequisite of hoshin kanri.

■ Daily management systems are managed visually.

■ Try to get your organization to focus on the world-class rates of improvement. This focus will help eliminate complacency when you are leading your peer group in performance.

Chapter 3

Leading Change— The Transformation Roadmap—Phase 1: "Get Ready"

Do not follow where the path may lead. Go instead where there is no path and leave a trail.

Ralph Waldo Emerson

Beginning the Journey

The content covered in Chapter 2, developing and deploying your Lean strategy, might seem a bit ambitious, or even overwhelming, depending on where you are in your improvement journey. For those of you who are just starting out to becoming a world-class healthcare enterprise, great lessons can be learned from the organizations that have gone before you. Keep in mind that the road to Lean transformation is now over sixty years old. Organizations large and small, public and private, union and nonunion have "left a trail" to follow.

A word of caution as you begin this journey: The road to enterprise-wide transformation is *very* long and will take ten to twenty years to complete.

Transformation is not a three-year plan. It is not a project nor is it a toolkit. Transformation is a process where the culture slowly and consistently changes, one team at a time, one unit/department at a time, one program at a time, and one system at a time. There is no silver bullet and there is no "easy button." In my nearly thirty years of experience working in either operations or in consulting, I never once met a management team that would be honest about this fact. Most organizations set out to "transform" in two years, with three years at the high end of their timeline. This is not a realistic target and you will do yourselves well to not make bold claims of transformation to the staff or to the board in this narrow period of time.

One must always remember that the Lean enterprise transformation has only one goal—the pursuit of perfection. Even Toyota is still striving for "perfection" and they have been competently working their Lean enterprise transformation for over sixty years. Organizations that are successful in their transformations have radically improved measures and metrics that were targeted and have improved safety and quality in leaps and bounds. But, the true Lean organization continues seeking improvement, forever. It is a way of life, not a trend. When in the fifth or sixth year of a transformation, one never hears "we need to fix this." Rather you will hear "we need to Lean this." You will not be the same organization or individual.

Implying that transformation is a long process, however, does not imply that you should have to wait a long time for results. A properly trained team with the right measures and the right improvement process can generate local improvements in a week. Recall the discussions on the world-class rates of improvement; performance is what is possible, but not with your current improvement infrastructure, organizational structure, improvement focus, improvement process, and management practices. Each of these will change over time. Fortunately, you will not need to change all of these at once.

There are three phases to transformation. The first phase is the "get ready" phase. In this phase, you will need to establish the basic infrastructure to begin improvement. While you do not need a massive infrastructure to begin creating a culture of improvement, you also cannot start with nothing. I will explain the roles in the improvement process that need to be filled as well as define a few tasks that will help you to prepare your organization for change and manage the issues that will arise as you begin your improvement journey.

The second phase is the "acceleration" phase. In this phase, you will identify where to begin your improvements, deliver on your operational improvements, sustain those improvements, and then spread those improvements across your organization. It would be helpful to refer back to Chapter 2 where it was discussed in detail how to link your improvement initiatives to your strategy. For those of you that are just getting started, I will offer an approach that utilizes

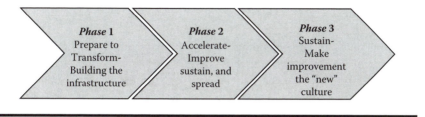

Figure 3.1 Three phases of transformation.

a blend of objective and subjective tools to identify a few key "value streams" to help you get started on improving quickly. An explanation on delivering, sustaining, and spreading improvement will follow. A special emphasis will be placed on sustainability because this is where all organizations struggle and some even fail. An organization's commitment to the Lean process and Lean thinking becomes transparent in this phase.

The third phase is the "sustain" phase. In this phase, I will discuss how to anchor the changes into the organizational culture. Through these activities, you will establish and cement your "new" culture. The focus will initially be on capacity building and using this capacity effectively. Explanations of taking your improvement approaches to support areas, business systems, and even outside your four walls follows. It is in this phase where you challenge yourself to include all areas of the organization both clinical and administrative (Figure 3.1).

In this chapter, I discuss the "get ready" phase of transformation.

Phase I: Preparing to Transform (Get Ready)— Building the Infrastructure

I am often asked if an organization is ready to take on a cultural transformation. Is there some type of readiness assessment that can be taken to determine if a cultural transformation is right for the organization? I can answer this in the most simple of terms. When the pain of change is less than the pain of staying the same, your organization is ready for a cultural transformation. It is that simple. No one organization is better prepared than another to take on change. The factor that makes the difference between success and failure is having the will to not fail. Notice, I specifically did not say the will to succeed. Lou Holtz, a retired Hall of Fame college football coach, now turned college football analyst, was once giving a motivational speech. He was talking about the difference between winning and losing in college athletics. There is a famous saying about winning, implying that "the team that wants to win 'more' finds a way to win the game." Holtz said that this statement is dead wrong. Everyone wants to win. However, winning teams hate to lose and do all the little things it takes not to lose. This includes game planning, preparing, practicing the right way, conditioning, etc. The team that wins the game is the team that refuses to lose.

My readiness assessment consists of having the senior leadership team answer a single question: "Are you prepared to do what it takes *not* to fail in your transformational efforts?" If you can answer "yes" to this single question, then your organization is ready. It will not matter about your size, infrastructure, funding model, level of capitalization, patient population, public or private, union or nonunion, etc. Having the will not to fail is the single readiness assessment question you will ever need to answer.

Once you have firmly decided to move ahead, there are some steps you can take to prepare your organization for success. Such steps include identifying your champion, finding a coach, preparing your infrastructure, deciding on a governance model, and training your team. While this list might not be exhaustive, the steps taken to prepare your organization to transform include

1. Select your change agent
2. Get informed
3. Get help
4. Establish a steering committee
5. Train your internal experts
6. Develop and deploy a communication campaign

Let's review each of these steps and provide an explanation of these terms in more detail.

Selecting Your Change Agent

Of all the steps in preparing your organization for change, perhaps none may be more important than selecting the right change agent. The change agent is the person, internal to your organization, who will lead the transformational efforts. This person will orchestrate and guide the transformation efforts of your organization. Not just anyone can do this work; there is a special skill set required to lead a major cultural transformation. The three requirements of a change agent include

1. Commanding the respect of the organization, both front line and management
2. Ability to navigate around and through cultural and organizational barriers
3. Ability to manage a room

The change agent will need to energize large groups of diverse people with different interests, talents, and goals toward a common vision. This is not likely delegated to a junior person or a new hire within the organization. The best change agent is a senior, executive-level position with a proven track record of results. This person will need to be trusted because your organization will be going to a place it has never been before. All of the answers will not be known, the risks will not be identified, and the outcomes are not guaranteed. Conversely, the organization will need to identify a person it trusts to lead the transformation. Steven Covey, a famous author of several books on leadership and management, wrote, "The first job of any leader is to inspire trust. Trust is confidence born of two dimensions: character and competence. Character includes your integrity, motive, and intent with people. Competence includes your capabilities, skills, results, and track record. Both dimensions are vital."[*]

The change agent also needs the political clout or savvy to navigate around or through organizational barriers. In many cases, this means seriously challenging the status quo and dismantling the bureaucracy that prevents real change. Every organization, including yours, is perfectly designed to achieve the results it delivers. So, if you want to change your results, you will need to change your organization. Waiting three weeks for a purchase order to be placed, sitting in the queue for two weeks for your maintenance work order to be processed, completing a five-page document for an information technology (IT) change request, and waiting six months to get a form through your forms committee are all symptoms of a sluggish bureaucracy, not an organization that will enable rapid change of performance and culture. The change agent must navigate these wickets in order for the teams to make change rapidly and effectively using A-3 thinking and Lean principles.

Are you going to make some people angry while you jump the bureaucracy queue, expediting the change processes needed to transform your organization? Count on it. A phrase that comes to mind that may not be politically correct, but is accurate: "shine the Lean flashlight on the process and the cockroaches will run for darkness." This is why I encourage organizations to have a senior executive in the change agent role. In the majority of the organizations delivering world-class rates of improvement, the change agent was the CEO. In none of these cases was the change agent a project manager or a midlevel manager. Not that these roles are not important, or that these change agents were not skilled individuals, but these roles simply do not carry enough organizational horsepower to bust through the barriers needed to transform an organization.

---

[*] Covey, S. 2009. *How the best leaders build trust.* Online at: http://www.leadershipnow.com/CoveyOnTrust.html

Improvement in performance and change in culture comes from breaking down the functional silos of the organization and enabling information and value to be delivered seamlessly across the organization. Turf protecting behaviors that discourage or prevent collaboration at the expense of a departmental budget, or foster a "that's the way we do it here" mentality have got to be eliminated.

Questions that you must begin to ask yourself at the outset of transforming your organization include

- Do the human resource policies support a rapidly changing organization?
- Are the payroll and scheduling systems enabling change and reducing waste in the system, or are these processes squelching creativity and sapping time from the manager that could be spent on improvement?
- Do the fiscal policies and activities provide meaningful managerial data and analysis needed for improvement, or are you stuck in the 1950s, spending all of your time providing GAAP (generally accepted accountability principle) reports that satisfy the financial reporting requirements, but deliver little valuable data to improve the business?

Improvement also comes from changing the way an organization responds to change. One real-life example I have encountered on more than one occasion is the change cycle associated with updating a form or a computer screen. Let's assume one of the kaizen teams has developed a new way to document the initial inpatient nurse assessment. This new approach requires half the effort, yields better results, and takes half the time. I have seen this great idea languish for six months or more waiting to get approved by the forms committee. The change agent needs to be prepared to take on this challenge and likely several others. Processes that can stifle change include small capital approval requests, small expense requests that take a week or more to get through purchasing, and small IT changes that demand a requirements document that takes longer to complete than the programming change. Although I'm not advocating that we eliminate all the controls that are in place to manage risk and help prioritize the organizational needs, the teams need to be supported with a "fast track" approach that usually is driven by the senior-level change agent. The change agent has to be prepared to take on all the "sacred cows," or "white elephants," or any other name you choose to call these barriers, to enable improvement of performance and culture. This might be the single, most important requirement of the change agent. With this attribute, great myths can be eliminated, but only if the organization is willing to support the change agent.

The third requirement of being a successful change agent is the ability to carry a room. What do I mean by the ability to carry a room? This is the skill of inspiring and engaging others in a team or group setting. Great change agents exude confidence and charisma. They are skilled in public speaking and great communicators. You will be taking your organization on a new journey, one that no one, likely, has been on before. It will require a high level of targeted communication to inspire people to follow you through this change and to let them know that the "other side" will be better for the patients, their families, the staff, the organization, the board, and the surrounding community.

I have personally witnessed some change agents that were very well respected in the organization and had the ability to navigate the organizational barriers, but lacked the group communication skills needed to inspire the team to put in the effort to change. In the end, the change agent was unable to create the mass momentum necessary to transform the organization. This is why the "ability to carry a room" has been added to the list of requirements desired in a change agent. Much of the success of the change agent is that their leadership style is such that people will follow on faith. This is not a universal attribute of all in leadership positions, so choose carefully.

Get Informed

Once you have selected your change agent, you need to get informed. In other words, you need to have your leadership team gain some knowledge about Lean—Lean in healthcare, and enterprise-wide Lean transformation. At this stage in your improvement journey, you are not required to be an expert on Lean tools, applications, and techniques, but you do need to understand, at a minimum, what is required to transform your organization, what resources are required, and what behaviors are needed from the senior leadership team to enable your cultural transformation to be successful.

There are many ways to get informed on Lean healthcare. Table 3.1 lists a few of these approaches and the advantages and disadvantages of these approaches.

If you are just getting started, my recommendation on where to begin would be to pursue all of these options, preferably in the same sequence as I have listed the alternatives. Begin with some reading. You can research a specific area, like perioperative services, or you can choose enterprise-wide transformation. There are hundreds of thousands of webpages and blogs that support Lean healthcare and hundreds of books. "The Resource" for Lean healthcare literature is Productivity Press, part of the Taylor & Francis Group. Their catalog of books can be found at www.productivitypress.com. Productivity Press has a series of books on healthcare management and leadership and a series of books on healthcare process improvement. In fact, my first book, *Taking Improvement from the Assembly Line to Healthcare* (CRC Press, 2011), can be found at this site. The plethora of books is an indicator that the Lean improvement process, while not easy, is a proven methodology for delivering real results and is not a "flavor of the month."

Table 3.1 Getting Informed

Approach	Advantages	Disadvantages
Read Internet articles	• Lowest cost • Can be targeted to your area of concern • Instantaneous access	• No ability to ask questions/not interactive
Read books/white papers	• Lower cost than remaining alternatives • Many reviews available to assist in your selection • More comprehensive than Internet articles • e-Book options are now available	• No ability to ask questions/not interactive • Multiple copies might be needed
Attend a Lean conference or Lean training	• Many options are available with various length, pricing, and topics • Ability to interact with presenters and attendees • Conferences are available in regional, national, and international forums • Training topics can be held onsite or offsite • Topics can be tailored to directly meet your organization's needs	• May require travel • Conference fees can be pricey • Cannot always validate the content of the presentations or the break-out activities • Lean healthcare conferences are improving, but the best Lean conferences currently are not exclusive to healthcare and provide Lean examples from a wide variety of industries • Training will likely require some type of fee payment

Visit another Lean organization	• Ability to see what a Lean organization looks like • Ability to ask questions and get real time feedback • Can target specific areas or choose an organization that is undergoing organizational wide transformation • Allows you to see visual management systems in action	• Some organizations charge a fee for this service • Likely will require travel and living expenses • Numbers of people you can send might be limited • May not get to see the specific area you are interested in seeing
Participate on another organization's improvement team	• Provides the opportunity to learn Lean with hands-on approaches • Ability to interact with others and ask questions and receive feedback • Limits distractions because you will likely be offsite • Limits risk because you will be working on someone else's project	• Requires a time investment of three to five days depending on the improvement activity • Likely will require travel and living expenses • Might not be able to participate on a team with the same focus as your organization

Read a common article or book as a team and hold a group review. What did you learn? What are the keys to success? What are the common mistakes organizations make? How did others get started, accelerate their change, and then sustain? Reflecting on such questions as these will help to build Lean knowledge.

Next, I would encourage the leadership team to attend a few Lean conferences. There are many to pick from and they all have something to offer. I personally prefer the conferences with break-out sessions because you can get detailed information on the topics of your choosing. At the time of this writing, I can recommend the following annual international conferences for their Lean expertise and knowledge sharing:

- The Shingo Prize International Conference
- AME Excellence Inside Conference
- ASQ World Conference on Quality and Improvement
- IHI Annual National Forum on Quality Improvement in Healthcare
- LEI Lean Healthcare Transformation Summit

There are dozens of other national, regional, and local conferences and training workshops held each year. Conferences are a great way to network and speak with others pursuing excellence. Remember, you are not the first organization to pursue enterprise-wide transformation, and you can learn a lot from others' experiences.

Training workshops are another way to get informed. There are a wide variety of public workshops held regionally and nationally each year. If you want to get the best experience, however, I encourage you to bring some training into your own organization. Holding the training onsite leverages your training dollars because you can have many people attend simultaneously with no travel expenses. Host a one-day Lean leadership workshop and have the following questions answered:

1. What is Lean?
2. How do you see waste?
3. How do you eliminate waste?
4. How do you get started in deploying a culture of continuous improvement?
5. What are the leadership behaviors necessary to drive change?
6. What are the key risks and how do you mitigate these risks?

If you can get a simulation included in this one-day workshop, even better. There is no better way to learn improvement than attending "dirty hands" university. Remember, we learn best by doing. Getting these questions answered will enable your organization to answer the readiness question: "Are we prepared not to fail?"

Following some research and education through reading, conferences, and training, visiting another Lean organization would be a great next step. There are hundreds of organizations deploying Lean improvement both within healthcare and outside of healthcare, although not all organizations are as successful as others with their efforts. The greatest Lean organizations in the world are not in healthcare, but rather in the manufacturing sector. However, that doesn't mean you cannot learn a whole lot from a "manufacturer." I would encourage you to conduct a little research on who has won The Shingo Prize, an award given to those organizations that deliver Lean excellence. The list of award winners can be found at www.theshingoprize/shingo-recipients.html. A tour of one of these organizations will show you what the pursuit of excellence in performance and culture looks like.

If you are committed to seeing excellence in Lean healthcare, then you should familiarize yourself with two organizations that have a lot to offer. ThedaCare, a ~6,100-employee community health system with five hospitals and numerous clinics, is headquartered in Appleton, Wisconsin.* Their body of Lean work is extensive and impressive. ThedaCare supports tours through the ThedaCare Center for Healthcare Value. Tour policies can be reviewed at http://www.createvalue.org/delivery/education/ceo-site-vists/.

Another organization with cutting edge Lean experience and results is the Virginia Mason Health System in Seattle, Washington, a nonprofit healthcare organization with 400 physicians and ~5,200 staff.† Virginia Mason delivers world-class rates of improvement through their Virginia Mason Production System. Training and facility tour information can be reviewed through the Virginia Mason Institute at www.virginiamasoninstitute.org. Anyone who has doubts of the value of Lean as a management system to create a culture of improvement will have fewer, after discussing improvement with either of these two organizations. There are many other great Lean healthcare organizations to visit. You would likely encounter several of these organizations at one of the Lean conferences recommended above.

The final recommendation on getting informed would be to participate on another organization's improvement team. In the spirit of scholarship, most all Lean healthcare organizations are happy to support outside team members. There are many things to be learned from being on an improvement team. Some of the key takeaways would include

- How did the team get selected and organized?
- How were the targets selected? Were the measures applicable to the organization?

* Online at: http://www.thedacare.org/About-Us.aspx
† Online at: https:www.virginiamason.org/workfiles/pdfdocs/press/

■ How was rapid change enabled in support of the team?
■ What was leadership's role in the change?
■ Did the change agent "own the room?"
■ What tools were used? How were they chosen?
■ How did the specific project get identified?
■ How did the team embrace change? How did the affected area embrace change?
■ What was the sustainability plan?
■ Were the targets met?
■ How were the physicians engaged?
■ Who attended the final presentation? How excited was the team at the final report out?
■ How long would an identical change take within your organization?
■ Did the follow-up and implementation plans appear realistic? Will the follow-up plans enable the organization to reach its future state?

Any organization seeking to get informed would benefit greatly by having each and every member of the executive team participate on another organization's improvement team prior to getting started. Surprisingly, your organization's and your individual penchant for Lean will be illuminated by this effort. It is through these experiences where you build an understanding of how to create the will to not fail.

Get Help

If we were entering the healthcare industry and we wanted to get an expert opinion on our heart, we would likely visit a cardiologist. If we needed expertise on diabetes, we would visit an endocrinologist. I don't know too many people that try to become experts on cardiology and endocrinology by simply reading a few Internet articles and attending a few conferences. As another example, did Tiger Woods gain his skill by reading "how to" golfing manuals? Yet, it is not uncommon for organizations to take an individual or two, send them to some basic Lean training and then embark on a culture of continuous improvement.

Just as you would find an expert in cardiology or endocrinology, you also need to seek out an expert in Lean enterprise transformation. In "Lean" circles, this person would be known as a sensei. Loosely translated, a sensei is a master or teacher. The sensei has many important roles to fill in a transformation including

■ Teaching your organization the Lean tools and concepts
■ Coaching your leadership team

- Helping to select the right areas of focus
- Assisting in developing the right measures
- Coaching on the development of your infrastructure
- Forecasting, managing, and minimizing risk
- Forcing reflection on how your organization is really performing
- Helping you develop your Lean business system
- Assisting you in managing the pace of change
- Providing you with lessons learned to shorten your learning curve
- To "call you" on some sacred processes
- To hold you accountable by ensuring you don't skip steps, and make sure your vision and actions are aligned

Bringing in some outside expertise to help with training, leadership development, infrastructure development, and team improvement is a wise investment for many organizations. External Lean expertise comes in many forms, from a Lean expert with expertise in one field to a Lean sensei that has expertise in many business areas.

A good external resource will shorten your lead time for results, accelerate the breadth and depth of your improvement, minimize your organizational risk, and assist in your development of management and leadership. Additionally, an outside resource is not tied to your political structure and organizational structure. This is a tremendous asset when it comes to the impartial ability to focus on process, rather than designing an improvement system based on personalities. I have one piece of advice should you wish to go outside for expertise. Pay attention to the experts who have practical experience in management development. The Lean tools, while potentially overwhelming at first, are the easiest part of improving. The most difficult aspect is changing the way management thinks, acts, and behaves. You will see a wide variation in Lean expert capability when you move beyond tools and into management/leadership development. The best Lean "sensei" are the ones that lead organizational change in one or more organizations as the change agent and site executive. These people are not only experts in the tools, but they can mentor senior leaders "eye to eye" having walked in the shoes of the person being coached.

To close this section on getting help, I will refer to Womack and Jones's *Lean Thinking*, one of the well recognized books on the application of Lean. In Chapter 11, the authors provide a step-by-step transformation process. Step 1, as we have discussed, is to identify a change agent. Step 2 is finding a sensei.* I am not aware of any organization that truly transformed to a Lean enterprise, inside or outside of healthcare, without a sensei. It's simply that important.

---

* Womack, J. and D. Jones. 2003. *Lean thinking: Banish waste and create wealth in your organization*. New York: Free Press, p. 249.

Establish a Steering Committee

When your organization begins to take on a large change initiative, there are two areas of infrastructure that need to be developed from the outset. One is the governance structure to manage and monitor the change, and the second is creating and developing your internal improvement expertise. Both are equally important, but I would like to begin by first discussing the governance process.

When you begin to see results from your first value stream, you will start getting requests from many areas of the organization to come and help them improve. As you should. After all, everyone has a need to improve quality, improve access, and lower costs, while simultaneously creating an inspired staff. Your organization may be asking about speed, scope, and results. How fast should you be improving? How many resources are needed? Are you getting a return on your investment? These questions are best answered by establishing a guiding coalition or a Lean steering committee.

The Lean steering committee has several key responsibilities in guiding your organization through the change process. The committee will:

- Establish the measurement systems and targets for monitoring success.
- Develop the rules for capturing results, and ensure that the results are being captured accurately.
- Use appropriate Lean tools to select the areas of focus (value streams) for the organization.
- Provide oversight that support staff, medical staff, and management are being developed. (They must be developing their skills through training and hands-on activity.)
- Remove the organization barriers. (These may be organizational structures, systems, people, policies and procedures, compensation programs, promotion policies, etc.)
- Monitor the pace of change. If you move too slow you will lose momentum and if you move too fast, sustainability of the program will suffer.

Many organizations do not want to set up yet another steering committee. Perhaps they feel that there are too many committees across healthcare organizations already. They prefer instead to add the Lean governance discussion to the existing strategy council, operations committee, or the quality council. I do *not* recommend this practice. In Lean improvement, there will be enough activity going on to warrant a dedicated committee's full attention. Remember that Lean is *not* a project; it is a management system of continuous improvement that results in the transformation of your organizational culture.

The steering committee meets at least monthly, and the length of the meeting is between ninety minutes to two hours. The committee is made up of eight to twelve people. My recommendation for the composition and roles of the members can be seen in Table 3.2.

Standard meeting rules are used. A timekeeper is established. Someone is assigned to take the meeting minutes. Minutes from the previous meeting are approved. A standard agenda should be followed. An example of this agenda is shown in Table 3.3.

During the meeting, action items are assigned and the team members are expected to complete their assignments before the next meeting. Accountability

Table 3.2   Lean Steering Committee Makeup

Position	Committee Role	Core Responsibility
CEO/President	Committee Chair	Leads Lean steering committee
Operations Executive for the Organization	Committee Co-Chair	Co-leads Lean steering committee
Chief of Medical Staff	Team Member	Drives the physician engagement strategy
Chief Financial Officer	Team Member	Drives the measurement capture and reporting from Lean savings
Representative from Human Resources	Team Member	Leads the redeployment policy discussions and actions
Leader of the Lean Program/ Department	Team Member	Leads discussion on improvement standard work and Lean improvement calendar
Corporate Leader for Quality, Patient Safety, and Risk Management	Team Member	Ensures Lean improvements are directly aligned with quality and safety goals for the enterprise
Representative from Marketing/ Communications	Team Member	Leads the communication strategy for Lean enterprise transformation
Various	Team Members	Assist in Lean transformation governance

Table 3.3   Sample of the Lean Steering Committee Agenda

Agenda Topic Leader	Activity	Length
Chair	• Check in and review previous meetings minutes	5 minutes
Value stream leader #1 (guest)	• Value stream results (YTD) • Countermeasures to address and gaps • Action plans for the next 90 days • Upcoming improvement calendar	15 minutes
Value stream leader #2 (guest)	• Value stream results (YTD) • Countermeasures to address and gaps • Action plans for the next 90 days • Upcoming improvement calendar	15 minutes
Value stream leader #3 (guest)	• Value stream results (YTD) • Countermeasures to address and gaps • Action plans for the next 90 days • Upcoming improvement calendar	15 minutes
CFO/Lean leader	• Corporate roll-up of Lean results	10 minutes
Lean leader	• Review and approve integrated Lean improvement calendar for the next 90 days	10 minutes
Lean leader/CMO or CMS	• Developing capacity • Review participation engagement statistics	10 minutes
Chair/Co-Chair	• Discussion of organizational barriers that need to be addressed • Updates from other team members	10 minutes
All	• Tour one area that had recent Lean improvement	30 minutes

Note: YTD = year to date.

for completing assignments is a prerequisite of effective meetings. This prerequisite is met by having a corrective action plan in place to address any shortcomings prior to the meeting. The meeting's purpose is to approve these plans to correct the shortcomings, not discuss solutions during the meeting. This group will provide oversight and governance for the overall Lean improvement journey for your organization. Establishing the governance structure for your organization is an important task in creating a successful infrastructure for improvement. This group leads the change.

Train Your Internal Experts

The next step in developing your infrastructure for improvement and in completing the activities necessary for the preparation phase for transformation includes developing your internal experts. Most organizations underestimate how much time it takes to improve. The preparation activities, the actual improvement team activities, and the sustaining activities all require skilled facilitation, which require some full-time resources in order to be done well. My rule of thumb is that you need one full-time person for each value stream you are improving. This person can be a dedicated resource or a seconded resource, but either way, he or she must be full-time. The correct Lean resources dedicated at the appropriate time will ensure actions plans and standard work have a higher likelihood of being sustained, resulting in significantly increased future gains.

The responsibilities of the internal expert are summarized in Table 3.4.

The data collection activities and the suite of sustaining activities require extensive amounts of time. Part-time resources generally are ineffective in completing these two specific activities well. Ineffective data collection leads to less than optimal results. Ineffective sustaining activities can lead to slow results or even project failure. Now that we have an understanding of how many full-time resources we need and what they will be doing, let's review what type of training is needed to get through the preparing to transform phase.

Over time, this group of experts will need to become skilled at both the science of improvement and the management skills necessary to be successful; however, in the preparation phase, we are mostly interested in improvement skill building. The visual management expertise, the management skills required for leading change, and the sustaining skills necessary to deliver real results will be built in the acceleration phase. We don't want to wait too long to start developing these additional skills, but they are not necessary to get started.

In the start-up phase, we want your organization's internal experts to become skilled in the scientific method. This starts with a thorough understanding of A-3 thinking and completing the A-3 form. In order to use A-3 thinking,

Table 3.4   Internal Expert Core Responsibilities

Role	Purpose
Become the internal expert on Lean improvement	Organizational leader for Lean tools, approaches, methods, and techniques
Leads improvement preparation activities	Uses standard work to ensure the team has the right team makeup, the right area of focus, the right measures/targets, and effectively uses organizational resources
Assist in the sustaining activities	Helps process owner to ensure standard work is in place and followed, and visual management systems and controls are used effectively
Teach visual management to the organization	Helps the organization understand the principle of managing visually: Being able to see normal from abnormal conditions that an intervention can be taken in real time
Coordinate the logistics for improvement	Ensures that everything is in place to allow the teams to be effective and use their time wisely
Develop additional team leaders	Builds improvement capacity for the organization
Assists in managing the improvement plan both at the value stream and corporate levels	Helps provide data for decision making that the improvement calendar is known, communicated, and followed
Train support staff and medical personnel on Lean principles, practices, and process	Builds improvement capacity for the organization
Facilitate the improvement activities	Helps the team to deliver improvement using A-3 thinking, build organizational capacity in the team members
Develop line management	Teaches line management the skills of Lean improvement to include A-3 thinking, leadership standard work, and visual management

Table 3.4 (*Continued*)   Internal Expert Core Responsibilities

Role	Purpose
Assist in managing the breadth and depth of improvement	Provides feedback on the proper timing for introducing new Lean tools, and to spread improvement across the organization
Assist in capture and population of the improvement scorecard	Teaches the process owner and assists finance in capturing and reporting the hard and soft savings associated with Lean improvement
Assist in the development of the visual management systems	Leverages the principle of visual management to create systems that help the support staff, medical staff, and management monitor and improve both process and results

an understanding of some improvement tools is necessary. At a minimum, I suggest the following training for your internal experts:

1. A-3 thinking and completing the A-3 form
2. Understanding the seven wastes
3. Understanding the five principles of Lean improvement
4. A working knowledge of the common tools to see and eliminate waste
5. How to prepare for a value stream analysis
6. How to prepare for a standard work kaizen event
7. Some basic facilitation skills

The skills utilized by the internal experts will be constantly growing and evolving. This initial training will get everyone on the same page and establish a common language for everyone to use. I would encourage as many executives as possible to also participate in this initial training. Over time, every executive will be expected to become skilled in the topics listed above.

Develop and Deploy a Communication Campaign

The final step needed to get through the preparation phase is to develop and launch your communication strategy. At this point, we want to communicate the "Why do we need to change?" question and the "How are we going to change?" question. Having everyone understand that the burning platform for change is an essential step in energizing the team toward change. Defining your burning platform for change answers the "why change" question. In healthcare, the burning platform should not be difficult to develop and communicate. There are several factors coming together that are creating a perfect storm for healthcare transformation. These include an aging population that creates additional demand on our systems, rapidly advancing technologies and therapeutics, an aging workforce leading to staff and physician shortfalls, lower revenues coming into our healthcare systems, and several chronic quality problems leading to patient harm. Each organization needs to create its own burning platform, but making the business case for change needs to be made early and often. The staff and medical staff need to be crystal clear on the reason for change and immediacy of this need. Without a sense of urgency, your transformational efforts will never get off the ground. Answering the "why change" question is an integral part of sharing your vision: a key leadership behavior.

The second big question that needs to be communicated is how the organization is going to change. The communication here needs to cover several key topics. First, you will want to answer why Lean was chosen as the preferred approach to change. There are several change management approaches in practice today, so why specifically was Lean chosen in your organization? More importantly, you might have to answer why other improvement methods were not selected. Next, you will want to answer what parts of the organization will be affected by change and when. Answering this question will be dependent on your pace of change. Are you beginning organization-wide or are you only starting in a few value streams? How were the value streams chosen? Why were other value streams not selected? When will change begin to affect the areas selected? What about the other parts of the organization?

In answering the "how" question, you will want to cover who specifically will be affected by the upcoming change (which programs, which functions, which teams, which physicians, which support groups, etc.). For each of these stakeholders, you will need to answer the "What's in it for me?" question (WIIFM). Actually, you will need to discuss how three different stakeholder groups are affected (Figure 3.2).

Each stakeholder group can impact the change process favorably and unfavorably, so in your communications, you will want to ensure that you have covered the WIIFM for each of the three groups.

While answering the "how" question, you will also need to cover what will happen for those support staff, medical staff, and management that do not wish to be part of the change. There will be a portion of the organization that does not wish to participate and having an answer for how the organization will deal with this group needs to be answered before beginning. I recommend that you have a plan for those that step forward and decline to participate up front (and

Figure 3.2 Three stakeholder groups.

provide this group a soft landing), and have a separate plan for those that don't step forward up front (and perhaps provide this group a less soft landing).

At a later time, you will expand on your communication strategy. You will want to highlight team results and the benefits of those changes to the patients, the support staff and medical staff, and the organization. At the start of your improvement journey, I do not recommend speaking about anticipated results; hold off on the success stories and overselling the change initiative until you have some tangible results. This is very difficult for most organizations to accomplish. The saying goes, "Do not oversell and underdeliver, but rather undersell and overdeliver." Answering the "why" and the "how" questions should be sufficient in the preparation phase of your transformation.

You will need to decide on your communication forum(s). I encourage you to use any and all vehicles to communicate and to continue with this approach as results begin to be realized. The various forums used by many healthcare organizations include

- Face-to-Face: Town hall meetings
- Department-level staff meetings, program-level staff meetings, and physician meetings
- Newsletters or e-newsletters
- Bulletin boards, posters, information posted on elevators
- Social media

I recommend you use as many forums as you can afford and keep current. Please do not underestimate the importance of the launch communication, because it is one of the reasons why some organizations fail to transform. Change will occur broadly and quickly using Lean approaches. We want everyone as informed as we can have them prior to the start. In the absence of information, staff make up their own information to fill in the holes. Sometimes this "fill-in" information is based on rumors and opinions, not facts. You may end up spending considerable amounts of time managing the issues created by the rumors and misinformation. A good communication strategy will offset this "fill-in" information with meaningful facts and deliver the vision of your change efforts.

Your communication campaign begins by answering the questions of why change is needed now, how the change will be realized, who will be affected, when the process will begin, and what the options are for those who chose not to participate. The strategy is deployed when the messaging is delivered to the organization through a wide array of forums.

Having now completed the key tasks of selecting your top-level change agent, getting informed on Lean and Lean transformation, getting help from a qualified sensei, establishing governance through the creation of a steering committee, training your internal experts, and developing and deploying your communication strategy, you should find yourself well prepared to launch and accelerate your Lean transformation.

Summary: Key Points from Chapter 3

An enterprise-wide Lean transformation will take one to two decades; transformation is not a two- to three-year project.

There are three phases to the transformation journey:

a. The *get ready* phase established the knowledge and infrastructure necessary to get off on the right foot.

b. The *accelerate* phase begins improvement in a part of your organization and strategically spreads improvement across the organization by building capacity and generating results.

c. The *sustain* phase makes change part of the new culture by institutionalizing the systems and processes to allow change to continue *forever*.

There are six key steps in the *get ready* phase to prepare your organization for change in performance and culture:

a. Find a senior-level change agent.

b. Get knowledge in Lean and Lean transformation.

c. Get help through an experienced sensei.

d. Create the governance structure for change by establishing a Lean steering committee.

e. Train your internal experts in the fundamental tools and concepts of Lean improvement.

f. Develop and deploy an effective communication campaign to let everyone know why change is needed now and who is affected.

Completing the six steps of the *get ready* phase will have your organization well positioned to deliver on meaningful change in both performance and culture, hallmarks of a Lean transformation.

Chapter 4

Chapter 4

The Transformation Roadmap—Phase 2: The Acceleration Phase (Improve, Sustain, and Spread)

Go to the people. Learn from them. Live with them. Start with what they know. Build with what they have. The best of leaders when the job is done, when the task is accomplished, the people will say we have done it ourselves.

Lao Tzu

Delivering on Preparation Efforts

At this point, your organization has covered a lot of territory. You have spent several months or longer getting ready to transform your organization. A change agent has been identified: a respected individual with an inclination toward change, the ability to challenge the status quo, and the charisma to lead a room.

Knowledge has been sought on Lean improvement and what is involved with an enterprise-wide transformation by you and the senior leadership team. You have found an experienced sensei, someone who has travelled the road you are now on. A governance process to manage the pace of change has been established through your Lean steering committee and this team will ensure organizational barriers to change are dealt with quickly. Your internal experts have been trained in Lean thinking with a base understanding of A-3 thinking, the seven wastes, the five improvement principles, and a working knowledge of the Lean techniques of value stream mapping and analysis, and kaizen improvement. You have launched your communication campaign to let everyone know why change is needed and who is affected.

The time has come to deliver on these preparation efforts. Your organization now needs to show some double digit gains in an area of high visibility to establish momentum. Nothing gets people more excited than *real* sustainable results. You will want to get some early wins to quiet the skeptics. Early wins won't shoo all the skeptics away, but it will keep them quiet long enough to give the transformation some wiggle room.

The improvement and corresponding measureable results will come from the repeated application of A-3 thinking within the value streams that you identified during strategy deployment. For each area that has been selected, a value stream mapping and analysis activity will be held. Recall from Chapter 2 that the deliverables from the value stream mapping and analysis include a future state vision and a detailed action plan for improvement. The action plan will include a series of quick wins, kaizen events, and projects that will be completed along a timeline using the scientific method guided and documented using A-3 thinking and the A-3 form.

Direct linkage should occur between the improve project measurable outcomes, the value stream key measures, and the true north measures of the organization. This ensures no improvement activity occurs (and the corresponding expenditure of resources) that is not directly aligned to your strategy. If you cannot directly see the correlation between the project outcomes and the true north measures, change the outcome measures or move on to a different project within the value stream plans. Time is too valuable to waste on activities that do not add up to strategic change. The use of resources on nonstrategic processes is one of the failure points of many organizations. This type of change is nice, but not necessary. The organization will not provide the attention and focus needed to sustain change in a nonstrategic area.

Once you have made the change and have realized some positive, measurable results, the focus of the management will need to quickly shift from making change to sustaining change. This shift happens by shifting the focus of management from results to both process *and* results; this shift will not be intuitive and it will not be easy. A thorough understanding of the principles of visual management and standard work is necessary in this transition. But, be warned, this is not Management 101. It will take courage, persistence, and tenacity at all levels of management to make this transition.

When a good understanding of sustaining improvement is developed, then your organization can discuss spreading the improvements to other parts of the organization. When I discuss spread, I am referring to spreading the improvement thinking, not spreading a solution or an artifact. Spreading solutions or spreading artifacts in lieu of spreading the thinking is one of the most common mistakes organizations make. The desire to spread allows management to feel that rapid progress is underway. In a culture change, we want to change the way people think, act, and behave. This shift is not helped dramatically by spreading solutions and artifacts. Spreading solutions creates the illusion of progress without changing the thinking of the organization.

To move through the acceleration phase of transformation, there are several key tasks that your organization will need to accomplish. Again, while this list is not exhaustive, the key tasks include

1. Ensure you have selected the right value streams on which to focus.
2. Establish value stream governance and set up your value stream performance system.
3. Utilize A-3 thinking to realize improvement.
4. Sustain the improvements and manage visually.
5. Capture the savings.
6. Spread Lean thinking across the organization.
7. Support your change with ongoing training and coaching.

Most every organization underestimates the time and effort it takes to make and sustain meaningful change. The result of underestimating is that the organization will be in too many value streams initially, launch too many A-3 improvements, and attempt to spread far earlier than the results warrant. At the end of the day, without sustaining change, there is no improvement. After a period of time, the leadership team will pull back and slow down the pace of change. To avoid this pull back, consider starting in only one or two key value streams. Once your organization understands the discipline, effort, and activity necessary to support world-class rates of improvement, you can move on to other value streams. This leads to the first key task—ensuring you have selected the right value stream(s) on which to focus your improvements.

Many organizations make the mistake of applying Lean medicine to a process "where it hurts." This is incorrect. All Lean improvement should be tied to the strategic outcomes as we discussed in Chapter 2. Selecting the critical few value streams that will leverage strategic change is important because if this is not done, senior management will view Lean as another tactical tool, not a strategic effort.

Step 1: Ensure You Have Selected the Right Value Streams on Which to Focus

Not every organization leads with strategy deployment. If your organization is committed to Lean quality improvement to deliver enterprise-wide transformation *leading to world-class rates of improvement in performance and culture*, then I would recommend you launch your initiative with strategy deployment. However, not every organization is ready to bet the farm on Lean as their approach to greatness and pursue an enterprise-wide beginning. Many organizations want to "dip" their big toe in the Lean waters and ensure the water is not too cold; this is understandable. And, if this is where your organization currently sits, then a different approach to selecting the key value streams can be taken. Simply follow the first three steps in strategy deployment to identify the key value stream(s) within your organization. Begin by establishing the organizational vision and developing the three- to five-year breakthrough objectives. Next, develop the annual breakthrough objectives and the top-level improvement priorities. From the top-level improvement priorities, you can select the one to two value streams that best leverage meeting your breakthrough objectives.

Let's assume that one of the top-level improvement priorities is to significantly improve the patient experience measured by patient satisfaction scores. In trying to improve the patient experience, we should go to an area of the organization where the patient satisfaction scores are low. For this example, patient satisfaction would fall under the true north dimension of service quality. If we are trying to increase access to services, we should focus on the areas with the longest wait times. One of the ways to analyze your organization is to use a histogram with data prioritized from highest to lowest (more commonly known as a Pareto diagram) to help make sense of your comparison data. An example of a Pareto diagram is shown in Figure 4.1. In this case, we are sorting support staff and medical staff satisfaction by program.

As you review these data, keep a few points in mind. The definition of a value stream is all of the activities, both good and bad, that make up the way we deliver value to a customer. A value stream is not a department, a program, or a unit. Analyzing our data by individual program makes sense because it is easy to understand geography, resource requirements, and budgets. In application, when we map a value stream, we see that the customer's experience actually crosses over several different departments. For example, one patient's trip to the emergency department

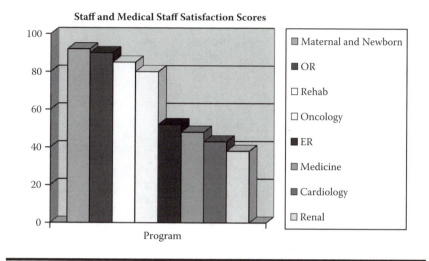

Figure 4.1 Pareto analysis of support staff/medical staff satisfaction by program.

can impact the ER staff, patient registration, laboratory, pharmacy, diagnostic imaging, and environmental services in a single visit. The value stream consists of all of the activities that span each of these departments during this episode of care. I want to reemphasize that a department or program is *not* a value stream.

Secondly, as we return to our discussion of identifying the key value streams, we ask how these data can be interpreted. In terms of improvement potential, clearly the leverage lies within the four areas circled in Figure 4.2.

With good data and an objective eye, identifying the first couple value streams is not too difficult. There are a few other considerations when selecting the place to begin your Lean improvement. First, make sure that you have solid leadership in place for both the support staff and the medical staff. Any weaknesses in management or medical management will be glaringly obvious when improvement begins. Solid management also implies that the key management positions are filled. I would not recommend beginning in an area with a vacant management position or a leadership position that is retiring, being promoted, transferring jobs, etc. Also, verify that no major disruptive organizational changes are scheduled in the near term. These disruptive changes can include launching a new IT system, major redevelopment, or a major organizational chart change. If these activities are far enough out, you can influence them significantly with Lean thinking and build the planning and improvement work into the value stream analysis. If the planning is 80% complete and the work cannot be influenced by Lean thinking, then hold off the launch until

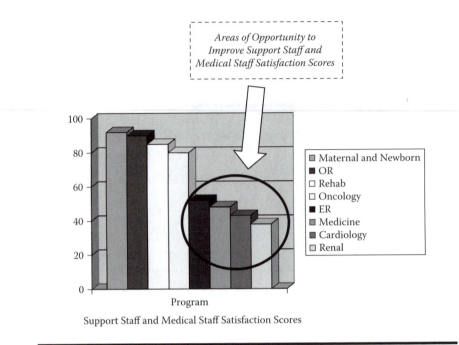

Support Staff and Medical Staff Satisfaction Scores

Figure 4.2   Areas of leverage to improve satisfaction scores.

these activities have been completed. Assuming that the leadership positions of support staff and medical staff are filled with strong leaders, and the disruptive technology will not be a factor in the near term, you can map your value stream and begin delivering improvement.

Step 2: Establish Value Stream Governance and Set Up Your Value Stream Performance System

Having selected your one to two key value streams, you will need a process to project manage the changes and govern the changes at a more local level. Recall that in the *get ready* phase (Phase 1), we established a Lean enterprise steering committee. A similar steering committee will need to be established at the value stream level, but with a different focus. The value stream steering committee will focus on value stream performance and deal with all the local issues that need to be addressed to enable change in performance and culture. The value stream steering committee has a smaller makeup than the corporate steering committee. Typically, the value stream steering committee will have co-leaders: an administrative practice leader and a physician champion. Starting out, the value stream administrative leader is frequently a director-level person and the physician champion can be the medical director or the program chief. The value stream steering committee also will have the process owners (managers) as members and the internal Lean expert. The vice president over the value stream is encouraged to attend, but is not a required member of the value stream steering committee. This committee will meet weekly and will manage the pace of the change (the improvement plans from the value stream analysis), managing the follow-up plans and results from the improvement A-3s and the value stream A-3, resolving any sustainability issues, ensuring standard work is being followed at the support staff and medical staff level, and managing the visual management systems of both process and results. A weekly meeting agenda would look similar to Table 4.1.

The value stream steering committee meeting should be a stand-up meeting held in front of the value stream performance wall. Management using the *wall* is a term for what is called managing the value stream performance system. This performance system uses all of our wisdom from visual management to make improvement a living and breathing tool for the chosen value stream. Figure 4.3 shows an example of the value stream performance system. Clearly, for the meeting to be effective and to meet the agenda timelines, it is vital that the information in the performance system be kept current.

The system contains the following elements: the future state value stream map, the value stream true north measures, the rapid improvement plan, and the status of open A-3s. As a result, the entire status of value stream performance is

Table 4.1 Value Stream Steering Committee Meeting Agenda

Activity	Lead	Length
Review value stream True north measures	Administrative and physician leaders	5 minutes
Review open A-3s (no more than 3) • Measures • Follow-up plans • Issues to be resolved	Process owners	10 minutes each (30 minutes total)
Review preparation for next A-3	Internal Lean expert	15 minutes
Other business	All	10 minutes
	Total	60 minutes

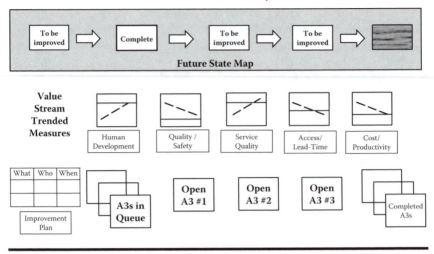

Figure 4.3   Value stream performance system.

known at a glance. The future state map highlights what areas have been improved and which ones have not. The value stream true north measures are trended so we can see the planned performance and the actual performance. The rapid improvement plan shows completed activities as well as the upcoming activities and the timing of those activities. The open A-3s show the three latest improvement efforts and details the status of those efforts using the eight steps of the scientific method.

You will want to make sure that you have not started too many improvement projects at any given time; I use the magic number of three. If you are working on more than three projects, the efforts get diluted and "activity" gets confused for "productivity." Your support staff and medical staff will try and keep up with whatever you decide to take on. It is the value stream leadership's responsibility to keep the team focused. It is much easier for the staff to focus if you simplify the number of new changes that are coming at them. It is also easier for you to manage three projects rather than five to seven or more.

At this point, your organization has identified the handful of key areas (value streams) you will be focused on, each directly aligned to your organizational strategy and selected to best deliver improvement on your organizational true north measures. In each of the value streams, you have performed your value stream mapping and analysis, and created a rapid improvement plan. Each value stream also has established a governance structure and created the value stream performance system to visually manage the improvements. Visual management is brought to life by tracking the value stream measures, detailing the improvement plan and showing the open A-3s where the Lean principles of flow, pull, defect-free, visual management, and kaizen are being utilized. From here, you will want to follow the scientific method for each discrete improvement and continue to execute your improvement plan.

Step 3: Utilize A-3 Thinking to Realize Improvement

The third step in the accelerate phase is to ensure all of the improvement projects continue to follow A-3 thinking. Lean organizations use A-3 thinking to create a community of scientists, focused on conducting a continuous series of small experiments in the spirit of improvement. Why would I mention A-3 thinking again as part of the accelerate phase? When your organization deploys your improvement strategy, you will likely uncover the several different approaches to improvement within your organization. Parts of the organization might be using the plan-do-study-act (PDSA) improvement science, others may be using project management approaches, yet another area may be using Define-Measure-Analyze-Improve-Control (DMAIC) process, which is the cornerstone to the Six Sigma methodology. There are countless other sciences. If you believe that Lean improvement is a toolkit, then continuing the use of multiple sciences makes sense. If you believe that Lean is a management system of continuous process improvement based on the themes of continuous elimination of waste and respect for all people, then you will quickly want to settle on a single science.

The greatest Lean organizations all utilize A-3 thinking documented on the A-3 form. It takes a lifetime to learn one science, let alone four or five. Additionally, like we expect for support staff and medical staff, we want to follow standard work for improvement. Standard work implies that you identify and select the best way known to accomplish any task. If the task is improvement, recognize that the greatest Lean organizations all use A-3 thinking as their standard.

A-3 thinking has an additional benefit beyond creating a standard for improvement. Following the steps in the A-3 *prevents* improvement teams from jumping to a solution before understanding the problem. The non-Lean approach to problem solving follows the following steps:

1. Discuss the opportunity/problem.
2. Identify solutions.
3. Implement solutions that may include adding resources, or some capital investment.
4. Repeat steps 1–3 when the problem returns with no clear plan or desire to end the issue *forever*.

A Lean organization will follow the steps in the A-3, where the problem-solving approach would look more like the following:

1. Identify the reason for action.
2. Define the problem statement by capturing the current conditions using data.
3. Define the target conditions using Lean principles.
4. Quantify the gap between current conditions and the target state by understanding the waste(s) and the root cause of the waste(s) causing the problem.
5. Generate solutions to eliminate the waste based on this information.

Following A-3 thinking would then lead to countermeasures and action plans to test the solutions to see if these solutions do indeed close the gap between current and target. A non-Lean thinking organization goes directly from step 1 to step 5. A Lean organization gets to the root cause of a problem *before* supplying solutions. A-3 thinking supplies a constant reminder not to go from step 1 to step 5 without completing steps 2, 3, and 4. As the organization gets more comfortable with A-3 thinking, the quality of the improvement projects will increase. Creating the improvement standard for your organization will shorten the learning curve for everyone. Through the hard work of the teams, guided by A-3 thinking, your organization will now be delivering improvement to portions of the value stream. Completing enough A-3 projects along the value stream will deliver overall value stream improvement. The key activity now is to sustain the improvements.

Step 4: Sustain the Improvements and Manage Visually

Step 4 in the acceleration phase is to sustain the improvements and manage the process *and* results visually. It is generally accepted by Lean practitioners that this step is the hardest in creating a culture of improvement. I tell organizations that all of the items we have discussed thus far—the strategy deployment process, selection of key value streams, establishing governance, and delivering improvement through A-3 thinking, the communication strategy, etc.—constitutes only 20% of the work; 80% of the work comes in sustaining the improvements. In order to manage visually, visual controls need to be established. At a minimum, visual controls are needed for both process and results, which is a shift in traditional thinking. Most organizations are familiar with tracking results, but visually managing process is a totally different paradigm. Recall that visual management requires the ability to *see* normal from abnormal conditions at a glance so that problems can be resolved in real time.

Every organization has some type of performance measurement system. This system of ratios, performance statistics, budget data, and scorecards is used to evaluate the effectiveness of the organization over a prior period of performance. The flaws in using only this type of reporting are twofold. First, the data are retrospective. At best, the data are usually thirty days old, the result of the prior month's efforts. Even worse, sometimes data, such as patient satisfaction survey results, lag a full fiscal quarter. It is very difficult indeed to make real-time adjustments to systems and processes based on data that is thirty to ninety days old. The second flaw is that the data are not very transparent. Typically, the reports are generated in an electronic spreadsheet or a series of hard copy reports. While useful to the manager or leader who has access to the information, data are frequently invisible to the support staff and medical staff. In creating a culture of improvement, measurement is used to motivate and make staff knowledgeable. This only happens if we give the staff access to the information.

To make information useful and to use it effectively, it should be provided in a timely manner. This enables decisions to be made in a window that allows for a change in performance within a narrow time horizon. It is not motivating to make a change that requires thirty days to see if any change for the better (or worse) was made. What does timely mean? For performance results, world-class organizations provide meaningful data on a daily basis. For process, world-class organizations provide data on a patient-by-patient or hour-by-hour basis.

Results do not merely happen, they are produced. Each process has a recipe or a formula that is followed to produce the results it achieves. Thus, if you want to change the results, you need to change the process. A Lean organization pays attention to both process and results. This is a significant shift in managerial culture over a traditional organization that waits for electronic reports to be generated showing how the organization is performing. In contrast, a Lean organization goes hunting for data. Within the workplace, process data are generated constantly. The process data are monitored frequently to ensure the "recipe" is being followed. If there is a deviation in the process, then necessary interventions are taken to get the process back on track.

5S: A Beginning Place for Visual Management of Process

Visual management of process has several different forms. In the workplace, visual management is guided by the principles of 5S. 5S (sort, set in order, shine, standardize, sustain) is a management system for creating a high performing workplace. The system is known as 5S because each of the letters in the five steps begins with the letter S. Table 4.2 illustrates the five principles of a 5S system.

Table 4.2   5S Definitions

Japanese Word	Principle	Very Loose English Translation
Seiri	Remove unneeded and unnecessary items from the workplace	**Sort**
Seiton	Organize the remaining items in a way that promotes standard workflow and enables standardized work	**Set in Order**
Seiso	Return the workplace to like new conditions	**Shine/Scrub**
Seiketsu	Create standardized consistent work practices	**Standardize**
Shitsuke	Personal discipline to maintain the previous 4Ss	**Sustain**

Beginning improvement with a 5S system can be valuable in several ways. First, 5S improves productivity and safety by ensuring that everything has a place and everything is in its place. One of the cornerstones of a great code blue system is a fully stocked, consistently organized cart to deal with code blue emergencies. Support staff and medical staff do not waste valuable time running around looking for supplies and medicines during a code blue. This would create a great loss in effectiveness and negatively impact the ability to provide urgent, safe care. In most organizations, the code carts are identical floor to floor and unit to unit. Why not provide this level of service and performance with all of your supplies and equipment? This is what 5S seeks to create—a high-performing work area where time is not lost hunting and gathering supplies, material, and equipment. Additionally, the supplies, materials, and equipment can be organized in a manner that promotes standard work. Your organization can help make sure that the proper process is followed by organizing the items in a manner that encourages following the "recipe."

Let's review a real-life example within a primary care clinic. Most physicians agree it is a good idea to track basic vital signs and capture weight and height of patients each visit. Surprisingly, the compliance with this data collection is not as high as you might think. Specific to capturing the patient weight, in one clinic, I'll call them clinic Z, the compliance rate for capturing patient weights was running 60% in adults. A team from clinic Z decided to figure out why the capture rate was so low. After observing 100 patients without the weight recorded, the data for the reasons in which staff failed to capture weights broke down to the following:

■ 55%: Patient refused to get on scale
■ 30%: Medical assistant forgot to capture the weight
■ 15%: Other

After some problem solving, the root cause for patients refusing to get on the scale came as a result of the scale being located in the exam room hallway, in potential plain sight of other patients and staff. Said differently, the patients were embarrassed to have their weight displayed near the public eye. The countermeasure was simply to put the scale out of the public eye. In implementation, the team decided it best to place a scale in each exam room. The second problem was the medical assistant (MA) forgot to capture the patient weight. By locating the scale right near the doorway in the entrance of the exam room, it became pretty difficult to forget to capture the weight of each patient. Both the patient and the MA walked directly by the scale during every appointment. Moving the scale to an area that promotes standard work meets the spirit of the second S, set in order. This simple change increased the compliance of capturing patient weights to nearly 100%.

Figures 4.4 and 4.5 illustrate a couple of other examples of 5S in action. Figure 4.4 provides an example of 5S in action. The "after" demonstrates how to create a high performing work area in an inpatient clean supply store room.

Before   After

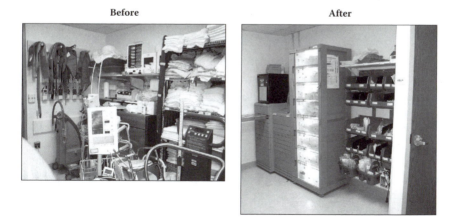

Figure 4.4 Before and after 5S, inpatient supply store room. (Courtesy of Spectrum Health.)

Before After

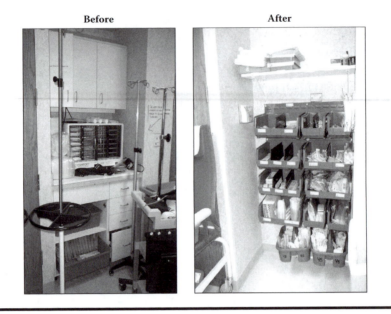

Figure 4.5   Before and after 5S. (Courtesy of Spectrum Health.)

How much staff time is freed up hunting and searching for supplies, materials, and equipment? Figure 4.5 shows another storeroom before and after 5S activity.

Another benefit of 5S is that it instills discipline in the staff. While it seems relatively simple to put things back when you are finished with them and clean up the workspaces, especially the common workspaces, after using items, these simple activities are difficult to sustain over the long haul. Maintaining a neat and organized workspace is a fundamental building block for what is to come later, namely heavy doses of standard work practices. I was taught very early in my personal (industrial-based) Lean journey that if a staff associate cannot put the broom back when they are finished with it, then our organization would have no chance in consistently following standard work. Amazingly, the 5S process demands that a specific location for the broom is identified. Two results immediately occur: (1) you know exactly where the broom is the next time you require it, saving the time of hunting and searching and (2) it becomes obvious, at a glance, if the broom is missing. This sounds elementary, but wasting time looking for an item is wasteful and impacts staff morale as well. Consequently, we spent a lot of time ensuring the small standards were followed.

So, let's translate this thinking to the realm of healthcare. Taking a short cut in how to maintain the discipline of the work environment leads to taking short-cuts in essential tasks required to produce high-quality, consistent healthcare work in a cost-effective manner. If a staff member can't put an IV pump back to its home when no longer needed, or return the vital sign station to its home space after vitals are recorded, what chance do you think there is that the staff will follow a complex, clinical pathway? A pathway is healthcare's standard work for the delivery of care. Compliance with pathways in the best organizations is difficult to achieve, let alone in an organization without discipline. 5S builds the discipline that is essential for what comes next, *standard work*.

Tying 5S back to step 4 in the acceleration phase, 5S allows an organization to manage visually. The system visually differentiates normal from abnormal conditions related to the location of material, supplies, and equipment, and allows problems (missing or excess material, supplies, and equipment) to be spotted at a glance. The abnormal condition can and should be corrected immediately. 5S is visual management of process; it highlights workplace conditions necessary to operate an effective work environment. We need a high-performing work area to assess, diagnose, and treat patients with less waste.

Using Visual Management for Process Control

Another example of visual management of process is the process control board. Process control aims to manage process, not results. Results capture can be automated and analyzed after the fact. However, process *must* be managed in real time. Process control allows for the entire team to manage the process on an hour-by-hour or patient-by-patient basis. This is not a typo. World-class healthcare organizations measure the performance of every single patient in real time, or they measure "output" of work every single hour. An example of an hour-by-hour process control board is shown in Table 4.3.

To qualify as a process control board, several conditions must be satisfied. The output of a process is based on takt time. First, we need to understand takt time. The process control board documents the completed units (in this specific case, patient exams are the output), but the units per hour are based on the takt time. If we need to "process" three patients per hour, then what is the takt time? In this example, the takt time is calculated as sixty minutes divided by three patients, or twenty minutes. The plan column is always the units per hour to be completed based on takt time. The actual column records the true number of patient exams completed within that hour. The takt time can change on an hour-by-hour basis, based on patient demand. The plan should change accordingly to reflect the change in takt time.

A process control board also requires real-time capturing of actual output. The actual column should be completed by the people who do the work each hour, based on the actual output. We are trying to see the difference between normal and abnormal. By capturing the plan versus the actual output, we can

Table 4.3 Hour-by-Hour Process Control Board for CT

CT Process Control Board			Date: November 3, 2012
Hour	Plan	Actual	Comments
0700–0800	3	3	No issues
0800–0900	3	2	Contrast not given prior to arrival
0900–1000	3	3	No issues
1000–1100	3	2	No patient to scan
1100–1200	3		
1200–1300	3		
1300–1400	3		
1400–1500	3		
1500–1600	3		
1600–1700	3		
1700–1800	3		

see abnormal at a glance. Seeing abnormal is important because it makes the waste visible. Once the waste is visible, we can intervene and get the work back on plan. It's essential to note that seeing the waste is only valuable if someone does something about it.

The next item required on a process control board is the capture of the sources of variation. Each time we have a deviation from standard, good or bad, we want to capture the source of the variation. These sources of variation are critical in performing future improvement, and they must be captured at the time they occur, by the people who do the work. We can create a histogram from the sources of variation, which is useful because the leading causes of variation are the most likely candidates for future problems. A beautiful aspect of Lean improvement is that every single deviation is an opportunity to learn and correct, not to hide. Consequently, leaders have two choices:

1. Select a measure that is easy to hit, cheating the organization out of a maximizing the opportunities for improvement or
2. Realign the thinking about how a target is selected. To learn that a missed target is a "golden nugget" in need of correction is a huge paradigm shift from a non-Lean organization

Let's review a common scenario. We were supposed to perform exams on twenty-four patients yesterday. At the end of the day, we worked an hour of overtime and only completed nineteen exams. So, we missed the standard time by an hour and we missed the target by five patients—or nearly 20%. Can anyone explain what happened yesterday? If we are lucky and the same staff happens to be scheduled, we might be able to recreate or capture part of the data. But, more likely, we will just absorb the variance and vow to "try" better today. Using a process control board, we can determine hour-by-hour what is happening. Maybe we can do something to prevent the hour of overtime if, by noon, we already know we are three patients behind. We definitely can capture the sources of variation to deliver valuable data in future problem solving. One of the powerful consequences of having reasons for delay is that the causes of these delays may well go beyond the scope of the managers responsibility, requiring leadership involvement to correct. How would these opportunities be documented today? Simply put, these delays would not be captured, but the guessing game as to why the area finished behind would start immediately. The key principle to visual management is to see normal and abnormal at a glance so we can take action.

Let's assume after a week of variance reporting, the staff generates the data seen in Figure 4.6.

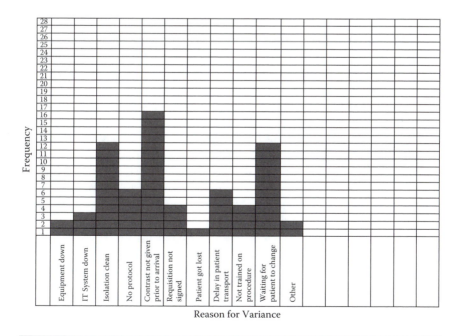

Figure 4.6   Variance histogram.

Which problem should we tackle first? Clearly the largest source of variation is that the outpatients have not been given contrast prior to showing up for their exams. This detail becomes a golden nugget that we can mine for further improvement. In *Lean speak,* a golden nugget is an opportunity. Each problem is a treasure of opportunity. How is that for changing the view of problems from a negative to a positive?

Process control data cannot be re-created accurately after the fact, it must be documented in real time. Sources of variation must be captured in real time as well. It seems that completing the data on the process control system is manual and time consuming. Does the staff have time to complete the system on a regular basis? In any environment, the staff, including physicians, have time to complete the process control board. A well-designed process control board should not take more than five seconds to complete, and we should be able to determine variance from standard in another five seconds or less. If filling out the board takes longer, we know that its design is too complicated, or that it's not easy to understand visually. The board can be automated, but I do not recommend you start with automation. In capturing the data, we aim to refresh adherence to standard work and to capture sources of variation, and these activities are difficult to automate. Also, your board and corresponding data are likely to change over time, so before you automate, take the time to become *very* clear about what you want. Lean organizations have found that staff will happily complete the board if management pays attention to the process and does something meaningful with the data. It is important to use the sources of variation (the data captured) for further improvement. Having staff generate data that are not used is not only wasteful, it's disrespectful. This action would violate the second theme of the Toyota Production System—respect for all people.

How does process control help sustain? First, the process control system makes all the data necessary to monitor the process on an hour-by-hour or patient-by-patient basis totally transparent. Secondly, sources of variation are captured in real time, thus, if possible, an immediate intervention can be taken. If not possible, the sources of variation can be summarized into a Pareto diagram so that the leading sources of variation can be addressed. Figure 4.7 illustrates how to take the data from the frequency chart and present the data in a Pareto chart format.

The Pareto principle holds that 80% of the problems are caused by 20% of the issues. With these data, the computerized tomography (CT) team, staff, radiologists, and management can now address the critical issues to improve safety, quality, access, and productivity. From this example, the key issues would be ensuring that the patients have been given contrast prior to their arrival in the CT department, developing a better process to have patients appropriately changed prior to their exam, and having a better process to clean the exam suite following testing for patients in isolation.

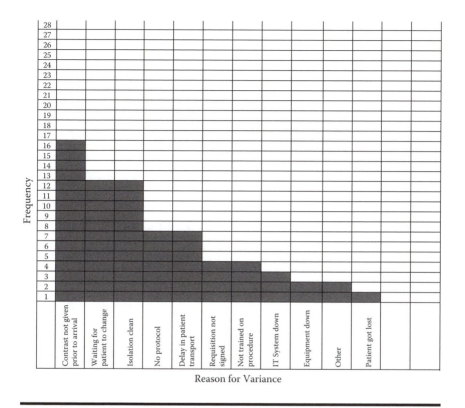

Figure 4.7 Pareto chart of the sources of computerized tomography (CT) process variation.

Process control also can be used to monitor a process on a patient-by-patient basis. An example of this is shown in Table 4.4. In this specific case, the process is discharge planning. For an admitted patient, the healthcare goal is to safely discharge the patient with the highest quality service, with a great outcome, in the least amount of time and with the minimum necessary resources. That's a lot to ask of any process, let alone a process with a complex medical patient.

Visual management is used to create total transparency of the discharge plan where the expected date of discharge is shown as well as all the relevant information leading to this discharge. The expected discharge date is the plan. On the dry erase board, any barrier to discharge is identified and documented with the person responsible and the due date for barrier resolution for each patient. This way we can ensure nothing is missed and ensure that the interprofessional team understands and can meet the plan. When the patient is discharged, the actual discharge date is captured so that the variance between the planned date and

Table 4.4   Patient-by-Patient Process Control

Patient Initials	Primary Diagnosis	Target Length of Stay (Days)	Actual Length of Stay	Variance from Target	Comments
F.W.	COPD	5	5	0	No issues
E.S	CHF	5	6	+1	No one to D/C on weekend
B.O.	Pneumonia	4	5	+1	Lost a day waiting on specialist consult

the actual date can be analyzed. This variance can be reported and captured on a frequency chart. The top reasons for missing the plan can be prioritized with a Pareto analysis and improved. Calculating conservable days, weeks, or months after the patient discharges is not helpful data, because it is not possible to reconstruct where the conservable day came from. Knowing in real time what the barriers are and resolving them is necessary to properly manage the discharge process for success. I have seen organizations using this visual management system for discharge planning reduce the average length of stay for patients by as much as 30% and reduce conservable days by as much as 75%.

The management of process is one of the fundamental differences between a Lean organization and a traditional organization. Managing the process is the key to getting fantastic results. In a Lean organization, the entire support staff and medical staff is in tune with what is happening on a moment-by-moment basis. Slight changes and adjustments to process are made repeatedly during the day to maintain flow. Real-time changes are possible because the visual management system makes it obvious to everyone, at a glance, that something abnormal is occurring. Standard interventions are in place to deal with abnormalities until a permanent solution can be found. Done well, the process (recipe) should deliver the correct results.

Using Visual Management for Improving Results: Managing for Daily Improvement

Every organization is concerned with results. Results are how we measure success and, frequently, pay compensation, and promotions are linked to the ability to deliver consistent performance. In a Lean organization, results are the outcome of following great, waste-free processes based on standard work and visual management. In a traditional work environment, all managers get monthly reports, budget summaries, and statistics that try to make sense of the prior period's activities, but correlating cause and effect is quite frequently very difficult.

Earlier in this chapter, we discussed the value stream performance system. This performance system is visual management in action. From this system, everyone can see at a glance the key measures for the value stream with target and actual performance, the improvement plan, and the key improvement initiatives (A-3s). Great Lean organizations take the visual management of performance to the unit level because only tracking performance is insufficient, and the goal is to improve performance. A Lean organization uses the measurement of performance to get better every day. That also was not a typo. A Lean leader will always leave the workplace in a better place than when the Lean leader walked through the door that morning. What could that look like in your organization?

The system used to get better every day is known as managing for daily improvement, or MDI. The MDI system visually tracks the key measures of the department, identifies and prioritizes variances from the plan, and develops and implements plans for improvement. This work is done daily by the entire staff. While management has the responsibility for the MDI system, everyone is expected to contribute toward the improvements every day. Imagine your organization for a moment. If you are a medium-sized healthcare organization, you might have a staff of 3,000. What could your organization look like if each of these staff members were engaged in improving your core processes on a daily basis? Would this daily engagement help change your culture? Having 3,000 staff members marching toward a shared vision can make a significant amount of change in a short period of time. Now compound this daily change over ninety days, six months, one year, five years. I think everyone can envision the end state. This is Lean healthcare in action.

MDI begins with a thorough understanding of the true north measures of the organization. These are the same true north measures that were developed through strategy deployment. The true north measures are cascaded to the value stream level and, next, to the department level. An example of the cascading of measures is shown in Table 4.5.

It is important that the measures are aligned to the organizational true north measures. Our role as a leader is to establish the vision, allocate the resources to

Table 4.5   Cascading True North Measures

Dimension	Organizational True North Measure	Value Stream Measure	Unit Level Measure
Morale/human development	Implemented suggestions for the enterprise	Implemented suggestions for the program	Implemented suggestions for the unit
Quality/safety	Reduce falls by 50% across the enterprise	Reduce falls by 75% across the program	Reduce falls by 80% on the unit
Service quality	Compliments received for the enterprise	Compliments received for the program	Compliments received for the unit
Access	Reduce conservable days by 50% for the enterprise	Reduce conservable days by 50% for the program	Reduce conservable days by 75% for the unit
Cost	Reduce the staff hours per patient visit by 10% across the enterprise	Reduce the staff hours per visit by 20% across the program	Reduce the staff hours per visit by 20% across the unit

accomplish the vision, and inspire people to take action toward this vision. Be sure you have aligned the staff toward a common goal. Managing for daily improvement establishes the local level vision, creates the infrastructure to accomplish the vision at the unit level, and inspires the staff to meet the vision. What a great system.

The tools used for MDI include a performance board, a daily huddle, and a project management system for managing the improvements. The performance board is shown in Figure 4.8.

Each individual true north dimension (staff engagement/morale, quality, access, and cost) of improvement has a set of four charts. The top chart displays the year-to-date performance updated monthly with both targets and actual performance. The second chart is month-to-month data performance updated daily with both targets and actual performance. The third chart is a histogram of the sources of variation between the month to date (daily) plan and actual, and the fourth chart is the improvement plan. Some organizations call the improvement plan the kaizen newspaper because it summarizes the kaizen (improvement) activity needed to ensure that the daily

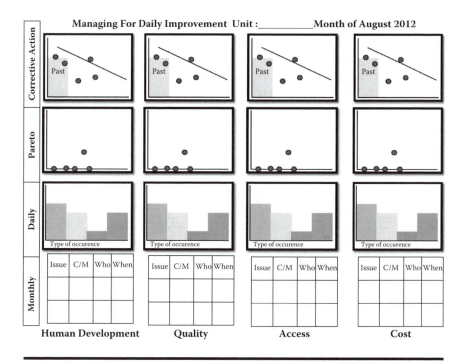

Figure 4.8   Managing for the daily improvement performance board.

target is met. The board is located in a common hallway where the entire staff can easily see the content. I actually prefer that patients and families can see the data as well, because it encourages questions from your "customers." For those of you concerned about the transparency of the data, what is so top secret that it needs to be hidden from the public?

The data in the MDI system are updated daily. I prefer to have a staff member update the data because they are able to engage in the process and it encourages them to understand both the measurement system and the supporting data. The assignment for who updates the performance boards changes weekly. Once a shift, the *entire* staff huddles in front of the board for a five- to six-minute meeting. The meeting will be held to this length if the agenda is scripted. The typical agenda is as follows:

- Morale measurement results, variance and action plans: 1 minute discussion
- Safety/quality measurement results, variance, and action plans: 1 minute discussion
- Service quality measurement results, variance, and action plans: 1 minute discussion

- Access measurement results, variance, and action plans: 1 minute discussion
- Cost/productivity measurement results and action plans: 1 minute discussion
- Unit level communication update: 1 minute discussion

After fifteen seconds of review for each of the different measurement dimensions, ideas for improvement should be solicited and documented on the improvement plan. Results of improvement projects from earlier assignments should be briefly discussed as well. It is important that the successfully implemented ideas be incorporated into standard work and used by everyone. The improvements can be as simple as a suggestion that can be tested, to a more formal PDCA project, all the way through a project documented on an A-3. The key is to be continuously engaging staff in improvement of the key measures of the unit aligned to the true north measures. Total transparency gives everyone an opportunity to be informed and to participate. It is through engagement and participation that the culture is changed. Some organizations hold the huddle at shift handover to ensure consistency in messaging and communication.

The daily huddle should occur at three different levels within an organization. The first huddle occurs between the staff and the staff line leadership, such as a charge nurse or a team leader. This huddle would take on the day-to-day challenges and improve the organizations performance through quick wins and small PDCA cycles of improvement. The second huddle would occur between the line leader(s) and the manager, administrative director, and medical leadership. This layer of the organization would take on problems that can be influenced at the value stream level. Solutions involving A-3 thinking and even kaizen events would be generated at this level. The third level of huddles happens between the value stream leadership and the executive team. This layer of leadership resolves barriers between value streams or barriers that need to be addressed by corporate policy. The cascading huddles change the focus of the organization from monitoring results to managing for action and improvement. The cascading huddles occur best daily and should only take a few minutes. Resolving the open issues can take much longer, but the key is trying to get better every single day.

Control Systems for Visual Management

Visual management is only effective with frequent audits of the visual tools. The 5S system needs to be audited to ensure that abnormal conditions are being identified and corrected. It also needs to be audited to ensure that as new items enter the workplace, or a change in existing supplies, material, and equipment, they are addressed on a timely manner. 5S systems need to be updated when changes in process and workflow occur. The process control systems need to be religiously audited to make sure variances from plan are identified and interventions are taken. Failure at this stage will result in waste creeping back into your systems and performance targets not being sustained. The managing for daily improvement systems needs to be audited to ensure that opportunities are being captured and addressed. Gaps in performance require action and these actions need to be assigned to the support staff and medical staff for resolution. Broader issues need to be escalated up the chain of command for action.

A great Lean healthcare organization never accepts that things are running as designed. Time and effort at all levels of management are spent "satisfying their curiosity that things are running as designed." Is this auditing being done because we do not trust the staff to do the right thing? Far from it. The auditing is completed to identify and fix the barriers that prevent the staff from delivering compelling value in the least waste way. The vigilance to focus on process is assisted by two techniques in a Lean system: leadership standard work and peer task audits. Let's first discuss leadership standard work.

Leadership standard work is the technique used by great organizations to ensure the focus of management and leadership is placed on continuous process improvement. Standard work is the step-by-step recipe followed to ensure a good outcome in the right amount of time. Leadership standard work is the routine and structure followed by management to shift the focus from process to results.*

There are a few key features of leadership standard work. First, the structure and routine given to a manager is process dependent and not person dependent.† A new manager can quickly come up to speed in his/her new role because the work is scripted to create the right focus. Secondly, observing who will and will not follow standard work makes it obvious which managers are not willing to make the transition to the new culture.‡ Knowing this is important because the line management role is essential in successfully creating a culture of improvement. You will want to deal quickly with those people who are "not on the bus." Please note: "deal quickly" needs to include retraining, and discussions as to why the manager is choosing not to follow the standard work, and then asking him/her for his/her improvement ideas. Every opportunity should be given to the manager to help him/her with the internal paradigm shift. After these measures have all been exhausted, then the manager needs to be given a final choice, that is, to follow the organization's standard work as a condition of employment. This is not

---

* Mann, D. 2005. *Creating a Lean culture.* New York: Productivity Press, p. 25.

† Ibid, p. 26.

‡ Ibid.

"losing a job to Lean," it is an employee who is being given the choice to follow an organization's rules and to actually participate in creating those rules. Finally, leadership standard work allows poor and marginal managers to quickly improve performance. Masaaki Imai, in his book, *Gemba Kaizen*, said that supervisors (supervisor, in this context, is another name for the line manager) do not know exactly their responsibilities.* In this excellent book on Lean management, Imai further states, "This situation arises when management does not clearly explain how to manage in *gemba* and has not given a precise description of supervisors roles and accountability."† Gemba is a Japanese word that loosely translates to "the workplace or the place where work is done." Leadership standard work makes the responsibilities and accountability clear for the manager.

Leadership standard work is a recipe for where to spend time during the workday. With the availability of electronic calendars and smart phone alarms, this seems pretty easy to accomplish. The concept is not difficult to understand, but does require tremendous discipline to accomplish consistently. Time is budgeted each day and specific tasks are designed to accomplish two things: focus on process and spending time on improvement. If we are honest, we must admit that most all of our days are spent on firefighting. The schedule needs to be adjusted to accommodate situations, such as a staff member calling in sick and not being available to work, a patient complaint that needs to be handled immediately, the budget is getting out of whack, a new accreditation standard that has to be met and the implementation is behind, your boss wants a report by 3 p.m. today, etc. Getting all this work done might feel rewarding. Heck, look at all the stuff I got completed today. But, it didn't advance the organization forward. You did not leave the workplace in better shape than you found it.

Key tasks in leadership standard work might include the following:

- Review the performance and process control boards and make interventions as necessary.
- 5S audit and intervention.
- Review the task card (*kamishibai*) audit results (this will be discussed later in this chapter).
- Review A-3s in progress and project manage actions needed appropriately.
- Review the suggestion system status for open projects.
- Audit standard work of staff and medical staff.
- Hold the daily huddle at the performance board.
- Take a Gemba Walk.

---

* Imai, M. 2012. *Gemba kaizen: A commonsense approach to a continuous improvement*, New York: McGraw-Hill, p. 105.
† Ibid.

■ Audit safe work and patient safety standard work processes.
■ Work on improvement tasks.
■ Root cause a new problem.
■ Work on any open follow-up plans on your A-3 improvement projects.

Actually, the list can continue on for quite a while. The key is to spend dedicated, focused time daily on improvement. If you do not budget your time to focus on improvement, the day-to-day firefighting will consume all of your time, treasures, and talents, and an opportunity will be lost.

How much time should be spent on improvement? After all, there are managerial and administrative tasks that need to be accomplished; important things like payroll, attendance management, scheduling, and budgeting. Table 4.6 lists the ideal time allocations to be governed by standard work by position in the organization.

It might be extremely difficult to "jump off" and begin scheduling and executing with this recommended amount of time per day at the different management levels of the organization. I would encourage you to start with some allocation of time, say an hour each day, and then build toward these percentages gradually over time. What are you going to have to give up or let go of in order to start spending time on improvement?

The following document is one of the better examples of leadership standard work. This specific example is for a nurse manager. The tasks are broken down by key time buckets during the day, and weekly tasks are documented separately. A mixture of tasks oriented toward both improvement and unit level administration are documented. Reasons why tasks are not met are captured, which allows for improvement of the standard at the end of each week. The leadership standard work should be discussed with the manager's superior on a weekly basis. Barriers to accomplishing standard work should be removed (Table 4.7).

Table 4.6 Time Allocated for Daily Standard Work

Position	Daily Time Dedicated to Standard Work (%)
Staff	100
Charge nurse or team leader	75
Line manager	50
Middle manager	33
Executive staff	20

Table 4.7 Nurse Manager Daily Leadership Standard Work Example

Time of Day	Standard Work	Deliverable
0730–0830	• General unit administration	Respond to e-mail and voice mail requests, payroll, scheduling, etc.
0830–0930	• Managing for daily improvement huddle • Walk the gemba and review visual controls	Team engagement, problem solving, and real-time intervention
0930–1030	• Attend bed meeting • Work on preparation or sustaining issues from past or upcoming kaizen activity	Alleviate bed-flow pressures as required, and prepare or sustain for improvement as required
1030–1130	• Attend managers' meeting or work on assigned committee work	Increase awareness and support organization as required
1130–1230	• Walk unit and monitor visual controls • Lunch	Team engagement, problem solving, and real-time intervention
1230–1330	• General unit administration	Respond to e-mail and voice mail requests, payroll, scheduling, etc.
1330–1430	• Walk unit and monitor visual controls	Team engagement, problem solving, and real-time intervention
1430–1530	• Meet with charge nurse to resolve open issues, plan for night shift, and review action plans from performance system	Planning, problem solving, and work time to improve
1530–1630	• Walk unit and monitor visual controls • Prepare for the next day • General unit administration	Team engagement, problem solving, and real-time intervention

How does this standard work compare with yours? Usually, the first big difference is that in a Lean organization, the entire day is not spent *bouncing* from meeting to meeting. In a Lean organization, the management and leadership, and physician leadership are not pinned down in their offices or in meetings all day. The management team will be seen in the workplace, problem solving and removing barriers enabling the delivery of the highest quality, in the shortest time, and at the least cost. Leadership standard work will get you out of the conference and into the workplace.

Peer Task Audits (Kamishibai)

Another control point for the visual management systems and standard work that leverages staff engagement is a system known as kamishibai. This daily audit system is used as a peer-to-peer feedback mechanism to reinforce the maintenance of operational standards. Kamishibai loosely translates to "paper theatre" and is part of a long tradition of picture storytelling, beginning as early as the ninth or tenth centuries when priests used illustrated (cartoon) scrolls combined with narration to convey Buddhist doctrine to lay audiences.* The Buddhist monks used the kamishibai scrolls to allow the audience a self-reflection to determine if they were living the correct Buddhist lifestyle. This system is wildly popular in Japan today with children, and the cartoon-based stories are used to teach behaviors, such as sharing and punctuality.

In a Lean organization, the kamishibai system is used to reinforce to the auditor that he/she is living a "Lean lifestyle." The kamishibai system is illustrated in Figure 4.9.

First, audits are created. On any unit, or in any department, many different types of audit cards can be created. For example, standards already exist for IV (intravenous) sight markings, hand hygiene, narcotic counts, and preventing ventilator-attributed pneumonia. Ideally, the audits are pictures that represent the key standards for the organization (Figure 4.10).

Once each day, every staff member conducts a single three- to five-minute audit using one of the cards created from one of the department standards. If the audit is passed, the green side of the card is slotted in the board. If the audit fails, the red side of the card is slotted. A red audit is dealt with in real time and the auditor discusses the result with the person being audited. Real-time feedback, both positive and negative, is the best way to change behavior (Figure 4.11).

Failed audits are trended based on frequency. The frequency of the failures can be summarized into a Pareto diagram for further action. The type and number of cards in the system is dynamic. Cards can be added and subtracted

---

* Online at: http://www.kamishibai.com/history.html

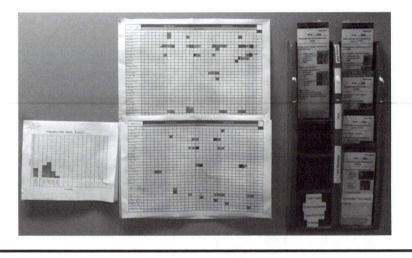

Figure 4.9 Kamishibai system. (Courtesy of Mackenzie Health.)

based on what is being found in the audits. For audits that fail frequently, more cards can be added into the system so these shortfalls can be reviewed more often. In the same light, for audits that pass consistently, cards of this type of audit can be reduced, thus they are audited less frequently (Figure 4.12).

The key point of kamishibai is that while completing the audit, the auditor is reinforcing their own understanding of the importance of following standards. It is through this self-reflection that the staff assesses if they are following a Lean lifestyle. A Lean lifestyle is one where everyone follows standards until a better standard can be created.

Two common issues that every organization faces when implementing a culture of continuous improvement include getting everyone to follow standard work and creating the capacity to audit all of the standards that typically fall on management; kamishibai addresses both of these concerns. By having every individual engaged in the audit process, the entire staff is involved with auditing standards. The process of auditing is designed to have the auditor self-assess if they are following the standards. This reflection helps the entire staff support the new approaches to work that deliver improvement in quality, access, and cost. The process of getting everyone to follow the standards is the key to improvement sustainability. Secondly, by having everyone participate in the kamishibai system, the workload of auditing is shared by everyone. Audit work that might take a single manager two or more hours daily can be spread across all employees on all shifts in three- to five-minute increments. In addition to distributing the workload, having everyone engaged allows broader coverage of all the standards. Yet another benefit of kamishibai is that like the other management systems, the audit system is entirely visual. The audits to be

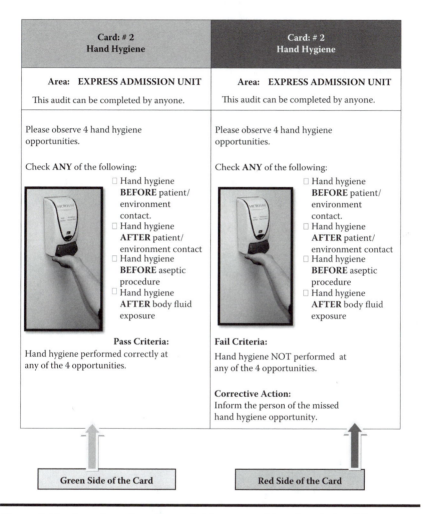

Figure 4.10   Sample task audit card. (Courtesy of Mackenzie Health.)

completed, the results of the audits, the pass/fail status of the audits, and the corrective action for failed audits are all posted for everyone to see.

Step 4 in the acceleration phase encompasses sustaining the improvements and managing the improved system visually. Using A-3 thinking, your improvement teams will be implementing flow and pull within your key processes. These teams also will be implementing zero defect systems to reduce errors. The new processes will be supported by standard work. The system is sustained by managing visually. Visual management involves many different approaches, but usually begins with 5S, a system to instill discipline while creating a high-performing work area.

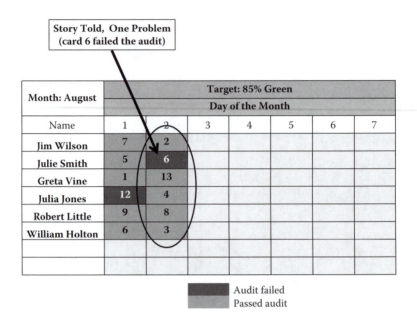

Figure 4.11 Telling the story.

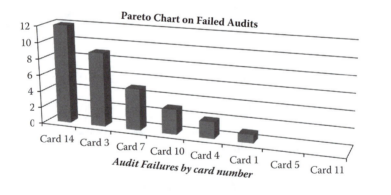

Figure 4.12 Pareto chart on failed audits.

Visual management of process, using a process control board and visual management of results, using a performance board then follows. The performance board is supported by managing for daily improvement, a system that endeavors to leave the workplace in better shape than when you arrived at work and engages all of the staff in improving your area's true north measures.

Visual management is supported by a control system. Two key levers of a great control system include leadership standard work and kamishibai. Leadership standard work shifts the focus of management from results to process *and* results. Kamishibai is a visually managed, audit system designed to allow self-reflection on following a Lean lifestyle. The combination of visual management systems and their supporting control systems is how Lean organizations not only sustain, but also improve on their improvements every day. These approaches support creating a culture of improvement.

Step 5: Capture the Savings

When A-3 thinking is used and then visual management systems are brought to life and improvements are sustained, you can expect double-digit improvement in your key measures. Results will start to be realized beyond anything you will have experienced in the past. Having a system that captures these results will be important for the long-term viability of your Lean efforts. Without a detailed understanding of the results, the improvement efforts will be viewed more as an expense than a benefit. It takes resources to support the kaizen teams, and the labor hours add up in a hurry. If you follow Step 4 diligently, your results will be at hand. The trick now is to quantify these results.

There are two main types of measureable results: hard savings and soft savings. Hard savings are those items that will show up on either your income statement or balance sheet. Said differently, these are bottom line and top line benefits that make their way into your financial statements and then into your budget. Soft savings are items that reflect elimination of wasted time and activity, but don't flow through to financial statements or budget line items. While not exclusive, some examples of hard savings found in healthcare include

- Increase in top line revenue
- Reduction in supply and material expense
- Reduction in therapies and pharmaceutical expense
- Reduction in labor expense
  - Fewer full-time equivalent employees
  - Reduction in agency costs
  - Reduction in overtime
- Decrease in utilities and energy consumption
- Reduction in facilities repair and maintenance expenses
- Reduction in inventory

These items result in benefits that can be incorporated into the budget in future years. Savings from this category result in lower costs per unit of service, increased operating margin, and also improved working capital and increased cash flow.

Some examples of soft savings include

- Reduction in steps travelled
- Reduction in handoffs of information
- Reduction in approvals or signatures
- Reduction in square footage utilized

There is a third category of savings that can turn into either hard or soft savings depending on what happens with these results. This category is called cost avoidance. Examples of cost avoidance include

- Capital avoidance (equipment, square footage, IT terminals, etc.)
- Improvement in quality and safety indicators (infection rates, complications, etc.)

The savings should be captured and reported by the finance department for two reasons. First, nothing is going to flow through to either a financial statement or the budget without finance's blessing. More simply, finance will allow the savings to have credibility within the organization. Secondly, finance needs to be engaged in the improvement process and is the area most capable of understanding and extracting the value derived from improved staff morale/engagement, improved quality, improved delivery/access, and reduced cost. If finance is not capable of extracting the value, then capture the successes as soft savings. Great organizations work collaboratively between operations and finance to convert soft savings to hard savings.

The process used to capture savings does not begin after the change is made, but rather when the first three sections of the A-3 document are developed and documented. Finance should be a partner in developing the reason for improvement, the current conditions, and target conditions. Most importantly, finance should be a partner in developing the key measures for the improvements. Such questions that may be asked during this process include

- Which key measures can be converted into hard savings?
- How will these measures be captured?
- Who will capture the baseline and target measures?

Transactional activities and financial report development are *not* the main focus of the finance department in a Lean healthcare organization. Finance is a partner in the improvement process and consults with the areas of focus to develop meaningful measures, and assists in the analysis and financial calculations that deliver the bottom line results every organization craves. Thirty days following the implementation of any new standard work and the visual management systems used to sustain the improvements, finance can provide their initial snapshot of the projected savings. This savings audit also is completed at the sixty-day point, and then, finally, at the ninety-day point. At the ninety-day point, the results should be incorporated into the budget to institutionalize the new process and hardwire the savings. A summary of all of the savings should be rolled up into an improvement scorecard. A sample scorecard of this summary is provided in Figure 4.13.

Hard and soft savings can be captured at three levels. First, capture the savings on an A-3-by-A-3 basis. Said differently, capture the savings for each individual project. Secondly, roll up the savings within each value stream. Finally, roll up the value stream results into an enterprise total.

What level of return on investment (ROI) should you expect? The general rule of thumb is that the return on investment in the first year should be a minimum of exceeding the breakeven point. Personally, I like to see the first year positive, but there are some investments in the first year that do not provide a hard return. These investments include setting up the infrastructure, establishing your true north measures, training your internal experts, contracting your sensei, and buying supplies to operate the performance system and strategy wall. Your first few value stream mapping and analysis sessions do not return any hard savings, either. These are planning sessions designed to create shared vision of the future and develop the improvement plan. These one-time expenses should quickly give way to meaningful results in quality, access, and cost that should reach the bottom line, once the A-3 improvement has started. Done well, the first year can return a positive ROI. In years two and beyond, the general rule of thumb is a return on investment of 3 or 4:1 for every dollar invested into Lean improvement. How much money would you invest in the stock market if you get a 3:1 return on your investment? Another key point in consideration of understanding ROI is that the organization should have clear understanding of the goals it has selected and how they could impact ROI. How many dollars does higher patient satisfaction, or staff satisfaction, deliver to the income statement? These goals might be paramount to the organization and yet might not be dollar driven. Know and understand the ROI relationships with each measure. That being said, do not select so many nonfinancial measures that ROI isn't important. That statement is fine until money gets tight and times get hard. Without a great ROI, Lean quality improvement is at risk.

There are some common causes why organizations do not receive a great return on investment for their Lean efforts. The most common causes for failure to deliver a return include

■ Failure to sustain improvements (standard work not followed, visual management systems not utilized, management control systems not utilized)

$'s in 000's	Hard Savings (Annual)								Soft Savings (Annual)					Capital Avoidance (Annual)		
	net FTE's	Overtime	Agency Cost Reduction	Increase in volumes	Increase in Visits	Supplies	Drugs and gases	Diagnostic and Therapeutic	Hours free up for other services	Hand-off's reduced	reduction in patient steps travelled	reduction in staff steps travelled	increase in patient satisfaction	construction square footage reduction	Cancelled capital $	improvement in quality/safety
Value Stream: Peri-Operative Services																
A3 #1	$75	$175										14,000				
A3 #2			$32	$300												X
A3 #3				$37							24,000	26,000				
A3 #4						$42										
A3 #5													+ 10 pts			
A3 #6				$67							47,000				$300	
Value Stream Totals	$75	$175	$32	$404	$0	$42	$0	$0	0	0	71000	26000	N/A	$0	$300	
Value Stream: Emergency Services																
A3 #1		$36							22,000		75,000	112,000				
A3 #2			$22		$1,100						110,000	210,000		$250		
A3 #3							$13								$300	X
A3 #4										14,000						
Value Stream Totals	$0	$36	$22	$0	$1,100	$0	$13	$0	22000	14000	185,000	322,000		$250	$300	
Value Stream: Recruiting Cycle																
A3 #1	$55	$475							1400							
A3 #2			$300													
A3 #3										47,000						
Value Stream Totals	$55	$475	$300	$0	$0	$0	$0	$0	1400	47000	0	0		$0	$0	
Enterprise Totals	$130	$686	$354	$404	$1,100	$42	$13	$0	23400	61000	256000	348000		$250	$600	

Total Hard Savings =   *$2,729,000*
Total Capital Avoidance =   *$850,000*

Figure 4.13 Savings Capture Spreadsheet

- Finance not being involved with measurement development, leading to measures without hard savings potential or the inability to convert the results to hard savings
- No system in place to capture results
- Focusing on the wrong measures
- Measures with low expectations (no double digit improvement)
- Line management and/or physician leadership fail to implement/execute the changes

It will take great leadership to steer the organization through all of the issues to create and capture bottom line results. Sustaining the improvements, engaging finance, and learning how to convert soft savings to hard savings are great places to begin.

Step 6: Support Your Change with Ongoing Training and Coaching

The more the world learns about Lean improvement, the more we understand what we don't know, and there is a *whole* lot we don't know. As you remove waste from your operations, new wastes will emerge that you didn't even realize you had. In Lean circles you will hear the phrase of "lowering the water level to a point that new rocks appear." This means that many of the wastes in your process are masked by your current processes and expectations. These "hidden" wastes, when finally identified, will be more difficult to remove and will likely require more sophisticated tools to help you see and eliminate these wastes. Consequently, great Lean organizations constantly augment their improvements with ongoing Lean training and coaching.

Lean Coaching

If you were going to undertake flying a plane, would you read a few articles online, attend a few seminars, play an online flight simulator, and go fly? Not likely. You would probably begin by finding an expert and asking many questions. You might find some other pilots with flying experience and pick their brains as well. If you are still interested, you would sign up for a ground school, complete the course work, make some instructor-assisted flights, and eventually fly solo. After approximately eighty hours of training, frequently spanning weeks or months, you might be ready to pass the skills exam and receive your pilot's license. Even then you would be a novice pilot and would benefit from some further instruction and coaching.

If you want to be great at improvement, you might consider a similar track. I'd find an expert, talk to others who have the walked the road before you, and then seek out extensive coaching. Finding a sensei was covered briefly in Chapter 3, and the role of a sensei in providing coaching will be expanded upon here. There are Lean sensei available who have mastered Lean improvement and who are capable of guiding you and your organization through the improvement processes and change management issues. Having a Lean sensei teach your organization improvement tools and approaches, train your infrastructure, minimize your risk, coach the senior leadership, assist you with your change management, and keep you focused on your journey is a step I would not recommend you skip. To find a Lean sensei, find another organization (either within or outside healthcare) and find out who they use as their sensei. There is a difference between a Lean sensei and a Lean expert. The question you want to ask, to differentiate between a "Lean expert" and a sensei, is: "In how many industries have you provided Lean expertise?" Virtually every world-class organization has used a sensei for many years (often twenty years or more). Their goal is not to improve on their own, but rather use the experience of a master to strengthen their journey and continually have their approaches to improvement challenged. The coaching aspects of Lean are multifaceted; there are dozens of areas of specialization for Lean coaching and several in particular that are used in simply "getting started." The key areas that will require coaching are listed in Table 4.8.

As your journey continues, you will begin to identify new and exciting opportunities to see and eliminate waste. The improvement concepts of flow, pull, defect-free, and visual management offer many tools and improvement techniques you can use. The good news is that, because many organizations have been using Lean for decades, the advanced tools we need already exist. The bad news is that there are hundreds of tools to choose from, and knowing which one to use and when can take some time to learn.

As your organization gets better with the fundamental tools of improvement, you will soon be ready for some more advanced approaches to eliminating waste. Some of the more advanced tools are shown in Table 4.9. Keep in mind that there is no common definition of basic and advanced Lean tools, so what I am calling advanced, others may call basic and vice versa.

In addition to expanding knowledge in new tools and approaches, the staff and medical management and senior leadership at your hospital will need ongoing training to understand and apply Lean. Everyone will need to be grounded in the five principles of improvement, the seven wastes, and A-3 thinking. Over time, we expect everyone to become competent in the common tools for seeing and eliminating waste and in the team-based improvement techniques of value stream mapping and analysis and kaizen improvement.

While learning by doing is encouraged, training of this breadth and depth will eventually require a more formal plan. World-class organizations begin by educating the senior leadership and then having this team train the organization.

Table 4.8   Sample of Year 1 Lean Coaching Topics

Coaching Activity	Description
Infrastructure coaching	Helps in defining your resources for improvement, including internal facilitators, improvement governance, and deployment planning and execution
Gemba walking	Model to learn based on a master/apprentice approach; gemba walking involves walking the work area to review the visual management system and management actions to support improvement
Management coaching	Supports line, middle, and senior management in learning how to manage in a constantly improving environment
Managing for daily improvement (MDI)	MDI coaching teaches an operation to stabilize the Four Ms (manpower, methods, mother nature/environment, and materials) for daily improvement
Problem solving	Using a blend of cause-and-effect diagrams and 5 Whys, real-time problem-solving approaches are learned
Visual management	Coaching on the management of 5S, process control, and results management; can cascade to include program-level improvement and enterprise-wide improvement
Kamishibai	This system uses a series of cascading audits to teach your organization how to live a Lean culture
Management development	Coaching on the fundamentals of management to include setting/maintaining standards, improving standards, and developing people
Kaizen standard work	Coaching preparation, execution, and follow-up activities and improvement standard work
Measurement capture and reporting	Establishing the infrastructure of capture and report hard and soft savings
Cascading leadership standard work	Learning the Lean approach to developing, executing, and improving leadership standard work to create a culture of improvement
Dealing with difficult employees	Group or individual coaching on engaging and inspiring the staff

Table 4.9 Sample of Advanced Lean Tools

Tool	Description
Vertical value stream	Lean approach to world-class project management; used for construction, IT deployment, and spread of Lean improvement, or anywhere else a project plan is needed and used
Quality function deployment (also known as the voice of the customer)	A structured process to develop the voice of both the customer and internal stakeholders when developing a new product or service; QFD is used to determine which features provide the greatest leverage in a new concept and also helps identify project risk and trade-offs that might need to occur during the development phase
3P	Production Process Preparation: New product/ process development technique that invents new capability
2P	Process Preparation: New product or process development technique that delivers new capability using existing technology
Heijunka	Involves leveling volume or mix of work to prevent batching and enable single item flow
Hoshin kanri	Technique used to deploy a strategic plan; powerful senior leadership approach to aligning the strategy horizontally and vertically across the organization to deliver sustainable results; monitors process and outcomes of the strategy to deliver world-class rates of improvement
Problem solving and corrective action	A process to understand a difficult problem and use a series of quality tools to get to the root cause of the problem, develop a series of countermeasures, test the countermeasures, and hard wire a solution; frequently uses A-4 thinking captured on the A-4 form
Statistical process control	Statistical tools used eliminate variability from a process; these will need to be introduced when defect rates approach defects per million
Kanban	Lean supply chain management system

Because it is very difficult to master all of the tools, expertise (tool and technique mastery) is usually divided across the leadership team. For example, one leader will become the expert on flow, another on pull. One person will become the internal expert on 5S and another on visual management. Over time, the responsibilities can be rotated so each member of the team can continue their own personal development and develop expertise in multiple areas. A great Lean improvement system will provide support for ongoing coaching and training. Continuous improvement takes a lifetime to learn, so in the acceleration phase, your organization will want to have both a training plan and coaching plan in place.

Step 7: Spread Lean Thinking across the Organization

If you have made and sustained improvement in one or more value streams, have captured the savings, and are now augmenting your improvement with the needed coaching and training to further develop your improvement skills, you are ready to "spread" some of your improvements; that is, extend your improvements into additional areas of focus. All organizations want to go faster in their rates of improvement, but you can only go as fast as you can sustain. Taking improvement across the organization should follow a very calculated approach. The pace of spreading improvement should be based on meeting outcome criteria (goals or milestones), and *not* on meeting time targets in a plan. When we talk about spread (sharing our improvements), there are two different types. In one type of spread, we take artifacts, products or solutions developed in one area, and move them to another area. For example, maybe we have developed a great way to manage glucose testing on an inpatient unit. It's such an effective solution that other departments will want to replicate this new "best practice."

However, another type of spread means increasing the breadth of value streams that are being improved by the organization. In this form of spread, new areas of the organization are introduced to Lean improvement for the first time. For example, let's assume we began our improvement in the laboratory and in the endocrinology clinic. These two areas have completed their value stream mapping and analysis sessions and have begun to deliver improvement by following A-3 thinking, and establishing standard work and visual management. The results have been sustained and the organization now wants to add two additional value streams for improvement. Perhaps we want to now venture into the cardiac catheterization lab and emergency services, starting as always with value stream mapping and analysis sessions and continuing the improvement process accordingly. These two approaches to spread require different strategies. Before we talk about the strategies, we should differentiate between the two approaches. Table 4.10 evaluates the two spread alternatives.

Table 4.10   Spread Approaches

Spread Approach	Advantages	Considerations
Introducing additional value streams	• Buy-in from the start as current conditions, future conditions and action plans are generated • Engages many more team members in improvement • New innovation with each opportunity • Tailored improvement plans for each value stream	• May be more resource intensive than replication approach • Can take longer than a replication approach • Requires more infrastructure (skilled facilitators) within your organization
Replication of tools, process, and artifacts	• Leverages tested solutions • Training key points are defined • Solutions are based on Lean principles • More rapid approach • Design resources are not consumed	• Usually we are replicating a product and not the thinking • Less buy-in to someone else's solutions • Limits new ideas and innovation • Difficult in "not invented here" environments • Project management resources are needed to manage the change

In most organizations, we are not faced with choosing one approach or the other because both approaches will eventually be utilized to spread the improvements. Let's review both approaches in detail.

Replication of Artifacts, Products, Solutions, and Process

This approach is used when we want to adopt a solution from one area to another in its exact form (or in a form very close to the original). Perhaps you have piloted a new standard process for cleaning a room on one unit and now want to take that process hospital-wide. To successfully achieve this replication, you will want to use a project management-based technique. Lean organizations use a tool known as a vertical value stream to manage projects. A vertical

Time	Customers		Project Team					Suppliers		Standard Work
	X	Y	MGR	RN	PM	HR	TL	D	E	
					Task	1	1	1		not in place
5 days			Task		2		2	2		in place
			Task		3					in place
			4		Task					in place
3 days					Task	5	5	5		in place
1 day			6		6	Task	6			N/A
3 weeks			7	7	7	Task	7	7		not in place
3 weeks	8				8	Task		8		draft
	9			9			Tollgate Review	9		
						Inputs		Outputs		

Phase 1

Figure 4.14 Vertical value stream example.

value steam is like a vertical Gantt chart. Using such a system, the project moves through several different phases and passes clearly defined "tollgates" before moving to the next phase. A simple example of a vertical value stream is shown in Figure 4.14.

Listed below is a simple overview of how you can use vertical value stream mapping to spread your solutions.

1. Identify a representative sample of the key stakeholders affected by the change.
2. Thoroughly review the known solutions so the entire team has an understanding of the process, tools, and visual management systems.
3. Assign an end date for the project.
4. Develop the criteria for passing each milestone. Criteria are measureable outcomes of process and/or results that must be met before moving to the next phase of the project. A project may have dozens or hundreds of input criteria depending on the size and scope (Table 4.11).

Table 4.11   Example of Spread Plan Tollgates and Criteria

Tollgate	Input Criteria
Launch preparation tollgate	• All materials and equipment have been purchased • Resources to perform the work have been hired • Pilot location is identified • Subject matter experts are available on the required days for support • Standard work is written and posted • Unit 5S is complete
Project completion tollgate	• Kamishibai system shows 90% compliance to standard work audits • Corrective action and problem-solving system is in place and operational • Edits to standard work have been made and posted • Unit is meeting planned volume and cost projects and has sustained them for 90 days • Daily huddles are being held and all staff is engaged in problem solving

 5. Determine the tasks needed to pass the tollgate.
 6. Assign accountability for the tasks to meet tollgate criteria. (The tremendous impact of the vertical value stream is the visual map that is presented that clearly details exactly who needs to be involved with each key step.)
 7. Execute the tasks needed to meet the tollgate.
 8. Hold a formal review to confirm that the tollgate criteria have been met before beginning the next phase of the project plan.
 9. Capture lessons learned from the tollgate reviews to improve the organizational knowledge.
10. Repeat Steps 8 and 9 until the project is completed.

If you ensure you have met the tollgate criteria prior to going to the next phase of the project plan, you will minimize rework later in the project. If you plan only the tasks necessary to meet the tollgate criteria, you minimize the number of steps needed to complete the project. The combined impact of these two design elements in your project plan can reduce the timeline for execution by 50 to 75%, while ensuring high-quality results at the end of the project.

Adding Additional Value Streams

Throughout this chapter, we have focused on how to deliver value stream improvement. In Step 2 of our Roadmap for Transformation, we discussed selecting and mapping our value streams. If we retained the notes we made during value stream selection, and the results are consistent with what was seen during the original planning session, we will find it simple to determine which value stream to select next. Using our chart from Figure 4.1, let's assume the baseline conditions have remained the same and we still are trying to improve staff satisfaction for our organization.

The graph in Figure 4.15 shows we likely started improvement in the value stream of Renal Services. If we were going to add another value stream, which one would we select next? The chart would tell us that Cardiology Services would be the next candidate. A word of warning: It will be *very* tempting to deviate from the data and embark on the value stream mapping in an area of "high pain" for the organization. However, we must remain strategic in our deployment of Lean. We need to stay focused on the areas that best help us meet our strategic outcomes. At times, the area of pain will impact your outcome measures, but often it will not—and if it doesn't, beware. You have an obligation

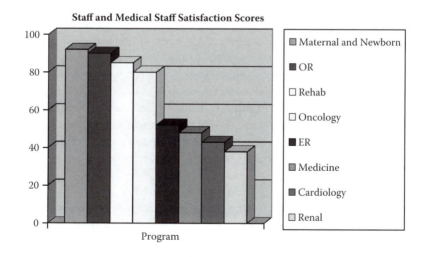

Figure 4.15 Pareto analysis of support staff/medical staff satisfaction by program.

to direct your critical few improvement resources on the most strategic areas. Many organizations struggle because they have a lot of Lean improvement, but not all of it is strategic, and, therefore, it does not add up to anything meaningful in terms of results.

Finally, I'd like to offer a few other key points on adding value streams within your organization:

- There is a limit to the number of value streams in which your organization can engage at any one time. This threshold is based upon several criteria, including organizational headcount, infrastructure (improvement resources), and your ability to sustain improvement. Only add an additional value stream *after* you have sustained improvement in the initial one.

- You need to consider administrative value streams as well as clinical value streams. While our business is healthcare delivery, the clinical teams can only absorb so much change. I have found that a ratio of 75% clinical value stream improvement to 25% administrative value stream improvement works well. Administrative value streams, such as recruiting and on-boarding, supply chain management and health records management (for example), can impact the pace of change within the clinical value streams. So, don't let your clinical improvement get too far ahead of your administrative improvement.

- Don't exclude any areas of your business from the value stream selection process. There is a Lean way to deploy IT, perform help desk and call center operations, execute strategic planning and strategy deployment, create a new service, or design a room, clinic, unit, or entire facility. There is a Lean way to perform parking services, volunteer services, and security services. One way to expand the breadth of Lean improvement and capability is to use Lean in areas that might appear (to a novice) to not be applicable. How about improving centralized scheduling and staffing, developing and implementing an evidence-based care map, improving foundation services (ending the waste in fundraising), and shortening the cycle for clinical research? Hopefully, you are getting the picture: *Anywhere* work is done, a Lean approach exists.

Once you are sustaining your gains, spreading your improvements and increasing your improvement pace, you are on your way to becoming a Lean organization. The improvement of multiple areas of the organization concurrently will help you drive improvement and achieve your strategic measurable outcomes.

Summary: Key Points from Chapter 4

■ Phase 2 in the transformation roadmap entails beginning organizational improvement, delivering improvement, sustaining the improvements, and then spreading improvement across the organization.

■ Improvement should be aligned with your corporate strategy. Ensure you are improving the "right" value streams.

■ Just as the organization requires some steering and governance, each value stream also will require governance. Be sure to have a physician lead and an administrative lead for each value stream, supported by an executive champion.

■ It takes a lifetime to learn any one of the many improvement sciences. While all of the methodologies are based on the scientific method, world-class Lean organizations use the A-3 form and A-3 thinking to deliver Lean improvement.

■ Visual management is the cornerstone to sustaining Lean improvement. Visual management systems are needed to monitor and improve process, results, and the work environment.

■ When standard work is in place, and visual controls are developed and utilized, it is possible to improve every day. This technique is known as managing for daily improvement.

■ Leadership standard work and kamishibai support visual management. These tools bring visual management to life through daily, hands-on engagement of both management and staff.

■ Expect double digit improvement in your key measures. Capturing savings is an integral part of the improvement process. Savings can be captured into three buckets: hard savings, soft savings, and cost avoidance.

■ The improvement journey is best supported with ongoing Lean coaching and development. Lean improvement is not intuitive and leadership and management will require ongoing support to create a culture of improvement. At a minimum, every organization will need to continue to develop new skills and techniques to remove the different forms of waste that are uncovered.

■ When results have been sustained, Lean artifacts and Lean thinking can be spread to other parts of the organization. Spread includes adding additional value streams as well as using Lean project management (through the vertical value stream) approaches to migrate improvement through an organization.

Chapter 5

The Transformation Road Map—Phase 3: Make Organizational Improvement the "New" Culture

If your actions inspire others to dream more, learn more, do more and become more, you are a leader.

John Quincy Adams

Changing to the New Organizational Structure

For many organizations, Phase 2 is both awesome and concerning at the same time. The ability to generate organizational results runs from easy to nearly impossible. For every two positive steps forward, there is one step backward. Fear not. Every organization that has embarked on a Lean transformation has gone through exactly the same experience. The ups and downs associated with progress are present because the old culture and the new culture are now at battle. The management systems and processes that have been developed or evolved over a period of years are not going to leave your organization without a fight.

The good news is if you have made it this far in your improvement journey, reflect on how many one-hour meetings it would take to complete the same level of work that a four-day kaizen event accomplishes. The estimates I normally get from a kaizen team is two to three years of meetings to equal the accomplishment of one kaizen event. The power of Lean is its velocity. So, hold on because the pace of improvement is not for the faint of heart.

The bad news is that it is not even possible to forecast where the resistance will come from. The key to successful transformation is to embrace the new culture and shut down the old systems as quickly as possible. An analogy for the transformational experience is like the phrase "get off your horse." At the turn of the last century, the car was an innovation that was not for the faint of heart. That being said, it was the future and that reliability, quality, and affordability improved exponentially over the next few decades. Still, the "few" would not give up on their "horse." It is time to create the atmosphere of "choice" for the reluctant cowboys. The organization must be firm in their commitment to the "car." Are you ready for this challenge?

A question is often posed as to why organizations fail to change their culture. Why is change so difficult to make on a large scale? While there are many opinions on the root cause of these failures, I believe the number 1 reason for failure is that organizations cannot sustain operating two different systems. It is simply too difficult on the leadership and management to balance old systems and new systems over a long period of time. Because managing in the old system is more comfortable, change fades away. So, how can an organization quickly shut down the old systems and embrace the new culture of improvement? The key lies in hardwiring improvement into the organization to make the change last. There are many support and administrative systems that have to be addressed to hardwire improvement. Several of these systems are shown in Table 5.1.

The core business of your healthcare organization might be research, prevention services, primary care, acute care, postacute, home care, etc. The important thing to understand is that without patients, none of the activities in Table 5.1 are necessary. If your core business is *healthcare*, then that is where your focus needs to be. All of the support areas exist to help the organization function. If the function of the organization is healthcare, then support areas need to ensure that they are supporting the frontline staff and physicians, and their corresponding management, not the other way around. Your organization never wants the "tail wagging the dog."

By this time in the transformation journey, you will be seeing substantial improvements in quality, safety, access, and cost. However, these results will

Table 5.1 Processes/Systems That Need to Be Changed to Support a Culture of Improvement

Department	Core Process
Organizational Development	• Capacity building for clinical and administrative staff, management, and physicians
Information Technology	• Help desk services • IT design, development, and deployment
Finance	• Accounts receivable management • Accounts payable • Payroll • Budgeting • Month-end close
Human Resources	• Recruiting • Job descriptions and competencies • Promotion criteria • Occupational health services • Lean management development
Materials	• Developing a Lean supply chain
Operations or Marketing or Facilities	• New process or new service development • Construction services • Project management
Senior Leadership	• Strategic planning • Strategy deployment • Improvement governance • Committee management
Medical Leadership	• Physician credentialing • Physician lead quality improvement
All	• Taking Lean improvement beyond your four walls to suppliers, customers, and partners

not continue without the support organization's improving at an identical rate. Lean is not just for direct care, it is applicable anywhere work is done. Any area of the organization that digs in and protects its turf defending processes that are no longer adequate to support a culture of improvement must be addressed. Aligning these processes in support of the clinical work will cement the improvements and changes into your organization. In order for an organization to transition into a culture that supports process improvement, every single person in every department must be dedicated to improvement and creating a positive culture. Lean transformation is like a tire, you must ensure that the entire tire is aligned, properly and equally round, and balanced or you will be in for a rough ride. Your organization is similar to a chain where the strength of the chain will be determined by the weakest link. It doesn't matter how strong the other links are. What matters is the weaker links because their lack of strength will ultimately determine the limits of the transformation. Let's review some of the processes that can be improved to help make change to the new organizational culture.

Lean Capacity Building

A culture of improvement cannot be created with only a handful of internal experts and a few leaders championing the change process; rather, everyone will need some skills in the science of improvement. Skills will need to be developed at all levels of the organization. Table 5.2 lists the management levels in a typical healthcare organization and a summary of the skills that you should build toward.

After reviewing Table 5.2, are you surprised that the highest levels of leadership require the most skills? In a world-class organization, the role of the senior leadership is to mentor and coach their subordinates. Mastery of Lean tools and concepts must occur to enable the leadership to become mentors. It is not expected that everyone take intensive training to become experts. However, a capacity building plan should be developed to ensure that the organization is constantly learning new skills relative to the application of Lean and the management of a Lean system. While the concepts are not difficult to understand, they also are *not* intuitive. In fact, the Lean approaches go against the many years of what determined success in management. Lean is full of contradictions from our past learning. For example, "doing things one at a time is better than doing work in a batch" or "you sometimes must go slow to go fast."

I would like to share a simple analogy as a final thought on capacity building: Learning Lean is like learning golf. It really doesn't matter how many books you have read or how many videos you have watched, golf is best learned by focused practice under the watchful eye of a professional. Golf is learned by doing. Lean

Table 5.2 Capacity Building

Support Staff and Medical Staff Affected	Skills Required
Everyone (including physicians)	• 7 Wastes • 5 principles of improvement • A-3 Thinking • Common tools to see and eliminate waste • 5S
Line management and physician leadership	Everything above plus: • Managing for daily improvement • Basic project management skills • Problem-solving skills • Value stream management
Middle management and senior leadership	Everything above plus: • Strategy deployment

is also learned by doing. Thus, any capacity building that occurs, must be application-based. Learn the tools, techniques, and approaches on real examples in the workplace. Lecture, classroom training, and simulations are all helpful, but the best learning occurs when the tools are learned and then immediately applied.

Lean Information Technology

Tremendous amounts of money are spent on information technology (IT). Integrated business systems that share databases for purchasing, inventory management, and accounts payable, and financial accounting are common and becoming more common every day. On the clinical side of the operation, large amounts of capital are being invested in electronic patient records, scheduling software, medication management, utilization management, and countless other systems. Data are captured and shared with the click of a mouse. Reports can be generated providing all types of statistics and trends, broken down by diagnosis, cost center, provider, etc. Nonetheless, there are differences of opinions on the value of IT systems within healthcare. A Harvard study in 2009 concluded that in an evaluation on 4,000 U.S. hospitals over a four-year period of time that the investment in installing and running hospital IT systems is greater than any cost savings.*

The financial impacts of an integrated IT system are debatable, but does IT make healthcare safer? Automatic pharmaceutical dispensing units that provide unit dose medications help with administration accuracy and reduce expired medicine obsolescence. Bar coding systems are used to verify the correct patient is being treated. Electronic patient medical records allow clinicians to quickly share information that could enable speeding up the time for decision making. I think everyone would agree that the use of IT systems creates the possibility to improve the quality of healthcare. What about clinical value? The integrated databases and corresponding reports definitely appeal to administrators, but what about physicians, nurses, and allied staff? In my travels, I have taken a straw poll on how well support staff and medical staff like their IT systems. The responses vary greatly from indispensible to total waste of time. Thus, I summarize current healthcare IT spending as an investment with a questionable financial return, some quality improvement capability, and mixed reviews on the value from the clinician's perspective. So, IT, in and of itself, is not the solution to all of healthcare's problems.

Regardless of my assessment, research firm BCC (Business Communications Company) estimates that the total clinical healthcare market is projected to grow from $7.4 billion in 2011 to nearly $17.5 billion in 2016.† This is an increase in spending of 136%. Lean organizations almost all use significant application of IT. The challenge is learning how to use Lean thinking to deliver compelling value from the application of the technology. Rather than debating the cost savings, improvement in patient safety and quality, and staff satisfaction associated with the use of the system, use the principles of Lean thinking to eliminate waste, and move the true north measures to accomplish your strategic outcomes.

The biggest problem that I see organizations make when investing in IT is that they bend their processes to fit the IT system and not the other way around. As a basic premise for IT requirements, ensure the process has been through the Lean lens before automating it. Taking a bad process and automating it merely makes for a "faster" bad process.

A Lean thinking organization will follow the steps in Table 5.3 when acquiring IT.

Many organizations first determine what is desired for the solution. For example, a new staff scheduling system is needed and they then proceed to jump

---

* Mearian, L. 2009. Harvard study: Computers don't save hospitals money, December 2. Online at: www.computerworld.com/s/article/print/9141428/Harvard_study
† Pham, T. 2012. 2012 Health IT Spending and Trends, On Line Tech, December 28. Online at: http://resource.onlinetech.com/2012-health-it-spending-trends/

Table 5.3   Acquiring IT for Healthcare

Step #	Activity
1	Initiate an A-3 and select True North Measures aligned to the organizational strategy.
2	Value stream map the end-to-end process.
3	Using creativity before investing in capital, execute the rapid improvement plan and redesign the process by creating flow and pull, making the process defect-free, and managing visually.
4	Determine if the improvement meets the strategic targets. If the new process meets the targets, you do not need an IT solution.
5	When incremental improvement can no longer meet the organizational targets, consider capital investment.
6	Determine if incremental investment on your current IT platform will allow you to meet your improvement targets.
7	If IT investment is determined to be the best solution, map the future state.
8	Evaluate process alternatives that enable the organization to meet the future state.
9	Investigate which IT solutions enable the future state process.
10	Perform a stakeholder analysis to be sure the solution accomplishes the following: • Meets the needs of patients and family members • Improves quality and access • Meets the needs of support staff and medical staff • Delivers clinical value • Reduces duplication • Minimizes errors • Is intuitive and doesn't require hours of training • Minimizes handoffs • Minimizes transactions • Remote access if necessary

(Continued)

Table 5.3 (*Continued*)   Acquiring IT for Healthcare

	• Meets the needs of the organization
	   • Does not increase the overall costs of the organization through entering transactions, keeping the system upgraded, etc.
	   • Can be supported
	   • Ideally is interoperable
	   • Is supported by process
	   • Compliance with statutory requirements
	   • Mitigates risk

11	Write the requirements document with the return on investment articulated.
12	Get capital approval.
13	Research alternatives.
14	Select an alternative.
15	Perform a vertical value stream analysis to develop the project plan.
16	Deliver the project in the least waste way.
17	Perform a postproject evaluation to evaluate the ROI and how well the project delivered value.

to Step 10. A Lean organization would begin by asking: "What is the problem we are trying to solve?" Then follow the steps in A-3 thinking to get to the root cause and develop a countermeasure. By starting with the solution, the first four steps in the A-3 thinking process are being skipped.

To close the section on healthcare IT, note that Lean thinking not only applies in the acquisition and deployment of IT, but also in the support systems of IT. Clinical informatics and decision support requests, as well as help desk services, can all be run in a Lean way. Standard work should be in place, balanced to the customer demand for services. Output (services and support) should be managed visually with a process control board. Results should be managed visually through the performance management system. Continuous improvement is expected in the areas of staff engagement, process quality, lead time for responses and services, and cost performance. Not having high performing IT systems will eventually have a detrimental impact on the ability to continuously improve in other areas of the organization.

Lean Finance

As part of their innovation series published in 2008, the Institute for Healthcare Improvement (IHI) created a whitepaper on the "Seven Leadership Leverage Points for Organizational-Level Improvement in Health Care." Leverage Point 5 is: Make the Chief Financial Officer a Quality Champion.* The general context of this leverage point is that CFOs (chief financial officers) are finding significant opportunities to improve patient care margins by reducing and eliminating error and clinical waste.[†] An important step in making change to the new culture is that process improvement work quickly shifts from an expense (funding teams and facilitators to make improvement) to an indispensable asset. Continuous improvement can create simultaneous, ongoing improvement in quality, access, and cost.

In a Lean organization, the CFO is one of, if not the biggest fan of continuous improvement. The CFO is a visible champion who can relay at a moment's notice the correlation between a culture of improvement and the corresponding favorable impact to the balance sheet and income statement. Because the CFO has major impacts on the budget and the allocation of corporate funds, having the CFO as a big fan is important. However, being a Lean organization and creating a culture of improvement goes beyond having a cheerleader. Lean leadership implies leading by example and every great Lean organization deploys Lean finance. Lean finance is about creating a system of continuous improvement within the core finance and accounting processes. Lean systems can be applied to the revenue generation cycle, accounts receivable, accounts payable, payroll, budgeting, month-end close, and health records management (billing and coding). Anywhere work is done, Lean can be applied, waste can be eliminated, and improvement can be made.

For each of these areas, the value stream mapping and analysis tool can be used to create an improvement plan. A-3 thinking can be applied to create continuous flow and pull. Within each of these processes, waste can be eliminated and lead times can be shortened for services. Defect-free principles can be used to mistake-proof the data going into and coming out of the work, ensuring a high degree of accuracy. Standard work can be created to support the new processes, and this standard work can be managed visually with process control and performance boards. Double digit improvement is expected year over year in the areas of quality, lead time, and cost performance. As an example, a 650-person

---

* Reinertsen, J. L., M. Bisognano, and M. D. Pugh. 2008. *Seven leadership leverage points for organization-level improvement in health care,* 2nd ed. Cambridge, MA: Institute for Healthcare Improvement, p. 20.
† Ibid.

healthcare community service agency with annual revenue of $250 million servicing 17,000 clients per month took a Lean approach to the month-end closing process. The current state process took twenty-two calendar days to close the books. The data quality was highly questionable and, because the statements came out so late in the month, the results were rarely used for decision making. In the current process, activity was bounced from accountant to accountant and between departments leaving little time for analysis.

To improve the month-end close process, value must first be specified. Who is the customer of the month-end close process? We could make the case that management is the customer because the data could be used for decision making. This is not really the case, however. Month-end reporting is a financial requirement necessary to meet accounting requirements and reporting laws. As such, the close doesn't really help patients. So, it is pure overhead and ideally should be as transactional as possible. The analysis of the reporting can be quite helpful in understanding where wasted time and activity is entering the business. The value add to the business is in this analysis. Summarizing the current state, the process delivered financial data necessary for reporting requirements, but delivered little management data for decision making and improvement. This is basically pure waste, allowing for the fact that reporting requirements are legally mandated.

After creating a new process workflow, the month-end reporting and analysis workflow was redesigned to seven working days with one and a half days built in for managerial analysis. The transactional activities were improved to create accurate data and the new financial analysis delivered business value add. Six-month plans were put in place to reduce the close time to three days with the long-range goal to have a one-day close.

Another example of a Lean finance would be an improvement in the revenue generation cycle. An urban teaching hospital with revenues of $1 billion and around 5,000 employees wanted to improve its top line and cash flow. This organization supports over 100,000 annual ER (emergency room) visits, 25,000 annual inpatient admissions, and 350,000 annual outpatient visits. Before applying Lean to this process, the organization had bad debt expense of 15.3%, and accounts receivable outstanding at fifty-two days.

Finance leadership led a value stream improvement from the point a patient registers in the hospital system to the point where cash is collected. A series of kaizen events using A-3 thinking followed in the following areas:

■ Patient access (Registration)
■ Collection of co-pays
■ Capturing preferred accommodations
■ Transcription

- Coding
- Billing
- Accounts receivable

Each process was improved and ended with standard work that could be managed visually. An analysis of variation from the standard was conducted daily, supported by the team huddle. Problem-solving efforts were applied to close the gaps between actual and target. In the first year, on an investment of about $100,000, the project returned over $5,000,000 while utilizing the current IT infrastructure. There were a few modifications to data fields and screens, but no major IT purchase was required. The improvement was the result of repeated applications of seeing and eliminating waste that changed the way work was done. The changes were supported by creating a culture of improvement to allow ongoing continuous improvement to the process led by the staff and managed visually. In addition to the financial returns, the streamlined registration practices led to a better patient experience (less waiting and duplication) and less waiting for the staff. The improvements in the health records cycle—transcription, coding, and billing—led to enhanced physician satisfaction due to less rework and delays in their payment/billing processes.

Lean Human Resources

One area of your organization that plays a key role in change and change management is human resources (HR). The employment life cycle is monitored through human resources. The life cycle of an employee can be seen in Table 5.4.

Any organization that wants to embed change as their new culture better be paying a *lot* of attention to the HR practices and policies. Your organization sends signals every time an employee action is taken. Promoting the manager that doesn't follow standard work over the one that does sends a signal. Leaving Lean training out of orientation and onboarding of new staff and medical staff sends a sign. Not having Lean skills as a competency for new hires outside of the organization sends a signal.

Likewise you can send positive signals. If you are having trouble getting physicians to participate in quality improvement, make the requirement part of the hiring process. Reward the team that best follows standard work. Every move related to support staff and medical staff is an opportunity to change the culture of your organization.

The long-term sustainability of your new culture is directly tied to your recruiting practices. Hiring people with multiple years of Lean experience

Table 5.4 Employee Life Cycle

Life Cycle Phase	Activities
Recruitment	Job descriptions and competencies
	Recruitment and sourcing
	Hiring cycle
Onboarding	Orientation
	Initial training
Retention and development	Ongoing training, education, and skills development
	Leadership and organizational development
	Personnel management—management of status changes
	Employer of choice programs
	Compensation and benefits
	Promotions
	Employee evaluations
	Occupational health and safety administration
	Labor relations
Separation	Planned and unplanned separation from the organization

is a plus, but not a requirement. Hiring people that can work in a team, be open-minded to team-based change, and can follow standard work is a must. The Lean skills and competencies you require should be written into the job description and follow along with the job posting. Don't underestimate the amount of work it will take to update the dozens (or hundreds) of job descriptions that exist in your organization. You can update the descriptions on an as needed basis when you need to hire or transfer someone, but start early.

Lean thinking should follow the HR practices used to manage an employee through their life cycle. This can be accomplished in two ways. First, Lean skills and attributes can be built into the various activities of the life cycle. For example, Lean training can begin at orientation, and Lean competencies can be integral to raises and promotions. Second, Lean thinking can be used to get the work done. Can waste be taken out of the orientation training? Can waste be taken out of the occupational health and safety practices? Can the hiring cycle time be reduced by 50%? Are the HR practices executed with standard work? Are they managed visually with clear targets and action plans? Is A-3 thinking evident and obvious?

Frequently, HR has the lead on creating people-based policies for an organization. One example would be the absence management policy. I have frequently heard HR department personnel say that the managers do not follow the absence management policy. Managers may skip steps in the administration of the policy or fail to document an absence in a timely manner. Certainly, the expectation is that everyone follows standard work, managers included. But let's look at the application of Lean from another perspective. This book is about leadership. HR leadership may be starting with the wrong problem. With regards to creating a culture of improvement, "clean up your own sandbox before you play in someone else's." Rather than changing someone else (i.e., the manager not following policy), a different approach might be to start by changing the HR work itself. Improve the hiring process and streamline labor relations. Optimize occupational safety and health services. Work with your own staff to create a culture of improvement and deliver value to the organization. When this is underway, the opportunity to engage others outside of your area of focus will be much easier.

Back to the absence management policy. I'm not inclined to let management totally off the hook. However, as Lean thinkers, we should use the Lean tools available to improve the process. A-3 thinking and problem-solving tools can be used to understand why the absence policy is not consistently used by management. Develop countermeasures to resolve the root causes and test the solutions. Engage management in the problem-solving process, and the chances of success will increase created by the increased understanding of the root causes of the problem and management ownership of the problem.

A community hospital, let's call it Meadowbrook, was having trouble sourcing and hiring nurses for the organization. This hospital had approximately 100 beds and a staff of 1,200. The hospital was state-of-the-art, with competent management and leadership. The commute was not excessive relative the "big city" competition, yet the hospital had a difficult time filling positions. Bob Broach, an experienced Lean consultant, once taught me that "the best people are on the market the shortest period of time." This makes sense intuitively, as the best people are always hired first. This statement also implies that a long recruiting cycle is not your friend. The best people will be off the market if a competitor can hire faster than you.

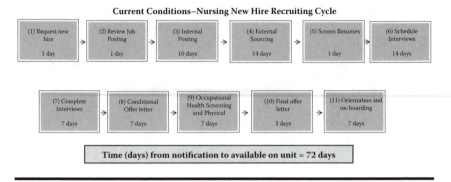

Figure 5.1 Current conditions recruiting cycle.

The organization decided to perform a value stream analysis on the recruiting cycle. The current condition showed a lead time for a new hire of seventy-two days. The process and timeline can be seen in Figure 5.1.

A series of four-day kaizen events followed, spanning nearly nine months, that included

- Improving the posting of positions
- Streamlining the applicant screening process
- Reducing the interviewing cycle
- Improving the offer letter process
- Improving the employee physical process
- Reducing the timeline and effectiveness of the orientation process

The final results reduced the recruiting cycle to forty-two days. This improvement of thirty days effectively solved this organization's recruiting issues. Qualified candidates now could be entered quickly and effectively into the recruiting cycle and hired in a timely manner. The net result for Meadowbrook was a reduction in agency/temporary staff expense of nearly $400,000 annually and a reduction in annual overtime premium of $280,000. Perhaps the bigger win for the organization was that, with the shorter cycle time, the better performers were now part of the team.

Another example of making change in the new culture involved improving management development and promotions. In many organizations, the best charge nurse or team leader gets promoted into the next open supervisor or manager position. In industry, the saying goes: If you take the best painter and make him/her your supervisor, I can't guarantee you got a great supervisor, but I can guarantee you just lost your best painter." The same goes for great clinicians. The best clinician doesn't always make the best supervisor, but it does ensure you just lost your best clinician. Does this mean we can't promote great clinicians or deserving people? Absolutely not, but a great Lean organization has the best clinicians in a position to succeed when promoted.

An urban hospital in a metropolitan area of approximately 3 million people wanted to improve the skills of their management team. This organization, that we will call Lakeshore Health, decided to establish some Lean-based promotion criteria. Any staff member that wanted to be considered for management had to take an eighteen-month position as part of the Lean core team. This program, known as the Lean management residency program, was designed to ensure that any new manager was an internal expert in Lean thinking before assuming his/her new role. Candidates were required to interview for these positions, and not everyone was accepted. Applicants needed to be in the top 20% of their peer group, be listed on the promotable watch list, be open minded to change, and have the ability to "carry the room." After an extensive interviewing process, the top candidates were accepted into the management residency program.

In the management residency program, the participants were given a value stream to improve. Their role was to learn and master A-3 thinking and apply the cycle of improvement to a series of areas within their value stream. In addition to the improvement activity, large amounts of time were dedicated to mastering the skills of sustaining improvement. By the end of the program, the residents were deeply exposed to Lean thinking and had dedicated, targeted, hands-on experience with

- 5S
- Value stream mapping and analysis
- The kaizen cycle of improvement including the standard work for preparing, executing, and sustaining a rapid cycle improvement using A-3 thinking and the A-3 form
- Standard work
- Visual management systems of both process and results
  - Managing for daily improvement
  - Kamishibai
- Improvement and sustaining project management
- A comfort with charts and graphs
- Experience with staff engagement
- Leadership standard work
- An understanding of true north measures
- Experience in working vertically and horizontally across the organization
- Linking local improvement to program and corporate strategy
- Driving double digit improvement in the key measures

When the first class graduated, the residents initially returned to their home area to make contributions to the program/department from which they came. This created an incentive for managers to encourage staff to participate in the program. When supervisor positions opened up, the interested candidates applied and frequently were given the new position. The results were dramatic. A typical resident, when compared to their peers, outperformed their counterparts in all measurable areas. The average increase in performance versus their peers against the key measures was 12–35% higher in any measureable category. These key measures include quality and safety, lead time and access, cost performance, the patient experience, growth, and staff engagement.

Having your promotable staff get experience as Lean thinkers before taking on a leadership assignment truly holds great potential for your organization. The assignment on the Lean core team taught the residents not only the skills to deliver and sustain improvement, but also a new way to manage. Improvement became part of the culture of their new departments/programs. As a young manager, there is a tendency to fall back on your experiences you encountered as a staff member. You manage as you learned to manage from your predecessor. A typical "qualification" in a non-Lean thinking organization may well be based on an individual's ability to handle emergencies or "firefighting." In a Lean organization, firefighting is an indication of a process not in control and in need of improvement. The firefighter qualification becomes less relevant and the Lean skill set becomes far more relevant. A period of time immersed in Lean thinking will create new and better experiences to draw upon. This eliminates the many months of trial and error a new manager must experience when new to the role. By promoting candidates from the residency program, your organization is sending a signal that Lean management is important.

Lean Supply Chain

A Lean process is one where nonvalue-added activity is continuously reduced. In creating a culture where change is the new way of business, the supply chain holds great promise. An area of frustration for support staff and medical staff is the proximity and availability of supplies and materials. The good news for healthcare is that the notion of Lean supply chain is well documented from sixty years of Lean industrial supply chain practices. A great Lean healthcare supply chain can yield the following benefits:

- Improved availability of materials and supplies
- Shorter lead times for replenishment
- Materials supplies near or at point of use

- More frequent replenishment of supplies
- Less obsolescence of materials and supplies
- Better ergonomics associated with material and supply presentation
- Improved inventory turnover
- Reduced supply chain costs (lower cost of goods sold, reduced administrative costs, reduced shipping/receiving/materials management costs, and reduced carrying costs)
- Safer care
- Improved support staff and medical staff satisfaction
- Improved patient experience
- Better supplier relationships
- A constantly improving and evolving supply chain relevant to daily requirements

How effective is your supply chain? There are many third-party vendors within healthcare that provide kitting and distribution services in very short lead times. Materials and supplies, with the exception of some hard to acquire pharmaceuticals, can be ordered and received within one to two days. Shorter lead times should lead to higher inventory turnover. Inventory turnover is the ratio of how many times an organization's inventory is sold and replaced over a period of time. Generally speaking, there are two calculations of this ratio. The easier formula to understand is

$$\text{Inventory Turnover} = \text{Sales \$/Average Inventory \$ on Hand}$$

As an example, assume New River Hospital (fictional name) has annual healthcare billings of \$400 million and carries inventory on hand of \$50 million. New River's inventory turnover is

$$\text{Inventory Turnover} = \$400 \text{ million}/\$50 \text{ million} = 8 \text{ inventory turns}$$

Eight (8) turns implies that the inventory dollars of New River Hospital turnover eight times per year. It is generally accepted that inventory turns across all industries range from the 8 to 12 annually.

Now, back to the healthcare supply chain. With the availability of supplies and materials in one to two days, we should expect inventory turns approaching 100. Why? Assume that there are 250 working days per year. Materials can be received every one to two days. Theoretically, we could turn over all of the inventory every two days. This would lead to 250 days/2 days average inventory on hand, which would equal 125 inventory turns.

My experience in working with North American healthcare organizations show the majority of organizations have typical inventory turnover numbers of four to twelve annual turns for storerooms and two to eight annual turns for surgical supplies. There is a big gap between 125 turns and 12. For a $400 million organization, 125 turns shows on-hand inventory of $3.2 million, while 12 turns has an on-hand inventory cost of $33.3 million. The difference of $30 million might eliminate the need to borrow for capital improvements, or prevent the delay of starting a new program.

In a Lean supply chain, materials and supplies would be pulled into the organization at the rate of the customer demand. The Lean word for a pull system with minimum inventory would be kanban. Kanban, loosely translates to "signboard or signal," and is a replenishment system based on signals that come from the true need of the customer. This is significantly different from a forecasting system, or a min-max system, or a reorder point system. A kanban system is an entire management system for operating the supply chain in the least waste way.

What does a world-class supply chain look like? I have been in a few of the tier 1 automotive suppliers and a few automotive assembly plants that routinely get over 1,000 inventory turns annually. This means the entire factory turns over all of its inventory dollars every four hours. While I'm not sure of any healthcare supply chain approaching 1,000 inventory turns, there are some programs starting to approach 50 turns!

As an example of the power of a Lean supply chain, one hospital system, we will call it Oak Grove Healthcare, wanted to improve its supply chain practices in the pharmacy. This particular pharmacy had 250 personnel that filled nearly 3.5 million orders annually. After completing a value stream analysis and series of kaizen events, the on-hand inventory was reduced from $3.9 million to $3.4 million. This freed up $500,000 in cash and represented a 14.7% reduction in overall inventory.

This improvement in cash flow is fairly typical using Lean approaches and A-3 thinking. In addition to the cash flow generation, one purchasing person was freed up from the ordering process and redeployed to work on other value-added inventory management projects. Three supply chain technicians were freed up as well from the pharmacy resupply process and redeployed first to improve the organization's receiving process and then to work on Lean supply chain projects on a full-time basis. The reductions in stock-outs lead to a reduced time to fill for new orders leading to many benefits including enhanced physician satisfaction, fewer substitutions (fewer phone calls going back and forth), and shorter times to initiating treatment.

Supply chain practices exist to allow the organization to function. In and of themselves, the supply chain creates *no* direct value to the patient. They exist to serve the support staff and medical staff in their delivery of value-added services. Because supply chain practices consume time, space, and resources while failing to directly affect the need of the patient, they are excellent candidates for elimination of process waste. Lean leadership of supply chain practices implies that world-class rates of improvement should be strived for along with the key measures of human development, process and product quality, lead time for supplies and materials, and productivity. It is not possible to provide world-class healthcare without a world-class supply chain. Remember that an organization is only as strong as its weakest link. Lean organizations understand this and create the vision, align the resources, and inspire the supply chain team for greatness.

Lean Project Management, Lean Construction, and Lean New Service Introduction

As you may now recognize, there is a Lean approach to all of the work done in any organization. Anywhere work is completed and value is created for a customer, waste is present. A Lean organization understands this and aspires every day to making the organization more waste free. Significant organizational dollars are spent in healthcare on introducing "new" things; earlier we discussed introducing new technology and IT systems. Project work is plentiful within healthcare. New quality procedures need to be put in place, new therapies are introduced, and accreditation standards must be met. Additionally, new programs are introduced. New services and clinics are made available to patients, and facilities are redeveloped or new construction projects are added.

In a Lean organization, regardless of the final value delivered either to patients or the organization itself, a similar approach is used: Lean new product/process introduction. World-class new product/process introduction management involves meeting two simultaneous objectives: (1) delivering compelling value to the customer and (2) doing the work in the least waste way. Table 5.5 shows a sample of the tools used in Lean new product/process introduction.

The vertical value stream approach to project management, part of the Lean planning system, was discussed in the deployment of IT projects earlier in the chapter. This project management approach can and should be used to manage any project. Lean project management is used to meet the customer specifications of any project, in the shortest lead time and in the least waste way. This approach has been used effectively in managing the following types of projects within healthcare:

■ Preparing for accreditation
■ Introduction of new therapies

Table 5.5   Lean New Product and Process Introduction

System and Organizational Management	Planning System	Execution and Delivery System
Business case	Quality function deployment	Concurrent engineering
System level architecture and standards	Voice of the customer	2P/3P design
Portfolio management	Vertical value stream mapping	Value engineering
Cost modeling	Obeya (big room) concept	Design for X
Knowledge management	Net present value analysis	Quality systems (mistake proofing)
Strategy deployment	Project risk analysis	Failure mode effects analysis
Visual management	Kano	Cause and effect problem solving

- Deployment of new medical equipment (diagnostic imaging, medical surgical, etc.)
- Facility redevelopment
- New construction
- Month-end close (financial)
- The budgeting cycle
- Spread of known Lean solutions to other departments and programs
- Introduction of new services (clinics and procedures)
- IT development and deployment
- Acquiring new businesses
- Capturing additional/new market share
- Development and deployment of new training curriculums
- Orientation of new employees

There are countless other areas for the Lean new product and process approaches to be realized. For those of you new to Lean, I think you can now see that a comprehensive enterprise-wide Lean management system is more that a toolkit to improve patient flow, reduce cost, and improve the quality of care. Lean is an entire business system that permeates every process in your entire organization. Respect for people and the elimination of nonvalue-added activity become part of every staff member's everyday job. Making change to the new culture implies continuously improving every system in your organization. From the list above, there are a number Lean tools and applications involved with new product/process introduction. Like all of the Lean tools and applications, they take years to internalize. Unfortunately, this set of tools and techniques is much more technical in nature and cannot be learned in a single session. A good Lean sensei will be able to teach your organization the new product introduction process or direct you to someone who can.

The Lean new product and process introduction system comes from the Toyota Production System approaches used to introduce new vehicles. Toyota can bring a new vehicle to market in about half the time of many of its competitors. It has developed this system over forty years of refining their new product introduction process that continues to evolve and improve today. As an example of a new process introduction, Crescent Moon Hospital launched a new service that provided short-stay rehabilitation services to adult medicine patients. Crescent Moon is a small community hospital of approximately 125 inpatient beds supported by approximately 800 employees and 300 volunteers. The hospital had challenges discharging patients from their acute care beds because the community services had a gap in their home rehab service offerings. There were long-term care choices and complex continuing care choices, and limited home choices, but no short-term rehab offerings within fifty miles of the hospital. Thus, the leadership team and medical program decided to develop and offer a sixteen-bed, short stay, rehab program to its patients.

The improvement process began with the creation of an A-3 to develop and deliver the required services. The improvement plans on the Short Stay Rehabilitation Unit called for a thorough understanding of the voice of the customer and a 2P (Process Preparation) design kaizen event was used to create the new service. The voice of the customer is the process where you gather the needs and wants of the customer. For a new process, we are concerned with the customer groups of the end customer, the staff, and the organization. The project closed with a vertical value stream project plan to acquire and deploy the people, equipment, and construction to launch the new service. A brainstorming exercise combined with stakeholder interviews was used to identify the voice of the customer and define the process requirements. An example of the voice of the customer documentation used is shown in Figure 5.2.

A portion of the key findings from the identification of the voice of the customer included maximizing customer service for the patient, reducing

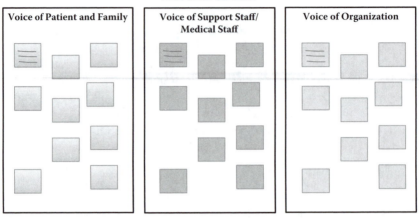

Figure 5.2 Voice of the customer for inpatient short-term rehabilitation services.

steps travelled for the staff, and reducing falls risk for all three customer groups. Once the voice of the customer was defined, the next step was to create the new process. In a Lean organization, the *entire* process is defined before any work is done. Process definition includes defining the following work flows:

1. Identification of the people required to do the work
2. Defining the work methods
3. Defining the materials, supplies needed to do the work
4. Defining the equipment needed to do the work.
5. Defining the information requirements to accomplish the work tasks
6. Defining the quality control systems to know the work has been done properly
7. Defining how quality and improvement will be communicated and acted upon within the work team

The 2P kaizen event is tailor-made to define the seven workflows. In addition to defining the process, the 2P kaizen event is designed to develop breakthrough improvement in the introduction of a new product or process. This specific event looked at several of the core processes that would occur within the unit on a regular basis and defined these seven workflows for each of these core processes. The core processes included unit admission, medication administration, development of an interprofessional plan of care, discharge planning, meal delivery,

Table 5.6 Seven Flows for Hourly Rounding

Product	Hourly Rounding
People	Unit nurses, physiotherapists, physiotherapist assistants, multiskilled attendants
Methods	Each hour ensure each patient is properly positioned, has all the items in the appropriate proximity, has their personal needs attended to, and has pain adequately managed
Equipment	Patient bed, patient table, mobility aids, remote control, patient chair, electronic chart, computer, bed pan or commode
Supplies and materials	Tissues, wipes, briefs
Information	Standard work for hourly rounding, hourly rounding visual management system, patient electronic medical record, standard work for hourly rounding
Quality	Visual management system for hourly rounding, variance report from missed rounds
Improvement	Action plans to improve the quality of the hourly rounding process visual management of results of the performance of the rounding process

rehabilitation treatment, patient care rounding, and charting. Obviously, there are other processes that occur on a daily basis on a rehabilitation unit, but these were considered to be the trouble areas for the organization.

Providing a further illustration of the seven workflows, Table 5.6 shows the seven flows for the hourly rounding process that was developed and deployed on the new unit. Before coming up with the final product, the 2P kaizen actually develops multiple ways to meet the customer requirements. A minimum of seven different ways are explored and evaluated against the customer requirements before settling in on a solution. The solution is then performed in a mock simulation to verify its effectiveness.

On this particular unit, the patient satisfaction results became the best in the hospital, and has been sustained in the 98th percentile against peer units. Additionally, as a result of the hourly rounding, the call bell requirements were reduced by 85% over other peer units. These types of breakthrough results are anticipated and expected from 2P improvement work.

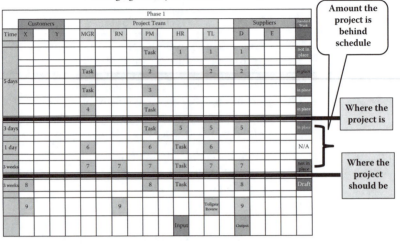

Figure 5.3   Managing the project schedule timeline.

This particular project closed with a vertical value stream analysis to develop the implementation plan. The team building the plan will stand in front of a wall and complete the step-by-step planning required to deliver compelling customer value from the project with the minimum amount of resources. Governance of the project plan occurs by meeting in front of the wall where the plan sits. I encouraged the development team to use two pieces of string to visualize the plan. One piece of string is used to show the actual date, and the second piece of string is used to show on which task the team is working. A large gap between the two pieces of string means the team is way ahead or way behind. Strive to make the two strings set at exactly the same point on the plan. In Figure 5.3, the left hand column of the vertical value stream map is actually a calendar beginning with the date of the plan at the top and the completion date at the bottom. The header of the column is identified with the word "time." The project plan shown in is behind schedule. The two pieces of string make this obvious.

There are some excellent features built into the Lean project management approach. One of the best benefits is the reduced timeline for the completion of the project. This occurs for several reasons including

- Minimizing the number of steps necessary to complete the project
- Building the collaboration in up front so time is not lost chasing down technical experts for their opinions and feedback
- Holding the discipline of the milestone reviews to prevent incomplete tasks to creep into the next milestone creating rework

Table 5.7   Features and Benefits of Lean Project Management

Enhanced Value is Delivered	Project Waste is Reduced/Eliminated
Maximizes the use of resources	Reduces the project timeline by 25–75%
Only defined tasks create work	Collaboration is scheduled
Standard methods are followed	Milestone discipline prevents errors from moving forward in the project
Continuous improvement is built in	Project is planned by a team not an individual
Gaps in current methods are known prior to beginning the project	Specification freeze points are built in
Project plans can be cascaded into nested project plans	Can be used for simple and complex projects

■ Standard methods are followed building on the organizational knowledge and best practices

A key point in the use of the Lean project management tool is that you will undoubtedly have most of the work at the beginning of the plan. The vertical value stream tool actually forces you to plan up front properly. This eliminates the rework and lost time caused by poor planning later in the project. Table 5.7 summarizes some of the additional benefits.

In many organizations, there are often multiple project management approaches. The **IT** team follows a project management discipline from the IT sector, **construction** follows a project management discipline from the construction sector, and **quality** follows a project management discipline from the continuous improvement sector. A lower-level manager now has to be moderately competent in at least three different approaches. In a world-class Lean enterprise, there is a *single* standard project management discipline followed: The vertical value stream approach to project management is the only approach used across the entire organization. This helps simplify the language and the concepts utilized for the entire organization. As a leader, it takes courage to create an organizational standard that breaks down the technical complexities of project management. This necessary step will help create the shared vision for the organization and align the resources on the journey to world class.

Lean Leadership Processes

Senior leadership in healthcare organizations will be heavily involved with many of the processes already discussed in this book. A valuable lesson learned is that if the senior management team practices do not change with the organization, then your specific leadership behaviors will drive the organization back to status quo. This will happen regardless of the competency of the Lean core team, the strength of the middle and line management staff, and strength of your profit-and-loss statement. **Senior leadership actions and behaviors are the single largest factor for delivering a successful Lean transformation.**

Many of the leadership practices will change by addressing the core processes discussed earlier in this chapter. Capacity building will require leadership to develop Lean thinking skills. HR policies will lead to the hiring of Lean thinking managers and physicians. Financial systems will use Lean thinking in the budgeting and financial reporting. Great Lean organizations actually eliminate the annual budgeting requirements and move toward a three-month rolling budget. In Chapter 2, the approach Lean organizations use toward strategic planning and deployment of the strategy was discussed in great detail. All of these processes will impact how leadership works within the organization.

There is one additional leadership process that is worthy of mention—meeting and committee management. Healthcare is full of meetings and committees, with often three to five times as many meetings and committees as to what I see in other industries. There are board committees, medical management committees, best practice committees, quality committees, professional practice committees, pharmaceutical and therapeutic committees, work-life committees, and a host of other standing and ad hoc committees in practice. Additionally, there is simply no comparison to other sectors when it comes to the volume of "required" meetings. It doesn't appear to be the value add of the meetings that make them desirable, it is the paradigm of involving everyone who will be remotely affected. What an efficiency killer this is. I have actually been in healthcare organizations where senior leaders must cancel two of three meetings that are simultaneously scheduled. The senior leaders start the day deciding what meeting not to attend. Not only is there waste in having to cancel 66% of the scheduled meetings, the one that is attended is of questionable value add. This indicates a "process out of control."

There is nothing wrong with committee work or value-added meetings. A focused group of committed individuals coming together as a team can get a lot accomplished. The challenge is that on many committees both the focus and the commitment is lacking. The process is further complicated by no clear committee goals, no standard agenda to follow, poorly run meeting etiquette, and less than stellar attendance. Additionally, homework between meetings is frequently not completed, leading to a lack of progress and a lot of wasted management hours.

Lean organizations use A-3 thinking to manage meetings and committee progress. Every committee must work from an A-3 form to lead and deliver on their goals. Imagine if every committee answered these four questions:

1. What is our reason for improvement?
2. Using data, how would we describe our current condition and what reflections do we have on our current conditions?
3. What is our desired condition?
4. How do we measure success?

Completing these four questions would enable the committee to document the first three sections on the A-3 form (Table 5.8). Following A-3 thinking, the next step would be for the committee members to quantify the gap between current and target conditions. Closing the gap would allow for solutions to be generated, which would constitute the working actions and small experiments of the committee members. Validated solutions would be rolled out across the broader organization through the follow-up plans; effectiveness of the solutions would be validated through measurement tracking. Progress of the committees would be reported simply by updating and reporting from the actual A-3 document.

Rising Sun Hospital had each of its committees go through A-3 thinking and create the improvement plans for their individual committees. In their current state, the hospital had fourteen committees. Seven were standard committees required by their bylaws and seven were ad hoc committees added to resolve a specific hospital problem or to manage a project. Upon completing their A-3 forms, the senior team had an opportunity to review the documents and the status of the committees. It became readily apparent that four committees shared similar goals and measures. The decision was made to immediately dissolve the four committees and create a single committee in its place. Two other committees were dropped when the improvement potential was quantified and it was deemed that the return on investment (ROI) for the committee work was insufficient for the investment in time and resources. The net result was a reduction from fourteen committees to nine (36% reduction), resulting in 1,440 hours of annual committee time returned to management and physician leaders. Additionally, standard work was created for managing the committee agendas, thus reducing the meeting length from one to two hours to a standard meeting length of fouty-five minutes. The standard agenda made the committees much more effective, and seven of the nine groups met their annual targets for improvement and their project timeline. This improvement saved management and physician leadership

Table 5.8 First Three Boxes of an A-3 for the Pharmacy Committee

A-3 Theme: Pharmacy Committee	*Date: 31 August 2012* *Revision #: 0*

Team Members: Bill Smith, Jean Mangum, Elliott Wilson, Samantha Todd, Jennifer Jones, Russell Kline

Reason for improvement:

- Live the corporate value: Improve the quality of care
- Be fiscally responsible
- Improve access to services

Current performance and reflections on current performance:

- Pharmacy spending is equal to $8 million
- Costs have gone up each year for 11 consecutive years
- No defined formulary utilized
- No formal process to introduce new medicines
- No process in place to practice antimicrobial stewardship

Target performance:

- Reduce overall spending per patient visit
- Establish a well-defined formulary that is followed by physician group
- Have a well-defined medicine testing and introduction process
- Antimicrobial stewardship is in place
- Introduce new drug therapies to reduce LOS

Dimension	*Measure*	*Current*	*Target*
Quality	Reduce infection rates by 2015	.022	.011
Delivery/access	Reduce I/P LOS	5.5	5.4
Cost	Reduce Rx spend	$8 million	reduce 10%

Anticipated hard savings: $800,000 in drug expense

Anticipated soft savings: Reduce infection rates by 50% in four years an additional 1,600 hours per year. Could your organization benefit from an additional 3,000 hours of management time?

Leadership processes should evolve over time. Lean-thinking organizations are constantly looking for ways to eliminate nonvalue-added activity. Because leadership processes generally do not directly meet the need of a customer, they are candidates for improvement. Those that do not deliver value should be eliminated, and the processes that do deliver value should be executed in the least waste way. No part of the organization can be skipped if you desire to become a Lean enterprise. Leadership engaging in improving their processes inspires the organization for greatness through leading by example.

Medical Leadership Processes

In a Lean healthcare organization, it is a requirement to have physicians that are engaged and inspired in their daily work. While physician engagement does not guarantee transformational success, failure to engage physicians *guarantees* transformational failure. Due to their specific role within the healthcare system and the wide scope of practice, physicians are in the unique position to stop quality improvements in their tracks. Physicians can create medical orders whether they are evidence-based or not. Physicians can choose to follow organizational clinical pathways or choose to deviate from them.

The process becomes even more complicated when we look at how the medical staff is employed and managed. Some physicians are employees of the hospital/healthcare system, and some are independent consultants with or without admitting privileges. Some physicians are part of a group that is hired to fill a specific medical role in the hospital. There are many groups in service that fill the physician jobs for diagnostic imaging and emergency services. The leadership of the medical staff is also distributed. Once you move beyond the board and the chief medical officer, there might be program chiefs, medical directors, and department chiefs. Each organization has a different degree of accountability within their physician management framework. Some organizations have unionized physician groups adding yet another layer of complexity to the management of the system.

A Lean organization works with some "knowns" and develops a plan to operationalize these "knowns." The following conditions must be satisfied to create a culture of continuous improvement:

1. Standard work needs to be defined and followed by all support staff and medical staff. Systems, programs, and units that are based on individual physician practice will *never* be able to transform.

2. Physicians need to take accountability for developing and following their own standards.
3. The measures and targets for the organization and the medical staff need to be aligned. In many organizations, the physician compensation structure drives the behaviors of medical practice. Administration and medical staff need to share aligned measures along the true north dimensions of staff development, quality, access, cost, and growth.
4. Physicians need to participate, full-time, on the kaizen improvement teams and use A-3 thinking to deliver results. Like the rest of the organization, the skills of improvement and the change of the culture are built using A-3 thinking learned in the structure of a kaizen event. Most organizations immediately default to going around the physicians or offering them a part-time presence on the team. These short cuts will prevent your organization from transforming.

The organization, thus, needs a plan to ensure all of these conditions are satisfied. The physician engagement plan needs to include the following items:

- Plans to create system level physician standards, created by physicians.
- An accountability framework to ensure standard work is followed by the medical staff (I have found this be extremely rare within healthcare organizations).
- Aligned measures and targets for administration and medical staff.
- Plans to ensure physicians can participate on the improvement teams in a full-time capacity.

What world-class healthcare organizations find is that when the physicians embrace Lean in a meaningful way, rapid progress in transforming the system can occur. Additionally, like all people, we tend to follow our own ideas. Thus, solutions generated by physicians have a much higher likelihood of being followed by other physicians. There are many healthcare "war stories" that exist about the time a change was made without physician input and how the change was perceived and followed by the medical staff. We want to avoid this phenomenon from happening during an enterprise-wide Lean transformation.

One of the approaches used by Lean healthcare organizations is to take advantage of the physician credentialing process to hire and credential physicians with a framework to help engage the physician group in Lean quality improvement. All healthcare organizations have hiring criteria for new physicians and an accountability agreement (or physician compact) that governs their employment. The best Lean organizations build the Lean behaviors and time commitments or improvement directly into the agreement. How much farther along could you be in process improvement if your physician agreements included some of the following statements:

- Participates, full-time, on a kaizen event team once per year.
- Follows department standards including standards for quality, clinical pathways, and order sets. Provides feedback for further enhancements.
- Assists in the development and deployment of physician department standards.
- Monitors personal performance against the true north measures of the department. Takes personal action and accountability to ensure measures are met.
- Participates in team-based quality improvement and patient safety.
- Leads one quality improvement initiative for the department using A-3 thinking each calendar year.
- Assists in peer audits of physician standard work.
- Demonstrates behaviors that encourage teamwork and continuous improvement of the department.

This list is not meant to be exhaustive, but rather to stimulate thinking on what can be done in your organization to make change in the new culture. **Lack of physician engagement is second on the list of why organizations fail to create a culture of improvement**, right behind senior leadership involvement. Building the physician behaviors and physician engagement leads directly into the hiring specifications, and the credentialing process can help ensure the organization is making change part the new culture.

Many organizations, while sincere about wanting to engage physicians, have a difficult time understanding where to begin. I offer the following suggestions for consideration in helping you get started:

1. Begin by standardizing clinical quality. Engage physicians in the development and deployment of consistent approaches to evidence-based care. Patients deserve the best possible care.
2. Standardize process. Develop plans for department-wide consistency and accountability. As an example, define standard start times, standard end times, consistent charting standards, standard rounding times, etc. What type of consistent information do you require from the interprofessional team? What time of day do you need this information? Variation in physician and staff practice in this area leads to significant levels of lost productivity and frustration from both parties. Build accountability, discipline, transparency, and repeatability into the department processes.

3. Develop solutions using the following approaches:
   a. Use creativity before capital. Do not default to more staff, more resources, more equipment, and more technology. These investments should be last.
   b. Be consistent with Lean principles. Solutions should create continuous flow, utilize pull, move forward to defect-free environment, and be managed visually.
   c. Use Lean tools, specifically follow A-3 thinking. Avoid jumping to solutions.
   d. Solutions should be nonpersonality based. World-class healthcare is not created by individual practice and preference. World-class healthcare is created by developing a system that is repeatable independent of the professional.
4. Involve medical leadership in the vertical value streams, value stream analysis, and kaizen improvement events that are going to affect their areas. Often they agree to attend to "protect their turf" and find out that Lean actually is "common sense on steroids."

Taking Lean beyond Your Four Walls

Healthcare is a system. You might be concerned that many of the activities that help make change in the new culture are within your organization's four walls. At some point, patients and caregivers will transition into or outside of your organization. To truly become world class, you will need to bring Lean quality improvement to both your customers and suppliers. It is easy to pull suppliers in and demand they improve performance. You own the contract. This is just the same because it easy for your customers to pull you in and demand that you improve your performance.

Both of these behaviors are not a partnership. World-class Lean organizations work together with suppliers and customers to take waste out of the system. This creates a win-win for all parties. Simply demanding one party improve their performance is potentially a win-lose situation. Taking waste out of the system creates the best possible outcome. When nonvalue-added activity comes out of the process, the customer wins. System quality improves leading to better outcomes and higher customer service, lead times for services decreases, and the total cost of the system goes down.

Earlier in the chapter, the approach to creating a Lean supply chain was discussed; the Lean supply chain is a customer–supplier relationship. The focus of this section is on the transitions of care. These transitions of care also are customer–supplier relationships to the sending party and the receiving party, but not to the patient. The patient expects that there will be no gap in performance and no gap in communication. Transitions of care happen frequently within healthcare. Emergency medical service patients transition to the emergency department. The emergency department patient transitions to an inpatient unit. Inpatient unit patients transition to home health or to rehabilitation services. Primary care patients transition to specialty care. The list is endless.

It is understood in healthcare that the handover of a patient from one professional to another or from one organization to another represents a time of increased risk. To be sure, patient consent and privacy legislation create some well-intentioned difficulties in the handover process. The medical complexity of some patients also creates additional challenges. A Lean look at the transition process, however, can bring new insights to a currently daunting challenge. Looking at the value-added activity from the patient's perspective cuts across all the organizational policy and funding barriers that make the transition process difficult. Lean leadership needs to provide the vision for the organization, and if seamless transitions become the goal, then leadership needs to allocate the resources and inspire all of the participating organizations for greatness. Leadership also needs to overcome the distribution of funding that makes sharing difficult.

There are many great examples on how healthcare organizations have partnered with other organizations to improve the transition of care, improve access to services, and reduce costs. Doorways to Care, designed to improve access to health and community services for seniors, caregivers, and families who live across the North York and York Region in a suburb of Toronto, is one example. A group of over twenty organizations developed a partnership to create a single point of access to a wide range of services including homemaking, transportation, social and recreational activities, nursing, and caregiver support.* Lean improvement approaches were used to create a common assessment tool, define the service need(s), locate the appropriate services within the geographical catchment area, and connect the client with the appropriate service provider(s) in the network.

Another example would be Virginia Mason Medical Center and its partnership with Starbucks™ on improving care for back pain. The net result of their Lean efforts resulted in the following:

> When it comes to back pain, going to a physical therapist first can significantly reduce patient downtime and cost of treatment. In fact, the savings in time and money can be as much as 50% over more traditional treatment routes, which include visits to primary care

---

* Online at: http://www.doorwaystocare.ca/

doctors, expensive MRIs and x-rays, visits to orthopedic specialists, and finally a trip to a physical therapist.*

Another example of taking Lean outside of the four walls of an organization to improve patient transitions include sixteen local long-term homes in a community we will call the Calhoun District, coming together to create a common referral package and intake assessment. This reduced the number of total forms used in one of their partner hospitals by sixty-four. By going to a single form, the errors dropped by 53% and over 400 annual nursing hours were eliminated in filling out and reviewing the different forms.

Another organization, named Awesome Rehab, realized that its admission process was a significant barrier to patient transitions. In the current condition, the rehabilitation hospital would only take admissions on Tuesday and Thursday afternoons. This led to many conservable days being accumulated in their acute care partners. Their joint Lean efforts led to an admission process that could happen seven days a week within a twelve-hour window, reducing the acute care length of stay by an average of 2.2 days. In addition to the reduction in conservable days, the rehabilitation hospital admission rate went up 7%.

The greatest Lean healthcare organizations routinely include patients, suppliers, and customers in their improvement efforts. By taking waste out of the system, for the benefit of the customer, all three parties get improved performance. When taking a traditional supplier–customer relationship approach, waste is often simply shifted from one party to another. This is not improvement, although one organization might show better performance numbers. This improvement would be offset by the other organization showing worse performance numbers. Unless the nonvalue-added activity is totally eliminated, and not moved around within the value stream, real improvement in performance does not occur. Lean organizations seek a win-win solution by removing waste from the system so both parties benefit.

This type of improvement is a bit more complex than improving within your own organization, which is why I left it for last in this chapter. High levels of trust must exist for improvement to be realized between organizations. Additionally, there needs to be a way for both organizations to share in the rewards including fiscal improvement. This can only work with transparency of costs that is sometimes difficult for parties to expose. If the real passion is on improving the patient/client experience, then this activity should become easier. It will take lots of leadership to truly accomplish your vision.

---

* Groves, J. 2007 (Jan. 17). Banishing back pain without breaking the bank. Online at: http://grovespt.com/uplimg/VirginiaMasonStarbucksWSJ2007b-Groves.pdf

Summary: Key Points from Chapter 5

- Transformation is difficult because the new Lean culture and the current organizational culture are at odds with one another.
- The new changes need to be hardwired into the organization to make change last.
- Processes and systems across the organization need to be updated to support Lean thinking. The majority of these systems will be within the support and administrative areas of the enterprise. Key areas to be improved include
  - IT systems and support
  - Financial systems and processes
  - Human resource policies and processes
  - Creating a Lean supply chain
  - New product/process introduction, project management, and construction services
  - Senior leadership processes to include strategic planning, hoshin kanri, improvement governance, and committee management
  - Medical leadership processes
- Support processes exist to allow the clinical staff and medical staff to better service patients and caregivers.
- Lean capacity building across all levels of the organization needs to be front and center in Phase 3 of the transformation journey.
- Your organization will now be ready to take improvement beyond the four walls of the organization to suppliers, customer, and service partners. This is a necessary step to take further waste out of the enterprise.

Chapter 6

Leadership Behaviors and Actions for Success

Don't ever settle for anything less than the spiritual and moral greatness the grace of God makes possible in your life. You'll fail; we all do. But that's no reason to lower the bar of expectation. Get up, dust yourself off, seek forgiveness and reconciliation, and then keep trying. But don't ever settle for being less than the noble human being—the leader—the exemplar—you can be.

Pope John Paul II

Leading by Example

Virtually every organization with which I have worked or talked has a vision statement, a mission statement, and a set of core values. The vision statements and values are created to guide the thinking and behavior of the organization. Because care for patients and clients is at the center of healthcare services, many of the vision statements read somewhat the same.

A sample healthcare vision might read:

- "To be the greatest community hospital in the state/province"
- "To be the worldwide leader in healthcare research and quality"
- "Providing the right care, at the right place, at the right time"

The core values have a common set of themes as well. Core values might include

- Patients and families first
- Teamwork
- Integrity
- Safe care
- Collaborative care
- Meeting patient needs along the continuum of care
- Respect

Having spoken with dozens of different healthcare leadership teams and their boards, each can articulate well the vision and values of their organization. However, in speaking with the different layers of the organization, first to middle management and physician leadership and then to line staff and medical staff, the clarity of the vision and core values frequently varies. Some organizations do a great job of continuously communicating their vision and values. The message of what the organization is trying to become and the values the organization will live by to get there are discussed frequently. Other organizations rarely speak of their mission and values, and the communication is only demonstrated in some vision and/or values posters scattered about the organization, and, perhaps, in a few slide presentations. The values are further degraded when the true actions of the organization, specifically the behaviors and actions of leadership and physician leadership, run counter to the values. For example, perhaps the core value of "patients first" in your organization is trumped by the strong desire to meet program/unit targets that drive access improvement at the expense of patient quality. One other consistent shortcoming is the ambiguity of the vision or goal. Imagine this: "To be the leader in healthcare by the year 20xx." This has so many different interpretations that making the vision is unclear. Does this mean that the organization implements a nationally recognized cancer center or do we start local with primary care clinics that reach out into every area of the community? An unclear vision creates no unity of purpose, and no light in the dark of the night. The statement is actually powerless and unfair to the organization. So, how do we move our organization toward our vision? It is in getting to our well-articulated and clear vision that our organization is transformed.

A few leadership behaviors adopted at the highest level of your organization will go a long way in ensuring your organization lives the right Lean values. If part of our vision is to become a Lean enterprise, then our behaviors should reflect this goal. Table 6.1 summarizes the leadership behaviors necessary to create a culture of improvement. In order to inspire the team to do their best, leadership needs to walk the walk, not just talk the talk. In leading by example,

Table 6.1 Lean Leadership Behaviors

Leadership Behavior	Why Necessary
Participate full-time on a three-day value stream analysis and a four-day kaizen event	• Demonstrates commitment to the approach • This is the best way to learn the tools • This is the best way to learn how the kaizen experience changes the culture while compressing the timeline for results
Learn the tools	• Everyone in the organization needs the ability to not think Lean, but to actually use the tools to see and eliminate waste
Walk the value streams Perform gemba walks	• Changes the role of the leader from "manager" to coach • Best Lean approach to develop subordinates • Gives leadership visibility in "gemba" to show importance to staff and medical staff • Gemba is the source of all facts; going there eliminates jumping to conclusions and problem solving in the conference room
Commit the appropriate resources to be successful	• Shows commitment to continuous process improvement • Reprioritizes less important activity, allowing management wiggle room for process improvement activities
Hold individuals and teams accountable (staff, management, and physicians) Address Antibodies	• Shows respect for people • Ensures standard work is followed Implementing and following standard work is the way organizations improve and sustain • Ensures consistency in how staff and medical staff are treated • Makes visible those who choose not to participate in process improvement activity • Separates personality-based actions and process-based actions

(Continued)

Table 6.1 (*Continued*)   Lean Leadership Behaviors

Leadership Behavior	Why Necessary
Redeployment versus unemployment	• Shows respect for people • Demonstrates that team members will not lose their job as a result of participating in process improvement activities
Demand and monitor results	• Aligns with the Lean pillar of continuous improvement • Shows respect for people by stretching their capabilities • Helps develop management and staff by staying involved with the process and results
Believe	• Greatness is available to everyone, but comes faster to those who expect it

or leading from the front, as the military would say, you demonstrate that change begins with me. This is the most powerful statement that leaders can make in an organization.

Participate

There is no better way to learn the tools, the change management approaches, and the questions you need to ask the improvement teams than to participate in the improvement activities like a value stream analysis and a kaizen event. Participation means to be a fully functioning team member. Being present part of the time and then skipping out for other management meetings and phone calls is not sufficient and demonstrates the wrong behavior. (Nor is sitting in the room, but spending a large portion of time scrolling through your smart phone.)

The true challenge to senior leaders is to leave your rank and title at the door. This is a prerequisite to success and respect. The humility of a senior leader being able to attend as a team member has a far reaching impact upon the organization. As a team member, learn to see waste by using the actual tools and then use the improvement principles to eliminate waste. At the senior leadership level, a commitment of one full improvement week per year would be a great start, and more is even better. The entire leadership team needs to participate, including the CEO (chief executive officer), vice presidents, COO (chief operating officer), chief of staff, and CFO (chief financial officer). It is preferred to have the leadership team participate in an event early on in the improvement journey as this demonstrates commitment to the transformational efforts. One great joy from this attendance comes later in the journey when a mid-level manager, physician, or staff associate gives a response that they are too busy for a kaizen event. This obstacle is overcome quickly when the response is that the CEO or the CNO (chief nursing officer) found the time. A final impact of attending a Lean activity is the growth in commitment of each individual leader to participate in future improvement activities.

Learn the Tools

Learning the tools is part of Lean capacity building as was discussed in the previous chapter. I cannot name a single organization that ever transformed to a culture of continuous improvement where the entire leadership team was not fully competent in the application of the Lean tools. When you learn the tools, you will start to use them in daily operations. (If you don't use the tools in daily operations, your understanding is insufficient.) The use of tools to see and eliminate waste leads to better decisions and different management actions. The collection of management actions is what shapes organizational behavior, and the collection of organizational behaviors is what defines your culture. As I discussed before, you cannot delegate Lean leadership, and changing the culture of an organization is not something that can be managed.

Leadership and management decision making, without a thorough understanding of Lean tools, will actually drive a wedge in your transformational efforts. Traditional approaches and management efforts will be in conflict with Lean management approaches. Great Lean organizations reduce command and control structures, a pillar of traditional management approaches. Information is transparent and variation in performance leads to real-time problem solving. Created through this transparency, one of the single best indicators on how the culture is changing is the velocity of "news." Does good and bad news travel at the same speed across the management levels? Bad news becomes an accurate tag as bad news is merely an opportunity for further improvement.

Lean organizations also engage all support staff and medical staff in process improvement using Lean thinking. To lead this effort, every leader must become a Lean thinker and be competent in the scientific method (A-3 thinking) as well as all of the supporting tools used to see and eliminate waste.

Beyond participating in improvement events, either within your organization or at someone else's organization, there are a couple of other ways Lean organizations advance the learning of the tools and their application at the leadership level. Such methods include: teaching of the Lean tools and their application, reading and studying Lean literature, and facilitating improvement. Let's discuss each of these in more detail.

Rotate Teaching of the Core Lean Tools

In the best Lean organizations, the leadership teams routinely take the time and effort to actively participate on teams and learn the tools for improvement. At some point, the leadership team actually begins to teach the organization specific tools. Typically, a handful of tools and techniques is identified, and the leadership teams invest time to master each of the highlighted techniques. A starting point might include 5S, problem solving, A-3 thinking, pull systems, managing for daily improvement, and one item flow. On a rotating basis, the leadership team holds workshops or "lunch and learns" with the organization to transfer this knowledge. In teaching the content and answering questions on the topics, a mastery of the subject matter is developed.

Book of the Month Club

Another approach used by Lean organizations is to continue the academic understanding of Lean. Each month, or every other month, a book on a Lean topic is indentified and the leadership is required to read this publication. On a monthly basis, a debrief session is scheduled and the reflections and learning from the book are shared. Key takeaways lead to changes in standard work and are tested in experiments using A-3 thinking. The ongoing exposure to new Lean thinking and new Lean approaches helps to not only learn the Lean tools, but to learn different applications of the tools. A Lean organization is a learning organization. Seeing and eliminating waste is a never-ending challenge. Forming a book of the month club reinforces the concept of continuous learning.

Become a Lean Facilitator

There is no better way to learn the tools than to be put in front of a kaizen team and lead the team through a cycle of improvement using A-3 thinking. The great Lean organizations that transform their cultures all have leadership that can apply the common tools used to see and eliminate waste. The common tools to see and eliminate waste are shown in Table 6.2.

Demonstrated understanding of the tools will show when leadership incorporates the use of the common tools in its daily work.

Table 6.2   Common Tools to See and Eliminate Waste

Tool	Application
Takt time	Calculation that shows the relationship between the available time to complete work and volume of work to be done. Shows the rate of inputs and outputs to a process.
Time observation	Direct observation used to quantify waste in time.
Cycle time/takt time bar chart	Tool used to determine staffing levels by showing the relationship between the cycle time to complete the work divided by the takt time.
Flow diagram	Process map used to show flow, connections, and waits.
Spaghetti mapping	Tool used to show the waste of motion and transportation.
Communication circle	Tool used to show information handoffs.
Standard work combination sheet	Form used to show the recipe for standard work by showing the work sequence and time associated with each task.
Standard work layout sheet	Visual depiction of the workspace showing people, workflow, and standard work in process.
Standard work in process	The amount of inventory required between workstations to maintain flow.
Process control	A visual management tool that shows the work plan and the actual work completed. The plan is based on standard work and meets the takt time calculation. Variation from the plan allows for management by exception and enables an immediate intervention.

Walk the Value Streams

Regular leadership rounds are another requirement. In Lean, these rounds are known as "gemba walking." Gemba walking is different from patient safety rounds or patient communication rounds or medical rounds, because they are designed to develop people. Keep in mind that a Lean leader is first a coach and mentor. Fortunately, participating on the teams and learning the tools will make you a better mentor and coach. Gemba walks are based on a master–apprentice model to learning. Just like in martial arts, the master (sensei) first leads by example, showing the student what to do. The next step is to have the apprentice practice. The third step is to have the master observe and provide feedback. This feedback is a combination of critique and encouragement.

In an actual gemba walk, the leader or manager, with their subordinate, will first walk the area and show the subordinate how to see waste, lead problem-solving activities, hold a daily huddle, or to manage visually, etc. Next, the subordinate gets a chance to practice. In an experienced Lean organization, gemba walks will occur weekly. In an organization new to Lean improvement, gemba walks can occur in time increments of less than a week down to a daily activity. Finally, in a future gemba walk, the leader observes the subordinate and provides feedback on the performance. The feedback should include opportunities for improvement as well as encouragement for the successes. Opportunities for improvement should be documented and managed visually. The action items that come out of a gemba walk should become part of the improvement plans documented on the visual management performance system. Gemba walks leave lasting impressions on staff. Asking the simple question: "If you could change one thing in your process, what would it be?" As a leader, you will find the responses illuminating, the staff will feel listened to and respected.

In addition to gemba walks, leadership models the proper behavior simply by walking the value stream. This behavior shows support for the improvement process, while allowing you to challenge the team when performance is off or not being sustained, and to recognize the team when a job is well done. Pay attention to the visual management systems and the results boards. What is important to you is also important to your team. When you show your team that you are interested in the visual management systems, they will take notice.

Commit the Resources to Be Successful

In addition to participating and showing commitment through involvement, leaders also can show support by committing the appropriate resources required to be successful. A successful improvement experience requires investment in three areas: facilitation, team resources, and improvement supplies. These resources can be considered "seed" money.

Facilitation

Many organizations underestimate how much time it takes to improve. The preparation activities, the actual improvement team activities, and the sustaining activities all require some skilled facilitation, which require some full-time resources in order to be done well. Generally, one full-time facilitator is necessary for each value stream being improved. This person can be a dedicated resource or a seconded resource, but, either way, he or she should be full time. The responsibilities of the improvement facilitator are summarized in Table 6.3. A consistent shortcoming of this requirement is that the organization has no problem providing a person fully qualified for this role. However, the organization has a HUGE problem allowing this individual to release his/her prior responsibilities. By default, the organization has forced two jobs on an individual: a leading indicator of burn out and suboptimal outcomes.

The data collection activities and the suite of sustaining activities require extensive amounts of time. Part-time resources generally are ineffective in completing these two specific activities well. Ineffective data collection will almost

Table 6.3   Improvement Facilitator Responsibilities

Carries the title of "internal expert" for Lean improvement by demonstrating a mastery of the tools, techniques, and application of Lean thinking	Trains support staff and medical staff on Lean principles, practices, and process
Monitors preparation activities to include logistics, correct membership, correct measures, improvement scope, and data collection	Facilitates improvement activities using A-3 thinking
Assists in the sustaining activities to include auditing, data capture, visual management monitoring, and training of support staff and medical staff in standard work	Assists in the development of line management through the teaching of visual management, and leadership standard work
Teaches the three dimensions of visual management to the organization: process, results, and enabling a high-performing work area	Assists in managing the breadth and depth of improvement (also known as the pace of change)
Develops and mentors team leaders and new facilitators	Assists in population of the improvement scorecard
Assists in managing the improvement plan at the value stream level. Participates on the value stream steering committee	Assists in the development of the visual management systems

always lead to less than optimal results, or results than cannot be measured. The sustaining activities, at a minimum, include supporting the process owner in the maintenance of the visual management tools and standard work documents.

Team Resources

In addition to facilitation services, investment will need to be made in improvement team resources. Lean is a process of the people and it is desirable to have everyone participate. Getting a team together to work through an A-3 or to work through a kaizen event means that team resources must be made available. Having the right team, working on the right project, with the right targets, is a fundamental requirement for success. Plan to allow staff and medical personnel time to be available to work on improvement. An improvement team will require between six and ten people to ensure that all key stakeholders are involved.

Middle Management Expectations

Additionally, middle management will need some "wiggle room" to improve. They need to have some dedicated time to focus on change management and building a Lean culture. They also need the freedom to "fail," and, to top learn from this failure and improve. Leadership needs to give management the freedom to fail and confidence to "try." Evaluate the priorities of your middle management. Are they focused on small projects that are less important to their departments than improvement? Good leaders keep those directly reporting to them focused on the right things. Deemphasizing the least important activities can go a long way toward ensuring success.

Supplies

Finally, you will want to allocate some resources to cover the supplies and materials needed to improve. (Note: A comprehensive list of the recommended supplies needed is available in my first book, *Taking Improvement from the Assembly Line to Healthcare* [CRC Press, 2011]). Office supplies are necessary to complete the improvement activities, and other supplies are needed for the visual management systems. Floor tape and label-making equipment are needed for your 5S system. 3 ft. × 4 ft (or larger) dry erase boards are needed for process control systems. These can be acquired on demand so there is no need to purchase them in advance. However, you should plan ahead by establishing a small budget to cover the cost of these supplies. Do not underestimate this step. I have seen teams "spin" for two days because no one in management knew who was going to pay for a $20 chart rack.

External Resources

It's also important to consider the resource of improvement expertise. Just as you are likely to consult a personal trainer to help you get in shape, or an accountant to help with your taxes, consider hiring a Lean expert to help you with improvement. Bringing in some outside expertise to help with training, leadership development, infrastructure development, and team improvement is a wise investment for many organizations. External Lean expertise comes in many forms, from a Lean expert with expertise in one field to a Lean sensei who has expertise in many business areas. A good external resource will shorten your lead time for results, accelerate the breadth and depth of your improvement, minimize your organizational risk, and assist in your development of management and leadership. Additionally, an outside resource is not tied to your political and organizational structures. This is a tremendous asset when it comes to the impartial ability to focus on process, instead of designing an improvement system based on personalities and organizational politics.

Should you wish to seek expertise outside of the organization, you must find experts who have practical experience in management development. Not the theory of Lean management development, but a resource that has led Lean management development in a Lean organization. Understanding the Lean tools, while overwhelming at first, is the easiest part of improving. The most difficult aspect of creating a culture of improvement is changing the way management thinks, acts, and behaves. You will see a wide variation in Lean expert capability when you move beyond tools and into management/leadership development. One of the great abilities in healthcare is the capability to share information between organizations. If honesty is what you seek, ask one of your peers at a different healthcare system for recommendations on great Lean sensei.

By providing the appropriate resources for improvement, including facilitation resources, team member participation, "wiggle room" (dedicated time and focus) for middle management, and a small budget for improvement supplies, you will greatly enhance your chances for success. Additional benefits can be gained by the use of outside Lean expertise, particularly with respect to Lean management development.

Hold People Accountable

For Lean to be successful, there needs to be accountability of all people involved. In many organizations, a healthcare team consists of a collection of individual contributors working at their own pace and achieving different outcomes. A great Lean system begins by creating team-based, standard work and then making sure that everyone consistently follows that standard. Ideally, everyone should follow the standard because they believe in the standard and are committed to the new process. Regrettably, that is not usually the place where you begin. Inevitably, following each improvement, there will be "builders" (5–20% of the group) totally committed to making Lean successful, "destroyers" (5–20% of the group) who strongly desire to see Lean fail, and the remaining 60–90% of the team will be "fence sitters" waiting to see which side will win.

The "frozen middle" is a term often used in Lean circles that refer to middle management and their lack of willingness to embrace organizational change. The frontline staff generally is excited about participating in the change process and being listened to. This group likes to be able to bring forth ideas that are embraced and implemented quickly. Senior leadership is generally pleased with Lean improvement because it brings about a sense of excitement in the organization, and it delivers meaningful results in a short time. However, middle management is caught in the middle of the change process. In a Lean environment, all of the existing management systems and personality-based processes are being eliminated. This is very threatening to the middle managers who have not yet developed their new management systems and do not yet trust Lean tools and approaches. Additionally, once visual management systems are in place, the manager's operation is completely transparent for everyone to see. Not everyone is comfortable with this visibility. An unpleasant phrase (to some) that accurately describes one aspect of the Lean process when properly applied is: "When the Lean flashlight shines in an area, the cockroaches run." A statement of fact is that some will not be able to accept Lean. They have done it "this way" for years and by golly, "I'm not changing." This is when the dedication of middle and senior management will be tested. You be sure, everyone in the organization will be watching intently. "What will management do?" This is the crossroads in every Lean transformation that must be crossed. There will always be the few that will challenge Lean and even after retraining and allowing for respectful input, refuse to comply. Then the question becomes: "Do we have organization standard work expectations or may everyone do it their own way?" How you answer will determine the ultimate fate of your cultural transformation.

As I reflect on my days as a middle manager, I remember being responsible for the work assignments, the work hours, the paperwork requirements, the process work flows, managing a budget, and much more. In a Lean environment, many of the systems and tools used in management are replaced by new Lean processes, standard work, and visual management systems. When the old systems are dismantled, managers feel very uncomfortable. What happens—often unintentionally—is that managers tend to hold on to the old systems and tools. This behavior is counterproductive in an improving environment and explains why Lean organizations refer to this behavior by middle management as the "frozen middle." Leadership needs to be very supportive of middle management during the change, but also needs to let go of the old systems as quickly as possible and embrace the new methods. It is understandable that our past experiences and habits will have us revert back to the known. Following the thoughts discussed in Chapter 5, making change the new culture will assist middle management by eliminating nonvalue-added activity in their administrative processes, freeing up time to focus on improvement. While leadership needs to provide middle management with training on the new system, middle management also needs to be held accountable for the both the process and the results. Just as we expect the staff to follow standard work, we expect management to follow the Lean management processes; these processes are management's standard work.

We also expect the healthcare organization to hold physicians accountable. While physicians certainly have much more autonomy than the rest of the staff, there are standards that should be met by the entire medical staff as well. These include (as a very small sample) start and stop times, standards for the timeliness and quality of paperwork and documentation, adherence to evidence-based best practices, and adherence to infection prevention and control practices. I have seen *many* great improvement efforts fail because the organization and the medical leadership would not hold the medical staff accountable in following the standard work.

I have one last thought on accountability. While we prefer the improvement experience to be a positive one for patients, medical staff, and support staff, at times it can be a difficult or even unpleasant experience. In the spirit of providing the best possible patient experience and outcome, sometimes improving means changing work hours or moving work from one resource to a different one. As leaders, we need to *always* do the right thing in service of the patient. On rare occasions, the staff might decide they do not want to follow the new process. If you are honest with yourself, you know some of the staff aren't following the work standards in place today. Evidence-based care is not used, documentation requirements are skipped, etc. It is your job as a leader to inspire your staff to follow the standard work. On even rarer occasions, an individual will need to be disciplined for not following the new process. While I do not want to anticipate the need for disciplinary action, I would be remiss if I did not acknowledge this possibility, even likelihood. As I tell managers, "There's a reason you're a leader." One of those reasons is your requirement and ability to hold support staff and medical staff accountable to maintain standards.

To emphasize this important point: If you are *not* going to have a culture of accountability, then you can stop with Lean improvement, or any improvement for that matter. You have *no* chance of being successful if the support staff, medical staff, and management will not consistently follow standard work. If there is no standard, there is no improvement. In simplest terms, a standard is a basis for comparison. If you cannot compare one activity against another, then you cannot validate improvement. Great Lean organizations understand this point. Once your organization understands that standards are no longer optional, you will see everyone start to accept accountability. However, your organization is a reflection of how you behave and if your organization doesn't hold support staff and medical staff accountable today, you have some work ahead of you.

Address Antibodies

One of the challenges you will face as an organization is how to deal with people who want no part of the change process. These people may be overt resisters and be extremely vocal about their displeasure or they may be passively opposed to change and simply uncooperative. These people can come from any part of your organization: staff, physicians, managers, directors, or even members of the senior leadership team. Experience shows that 5% to 20% of the organization will strongly resist change. This is not an insignificant number and you must deal quickly and effectively with this population, otherwise you likely will fail to change the culture. Lean organizations call these resistors of change "antibodies." The analogy is as follows: In the human body, when an infection invades your system, antibodies become active to preserve the status quo. The antibodies have the specific purpose to return your system to its normal state. The same is true when you try to change the culture of your organization. When change is infused into your organization, the antibodies will become active to preserve your existing culture. Is this a bad thing? Not with respect to the healing process but for a change initiative, the answer is yes, but follows with a short explanation. Not every antibody has ill intentions. Some antibodies become active out of great concern that the changes will be harmful to the patients, themselves, and the organization.

Unfortunately if not addressed, antibodies multiply. If you do not appropriately deal with the antibodies when they first become active, they will quickly influence other people in your organization. Left unchecked, this group can totally derail the change process and end your attempt at creating a culture of continuous improvement. The question is: How do we deal with the antibodies? The first line of defense is to make expectations very clear when you begin improving. Leadership must be crystal clear on the reason for change, what's expected from everyone, who will be affected, and the consequences for those who choose not to participate. These messages need to be tailored for the different levels of the organization. An "elevator speech" can be prepared for support staff, medical staff, and management to address the concerns of each of the layers. This speech should be delivered very early in the change process.

The next way to address antibodies is to get them involved in the change process. After all, are you more likely to accept your own ideas or someone else's? People generally like their own ideas and the more people that can be involved with an idea, the less resistance you can expect. The majority (80%) of your antibodies will completely change their position once they have participated in either a kaizen event or an A-3 improvement project. This change in people can often be very dramatic. On countless occasions, I have seen a staff associate or physician formerly labeled a troublemaker became a great Lean champion following an opportunity to participate in improvement. Is this not a great win for your organization? To take someone deemed "difficult" and turn him/her into a believer and practitioner of continuous improvement is a great feat.

On the rare occasion, participation is not sufficient to turn an antibody. In these cases, you will need to apply situational leadership, dealing with the support staff or medical staff associate on a case-by-case basis. The organization needs to be consistent in how it addresses antibodies. You don't want different standards for different layers or departments within your organization.

There is a phrase you will hear in Lean circles about changing culture: The fastest way to change the people is to change the people. Sometimes you have to separate an individual from your organization who not only fails to participate in improvement, but also fails to follow standard work, and who negatively influences others. Let's hope this is not a frequent occurrence, but it does happen.

In summary, antibodies become active to preserve the status quo of your organizational culture. Antibodies need to be addressed quickly and fairly to prevent them from negatively influencing other staff members. The best way to address antibodies is through clear communication and by getting them involved in the process.

Redeployment versus Unemployment

The primary focus of Lean is to create a culture of improvement. In order to foster this culture, we need to create an environment where the support staff, medical staff, and management trust the organization. One of the key areas of trust begins with job security. As wasteful activity is eliminated from your organization, personnel resources are freed up. If there is no meaningful work for these resources, it can be tempting to downsize the organization through layoffs, particularly if the financial position of the organization is not strong. Your staff deserves the assurance of their continued employment from the first utterances of Lean transformation coming to the organization. Rumors will likely persist, but the redeployment statement needs to be delivered clearly and frequently that no employee will lose his or her job as a result of Lean improvement. An employee may be required to change jobs, shifts, departments, etc., but employment is not at risk.

The fastest way to destroy your continuous process improvement journey is to lay off an employee following an improvement activity. In good faith, we bring support staff and medical staff together to eliminate wasted time and activity from the organization. In doing this, we simultaneously improve staff morale, patient quality, and safety. We increase access and we lower costs. We cannot "reward" our staff for this effort by asking them to find another job elsewhere. The first time you lay someone off as a result of an improvement, your chances for further improvement using an empowered staff are *zero*. No one is going to improve themselves out of a job. Why would they?

Lean organizations meet staff needs and organizational needs by offering employment security, not job security. If we identify a need for twelve registration clerks following an improvement, and sixteen registration clerks are currently on staff, what do we do with the surplus? Lean organizations use a term called *redeployment*. We want to redeploy these staff members to other open positions. Admittedly, those positions might not be in registration, they may require a shift change or other adaptation, but they allow the staff to be retained. Think redeployment, not unemployment.

Why is redeployment essential? The answer is simple. By far, most of your organization's expenses are related to staffing. Let's reflect on that statement. Your staff members certainly need salaries and benefits, but what are the other costs? Employees also need telephones, computers, parking spaces, personal lockers, and desks. They use materials and equipment, consume office supplies, and need break rooms, microwaves, and refrigerators. Many of these items require ongoing operational expense. Take a look at your budget. Try to connect each line item to your staff and you will likely be amazed to discover how much of your budget goes to supporting your personnel.

As leaders, we have a responsibility to use our resources wisely. If we can avoid adding resources by eliminating wasteful time and activity, we have a requirement to take full advantage of that opportunity. Likewise, if we free resources up, we should make them available to the rest of the organization through a redeployment strategy. This practice allows staff members the security in having a job, while meeting the needs of the corporation in filling an open position. In Lean organizations, this practice is followed even if the position requires significant retraining.

We can consider many alternatives to laying off staff, which I call the "redeployment hierarchy." Below is a list of possible redeployment strategies:

- Redeploy into other open positions.
- Retrain into other open positions.
- Reduce and/or eliminate temporary or agency staff.
- Implement a strategy to not replace any staff attrition.
- Reduce or eliminate overtime.
- "Insource" services that are being outsourced.
- Add new services with the freed-up resources.
- Run temporary improvement teams to accelerate improvement.

On the other hand, it may be too late for you to avoid reducing headcount. Perhaps your financial position indicates that you have no choice. Can you still deploy a Lean management system? Absolutely, but you need to address the personnel situation *first*. Any staffing adjustments need to be completed before you begin to improve. In this situation, the challenge you will face is that you must resource the improvement teams with a smaller staff. In some organizations, this can be a difficult proposition. However, if we want to show respect for all people, then we need to address our staffing issues in a fair and up-front way. It is disrespectful to use Lean continuous improvement to lay off staff to meet fiscal concerns. There are other approaches that more appropriately demonstrate respect for people.

You may be asking one additional question regarding redeployment: Whom should we redeploy? Should we redeploy the worst staff member, the best staff member, go by seniority, or leave it up to the process owner? If you are working in a unionized environment, the answer is straightforward. Any change in staffing will need to take place in accordance with the language in your collective agreement. In a nonunion environment, I suggest you use a new paradigm. Great organizations always redeploy their *best* performer. I realize this may come as a shock. Believe me, as a former manager, I came up with all kinds of strategies to retain (actually to hoard) my best people. You may be asking (as I did): "Now you want me to give up my best employee willingly?"

Lean organizations celebrate redeployment as a tremendous organizational success. When we redeploy, we are *rewarding* our best performer by giving him/her an opportunity to go and learn a new skill. We don't want to give this opportunity to just anyone. Our best and brightest should get the opportunity to advance and develop. The remaining team will survive in our Lean organization. Throughout the Lean improvement that preceded the redeployment, you created a new process with standard work and visual management. As a result of standard work, *everyone* will be able to improve their performance. And, with visual management, you have control of both the process and the results. There will never be a better time to release your best performer for their next exciting opportunity.

Monitor and Demand Results

This leadership lesson is about expectations. When you satisfy your curiosity and participate on a team, you will quickly validate that 95% of the work being done is nonvalue-added activity. In Lean, we want to eliminate and reduce nonvalue-added activity. When you see this for yourself, your expectations of what is possible should change. Using Lean, you can *expect* double-digit improvement in performance. Remember, we are trying to eliminate the nonvalue-added activity, which accounts for 95% of the activity. A well-run team should improve the key dimensions of staff morale, quality, access, and cost by more than 10%. If you are just beginning to improve, I expect that your results will be even better, because you will be eliminating even more waste. As a leader, you have the right to demand results using a Lean improvement system. Create a sense of urgency in the teams. Take an interest in the daily, weekly, and monthly performance. Expect improvement.

Believe

Throughout your transformation journey, never stop believing. As a leader, you need to monitor and demand results. If you do, your achievements will be significant. A Lean leader can take your organization to a place it's never been. It is a place where both support staff and medical personnel are excited to come to work, where patients get the world-class care they deserve, where access increases so that essential healthcare services can be offered to more people in your community every day. It is a place where these essential services can be delivered in a cost-effective way, so that your healthcare organization can maintain excellent fiscal health, year after year. Every Lean organization has the capability to be great. Creating the shared vision, aligning the resources, and inspiring people to achieve the vision delivers the leadership required to make this greatness possible.

Summary: Key Points from Chapter 6

- Creating a culture of improvement begins with leadership changing the way they think, act, and behave.

- Demonstrating proper leadership behavior brings the organization's vision, mission, and values to life.
- The key Lean leadership behaviors include
  - Participating full-time on improvement teams
  - Learning the Lean tools to see and eliminate waste
  - Walking the value streams and performing gemba walks
  - Committing the appropriate resources to be successful
  - Holding yourself, individuals, and team accountable for results
  - Addressing "antibodies"
  - Having and following a redeployment philosophy to absorb freed-up human capital
  - Demand and monitor results
- Believing in the greatness your organization is capable of achieving.

Chapter 7

Mitigating Transformation Risk and Avoiding Common Mistakes

It takes enormous self-confidence to be simple, particularly in large organizations. Bureaucracy is terrified by speed and hates simplicity.

Jack Welch
Author and former CEO of GE

Being Successful and Avoiding Failure

I would like to cover a topic most people would rather avoid—failure. There are a wide variety of statistics out there, but the general consensus is that most transformational efforts fail. For those of you that have been around the block a few times, I'm sure you can relate. The new organizational structure failed to deliver the intended results. The new IT system didn't lower costs. The new piece of laboratory or diagnostic imaging didn't meet its productivity targets. This doesn't imply that improvement was not made, or even that improvement was not sustained, but rather that the project didn't hit all of its projections. Failure from a Lean enterprise transformation perspective implies that the organization failed to create a culture of continuous improvement. In all organizations, some type of improvement work is taking place. Simply keeping up with new and changing accreditation standards, current evidence-based treatments and procedures, and new insurance requirements requires some type of ongoing organizational change and improvement.

A successful Lean enterprise transformation implies that *all* support staff and medical staff are engaged daily in eliminating wasted time and activity. With each iteration of removing wasted time and activity, the entire organization becomes more patient- and family-centered. Improvements, aligned to the organizational strategy, are met and newer targets are established. In a transformed organization, the key measures of staff engagement, quality/safety, patient/family satisfaction, access/lead time, cost and growth are *always* improving, forever. Delivering daily improvement becomes how the organization functions. Focus on improvement is embedded into all the activities of the organization. Leadership, management, support staff, and medical staff all understand that every process can be improved. Status quo is never accepted, even when change is difficult or unpopular.

As I like to say, getting to this place is living in "very rare air." My sensei used to tell me only 1 to 3% of all organizations get to world class. That implies that 97 to 99% of organizations never reach world-class status. So should we give up? The odds of getting to world-class status are not very good. The short answer is: Absolutely not. While only a few organizations get to world-class level, the odds of getting to great are better, and the odds of getting to better are almost guaranteed if you follow the roadmap described in the previous chapters. In creating a culture of improvement, the goal is to continuously get better. A great Lean organization understands that eliminating any nonvalue-added activity is good for the customer and all stakeholders, and each wasteful step eliminated gets the organization to "better."

As a leader, you will want to do everything in your power to give your organization the best chance to succeed. Seeing improvements in how care is provided is reason alone to transform. However, when you also see the changes to management, support staff, and medical staff culture and behavior, any leader quickly becomes a believer in a Lean management system. So, what are the actions that a leader can take to mitigate the risk of failing to transform or prevent excessive stumbling through the transformation journey? Many of these points have been discussed earlier, but I will consolidate and repeat some of these key topics and add a few new thoughts as well.

An early stumbling block organizations face when starting on a continuous improvement journey is that they fail to realize how much work is truly involved. Assembling a team, studying a problem, and developing and implementing a solution is a lot of work, but only about 5% of the work needed. The first 20% of the workload is simply properly preparing to improve. Selecting the right team, measuring the right things, and using the right tools and approaches make up this 20%. The common mistake organizations make is failing to gather the appropriate baseline measures. Without the baseline measures, it is impossible to show an improvement. There is no data to compare past performance against current performance. The routine causes for this include selecting the wrong measure, reliance on IT-captured measures, and failure to resource the data collection efforts. Many times the best way to gather the best information is to spend a fair amount of time in the gemba performing time observations. Even skilled facilitators often do not like this part of the job. Time observation work is not glorious, but enables your organization to not only see waste, but also see the sources of the waste and lost time associated with the waste.

The remaining 75% of the work is in deploying and sustaining the change. Why is sustaining change so difficult? It is because the culture of the organization will constantly be pulling the system back to status quo. If you think gravity has a strong pull, infuse change into your organization and see another law of nature in action. Your staff, volunteers, managers, board, and others will all behave in ways that promote the status quo. Your systems and processes will all drive your changes back to status quo. These can be overcome, but it will take a lot of work and effort. The roadmap for transformation and the Lean leadership behaviors were all developed to allow change to stick. Every step is choreographed to break the pull of gravity allowing your organization to develop a culture of improvement. Recall that the roadmap covers preparing to change, accelerating the change, and making change to the new culture. The leadership activities detailed within the roadmap are not "hard" to accomplish, but they are time consuming. How much time do you currently spend in the "gemba?" How difficult will it be to refocus your workday to enable you to accomplish your leadership standard work? Are you prepared to work through the personnel issues with the "antibodies"? Can you dedicate the time and attention to the Lean steering committee to govern the transformation? Each of these activities takes focus, time, and attention. However, each activity is necessary to create the culture of improvement for which everyone is striving.

There are a few common stumbling blocks organizations frequently encounter when embracing Lean improvement. We have already discussed the first of these, underestimating the amount of effort it will take to be successful. Other common mistakes include

- Don't waste the first 6–9 months
- Failure to monitor the breadth and depth of the change

- Failure to get everyone involved
- Failure to eliminate two management systems

Don't Waste the First Six to Nine Months

Many organizations want world-class results without doing the heavy upfront lifting. In an effort to change the culture, these organizations rush out and hire internal or external experts and jump into some type of Lean improvement. The initial burst of energy is refreshing and individual projects hold great promise. But, then change becomes more difficult and sustainment from the first few projects is very weak. Results are not being generated or are not being sustained. The reason is as we discussed, the organization is in the midst of a confluence of two methodologies: the old and the new.

It is somewhere in the six- to nine-month point that these organizations realize they have not built the proper foundation to improve and have to reset their improvement efforts. This is the second most common mistake organizations make when embarking on a Lean transformation. There are no short cuts to transformation. Each infrastructure creation activity and each improvement team deployed is a building block for future success.

Table 7.1 shows the various key steps required to transform your organization. Most organizations skip the initial steps and jump in at the step ***Deliver improvement***. I emphasize this step by using bold and italicized font. I didn't bold and italicize "using A-3 thinking" because most organizations fail to do that activity as well.

If all the steps in Phase 1 and earlier steps in Phase 2 are skipped, then somewhere between six and nine months, the process will deliver much less than optimal results. The key to sustainability is leadership standard work supported by visual management systems. By skipping all the previous steps, the foundation to sustain will not be in place. Many times the reason the initial steps were skipped is because leadership was unaware of the necessary foundation steps, or worse, failed to make the time and effort commitment to complete the activities. Essentially, the two most common mistakes organizations make are failure to understand the leadership time and effort needed and skipping the initials steps on the transformation roadmap, which are closely related. Regrettably, for many organizations this initial failure is enough to stop a transformation effort. In other cases, organizations significantly reduce their effort or funding, which leads to a slower pace of change or underfunded improvement effort.

I believe that every organization can overcome this loss of the first six to nine months, but it won't happen by delegating all of the initial leadership

Table 7.1 Transformation Roadmap

Phase 1 Preparing to Transform	Phase 2 The Acceleration Phase: Improve, Sustain, and Spread	Phase 3 Make Organizational Improvement the "New" Culture
Find your change agent	Ensure you have the selected the right value streams on which to focus	Build organizational Lean improvement capacity
Get informed	Establish value stream governance	Develop Lean IT processes
Get help	Set up your value stream performance system	Develop Lean financial processes
Establish a steering committee	Deliver the improvements using A-3 thinking	Develop Lean Human Resources systems and practices
Train your internal experts	Sustain the improvements and manage visually	Develop a Lean supply chain
Develop and deploy a communication campaign	Capture the savings	Develop Lean processes for project management, new product/process introduction, and construction services
	Spread Lean thinking across the organization	Create Lean leadership processes
	Support change with ongoing coaching and training	Create Lean medical leadership processes
		Take Lean beyond your four walls to suppliers, customers, and service partners

activities to a lower-level person in the organization. Leadership has to set the vision, align the resources, and inspire the team for greatness. Lead by example. Commit the time and effort to build the infrastructure, and be prepared to align the resources to sustain the improvements. Ensure that all the layers of management can focus their attention on leadership standard work and visual management. Remember, sustaining is 75% of the work in a transformation and being able to sustain your improvement is always the deciding factor in transforming your culture.

Managing the Breadth and Depth of the Change

The focus of healthcare is patients. There are hundreds of diagnoses and medical conditions with hundreds of tests and treatments to support these conditions. Because of this, virtually all healthcare organizations begin their Lean improvement in a clinical area. This makes sense, as the core business of healthcare is, well, healthcare. However, how many different areas of healthcare should we be improving at the same time? There are dozens to pick from: emergency services, cardiology, primary care, pharmacy services, etc. Also, when should we branch our improvement efforts off into the administrative areas? Again, there are dozens to pick from, such as billing, scheduling, hiring, financial close, supply chain management, etc. A common mistake organizations make when engaging in an enterprise-wide transformation is that they fail to monitor the breadth and depth of their improvement efforts. There is no magical formula to follow when managing the breadth and depth of organizational-wide change, but there are some guidelines that can be followed.

First, once you have completed your analysis and have selected your initial value stream, begin by creating a model "cell." A cell is a work area where the five improvement principles are all in place. You want to create one area in your organization that has one item flow, pull systems in place, zero defect systems, visual management of process and results including 5S, and leadership standard work. This area will be the place you send other areas of the organization to when you want to highlight what "good looks like" from a Lean perspective.

Following the model cell, the next step is to create a model value stream. A model value stream would have a series of cells that help create end-to-end flow within the value stream. As an example, let's review surgical services as a model value stream. Within this value stream, the following cells were created:

- Surgeon clinic visit where the decision to operate is made
- Surgical scheduling

- Preadmission testing
- Preoperation (day of surgery)
- Anesthetic blocks
- Case kitting (kit build, sterilization, and case cart build)
- Room turnover
- Phase 1 recovery
- Phase 2 recovery and discharge
- Sterile processing (rinse and wash)

For this value stream, the model cell selected was the preadmission testing process. In this cell, standard work was created for chart preparation, registration, nursing assessment and education, allied assessment and education as appropriate, lab and diagnostic imaging testing, and anesthesia consult. The patient went to a single room and almost all of the services came to the patient. The visit length was reduced from 3.5 hours to a single hour and the productivity improvement yielded an increase in visits from sixteen per day to twenty-six per day with two fewer staff.

Following the completion of the entire value stream improvement plan, the following results were generated:

- 16% decrease in the OR cost per case
- Increased OR cases by 21% over budget
- Increased prime time pre-op day surgery, PACU, post-op day surgery capacity by 30% thereby reducing overtime expense
- Improved OR on-time start times
- Redeployment of two staff

Completing a model cell followed by a model value stream allows your organization to now take your improvement both wide and deep. Following the completion of one pass through the surgical value stream, surgical services completed a new value stream mapping and analysis exercise. The creation of the cells helped create the future state from the original mapping and analysis exercise. The future state from that exercise is now the current state and a new future state needs to be created. Multiple cycles of value stream improvement, in a single value steam, is what is meant when Lean organizations talk about going "deep." Taking improvement into other organizational value streams is what is meant when Lean organizations talk about going "wide." Getting to world class will require a strategy that includes both going deep and wide in your improvement efforts (Figure 7.1).

The trick is to find out at what pace you want to be wide and deep. For your organization to get to the tipping point, everyone will need an opportunity

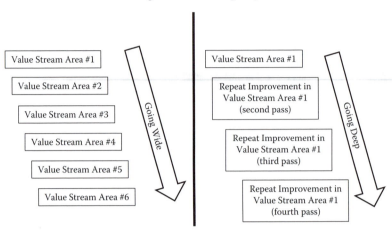

Figure 7.1 Going deep versus going wide.

Table 7.2 Pace of Change

Staff Population (Full-Time Equivalents)	Opportunity (50 weeks)	# FTE/Week	# FTE/Team	# Kaizen Teams/ Week
1,500	50	30	8	~4
2,500	50	50	8	~6
5,000	50	100	8	~12
10,000	50	200	8	~25

to be on a kaizen team. Assuming there are fifty available weeks in a given year for improvement activity, you can divide your total support staff and medical staff population into the fifty weeks to get a feel for how many team members are needed each week to get to the tipping point. Table 7.2 illustrates how this number can be easily obtained.

The flaw in this analysis is that it assumes that every participant on every team is a different employee. In reality, about one-third of the team will have been on a team before and only two-thirds of the team members will be newly exposed team members. You will want to be aggressive in getting everyone involved, but not so aggressive that managing the suite of organizational change creates chaos, or even worse, your organization cannot sustain the changes as they unfold. Never confuse activity for productivity; just because you are improving in four or more value streams simultaneously (activity) doesn't mean change is being sustained (productivity).

Leadership has to balance getting everyone involved with getting results. My philosophy has always been to start in two value streams and increase the number from there based on three factors:

1. Having the appropriate number of facilitation resources to lead the improvement activities. Assume one full-time resource per value stream engaged.
2. Ensuring the results are sustained all along the improvement process.
3. Maintain the following ratios of improvement activity:
   a. 10–20% of the value stream improvement work should be on their second pass of improvement (go deep).
   b. No more than 80% of the total work should be in the clinical areas. 20% of the improvement work must come from the administrative areas of the organization.
   c. No more than three value streams should be engaged per executive level sponsor. When managing more than three improving value streams, the ability for the senior sponsor to focus and remove barriers becomes very challenging.

If you do a careful analysis of the number of teams required to get everyone involved using Table 7.2, the number will likely appear quite daunting. Very few organizations start off at that pace of improvement. I encourage organizations to start small and create the model cell and model value stream, and then increase the number of value streams based on the factors discussed above. In the first year of improvement, leaders will get a feel for both the pace of change and their ability to manage and sustain change. The goal is to ramp up to everyone being engaged while sustaining all of the improvements along the way. The number of value streams actively engaged in improvement will change as you get more experienced. The breadth and depth of change is a topic to be governed at the executive steering committee (Chapter 3).

How long does it take to complete all the efforts identified in an improvement plan from a value stream analysis and mapping session? As a general rule, the action plans can span a timeline between one and two years. After completing this plan, there will be so many improvements that the work area operates totally different. It is now time to repeat another value stream analysis in the same area.

Leadership, Management, Support Staff, and Medical Staff Engagement

One of the roles of senior leadership in creating a culture of improvement is to remove the organizational barriers to enable improvement teams to make rapid change. Management's key role in the change process is to engage the staff in problem solving, to manage visually through leadership standard work, to hold staff accountable to following standard work, and to problem solve any barriers to standard work. The key role of the support staff and medical staff in the change process is to follow the steps of A-3 thinking to quickly see and eliminate waste and develop a new standard that can be managed visually. The staff will then follow, monitor, and improve the standard on a daily basis to create a culture of continuous improvement.

In order to get to this elusive culture of improvement, everyone must participate in the improvement activities. The common mistake organizations make when embarking on a Lean enterprise transformation is they fail to engage all of the stakeholders in the change process. Senior leadership will better be able to remove the organizational barriers if they understand A-3 thinking, and have participated on both a value stream and a kaizen event. Management will be better able to follow leadership standard work and manage visually following active participation on the improvement activities, supported with targeted coaching. The staff and medical staff will be much more supportive of change and following standards after they have been given the opportunity to participate directly in Lean improvement through a kaizen event or working through an improvement A-3.

Engagement is so important that I recommend you track your engagement numbers as an organization. Table 7.3 can be used to track event participation.

In a Lean enterprise transformation, participation doesn't necessarily equate to engagement, but it is a great place to start. Participation on improvement teams creates a structured environment for support staff and medical staff to engage. Tracking participation numbers also helps the organization understand where the lack of participation by a certain role will create a barrier to improvement in the future. The area of most concern is physician participation. We have many different professionals in a healthcare system: nurses, physicians, respiratory therapists, occupational therapists, and physiotherapists. We also have social workers, pharmacists, laboratory technicians, and imaging technologists. With all of these professional people engaged in healthcare, why are we singling out the physicians? Physicians are in the unique position of being able to personally choose whether to follow or not follow organizational standards. Physicians can deviate from standard order sets and clinical pathways, they can add or subtract diagnostics, they can add or subtract medication treatments, and decide when to discharge. No other staff function within the healthcare environment

Table 7.3   Sample of Event Participation Tracking

Role	# of People on 0 Events	# of People on 1 Event	# of People on 2 Events	# of People on 6 to 11 Events	# of People on 12–35 Events	# of People >36 Events
Senior leadership	6	3	1	0	0	0
Management	62	81	42	21	0	0
Support staff	2,100	1,100	540	62	14	0
Medical staff	400	75	8	2	0	0
Volunteers	800	240	63	4	0	0
Internal experts	0	0	0	6	2	3

is in the unique position to unilaterally practice with this autonomy. Is this a bad thing? Absolutely not. However, it's essential that physicians are engaged in our improvement work. By engaged, I don't mean popping into a room on occasion during an improvement activity. What we desire is a healthcare system that is physician-led. Who is in a better position to lead improvement than our medical staff? Clinical healthcare needs physician champions. We need to synthesize continuous improvement into practice, therapeutics, medicines, surgical procedures, and diagnostics to deliver (even invent) better evidence-based, best-practice care.

On many occasions, I have seen an interprofessional team collaborate with a physician to develop a clinical pathway. The pathway deployed the latest technology, protocols, order sets and treatments, and was evidence-based. After the team reached alignment in both process and format, the pathway was documented in a manner consistent with the requirements of health medical records. The work was piloted on a few patients with favorable results in outcomes. When presented to the physicians working in the department, what do you think the reception was? Typically, the pathway is received with skepticism, criticism, and an offer to make many changes. Rarely is the pathway adopted and followed. The question is why?

The likely reason is that physicians were not sufficiently invested in the change at the beginning of the process. The behavior of rejecting change is not specific to physicians. In any area of professional specialization, change is always easier to accept when you are invested in the change and part of the change. This becomes an opportunity for Lean organizations. Rather than "managing around" physicians, how do we inspire and engage physicians to lead quality improvement? Great organizations have a strategy to engage physicians. This strategy may include creating a value proposition specifically for physicians (that is, explaining to physicians the value of engaging in administrative improvement work, for example), holding special training and education sessions, leveraging the medical leadership, and, in some cases, providing some amount of funding to allow for full participation. Experienced Lean organizations even build improvement requirements for physicians into their physician agreements. I encourage you to engage the physician group early in the Lean improvement process so that you can build this strategy collaboratively.

Inability to Operate Two Systems

In Chapter 5, I briefly mentioned why many organizations fail to change their culture. My hypothesis is that organizations cannot sustain operating two different systems. A Lean healthcare enterprise runs fundamentally differently from a non-Lean healthcare enterprise. What management, support staff, and medical staff focus on, how they spend their day, the relentless pursuit of perfection, and the constant elimination of nonvalue-added activity do not resemble the traditional healthcare system. It is likely that your culture is not currently one of continuous improvement. Because of this, following a change, the many systems and processes in place today will always be pulling your culture back to status quo. The common mistake organizations make when embarking on a Lean enterprise transformation is they fail to realize this dual system phenomenon is creating havoc in the change process. It will require tremendous leadership and courage to take on the old systems.

These battles won't just be fought within the improvement teams, these battles also will occur at the senior levels of the organization. Finance will want to put in new controls that will add three days to the turnaround time for purchased equipment, negating the entire kaizen event team activity that was intended to streamline the approval process for new equipment. The new HR employee review system will now require an additional three hours a week per manager to execute, competing directly with gemba time for the manager. This list goes on and on. As the organization becomes more Lean, traditional solutions to problems will not be used as an overlay to previous Lean solutions, but it will take time to get to that point. The larger your organization, the more bureaucracy there will be. Size likes bureaucracy. The value streams that your organization is trying to improve will be bombarded with changes from other parts of the organization that do not yet have a Lean thinking mindset. The conflict of interest from these changes is demoralizing for the team and management and must be resolved at higher levels in the organization. These discussions are difficult to have. No senior leader likes having their corporate-wide project put on hold, or having an exception created for a single value stream. If consensus is reached, the resulting solution often takes the organization back closer to status quo, thus delaying the change process and the corresponding cultural transformation.

So, how does an organization reconcile the differences? The best way is to transform the organization *faster*. The more Lean thinkers and Lean processes that exist in your enterprise, the less likely a nontraditional solution will get implemented. This solution might be at odds with the earlier chapter discussion on managing the breadth and depth of change. Again, you only want to go as fast as you can sustain. But, all things being equal, changing at a faster pace shuts down your old system sooner.

Common Errors to Organizational Change Efforts

Change management expert John P. Kotter's book, *Leading Change,* was published in 1996. Following fifteen years of analysis of dozens of failed corporate initiatives, Kotter wanted to articulate why transformation efforts failed.* The summary of this analysis is that there are eight common errors to organizational change efforts including[†]

1. Allowing too much complacency
2. Failing to create a powerful coalition
3. Underestimating the power of vision
4. Undercommunicating the vision by a factor of 10
5. Permitting obstacles to block the new vision
6. Failing to create short-term wins
7. Declaring victory too soon
8. Neglecting to anchor the changes firmly in the new corporate culture

I thought it might be valuable to map the activities in the transformation roadmap described in Chapters 3, 4, and 5 to see if they provide any help in avoiding the eight common mistakes organizations make.

You can see that following the transformation roadmap (Table 7.4) will help assist your organization in avoiding the eight common mistakes organizations make in undertaking an organizational change effort. Many of the activities used in a Lean enterprise transformation, like visual management and leadership

---

* Kotter, J. P. 1996. *Leading change.* Boston: Harvard Business School Press, p. ix.
† Ibid., p. 16.

Table 7.4   Avoiding Common Mistakes in Organizational Change

Organizational Mistake	Lean Transformation Roadmap Risk Mitigation Activities
Allowing too much complacency	Establishing true north measures with double digit improvement
	Visual management
	Managing for daily improvement
	Kaizen rapid cycle improvement
	A-3 thinking
Failing to create a powerful coalition	Enterprise transformation steering committee
	Value stream steering committee
Underestimating the power of vision	Deploying hoshin kanri
	Communication strategy
	Value stream analysis
Undercommunicating the vision by a factor of 10	Communication strategy
	Measurement capture
	Physician engagement strategy
	Value stream and kaizen report outs
	Lean capacity building
Permitting obstacles to block the new vision	Executive sponsor
	Enterprise transformation steering committee
	Value stream steering committee
	Daily team leader meetings during kaizen events
	Leadership standard work
	Visual management
	Managing for daily improvement
	Enterprise wide engagement
	Gemba walks

(Continued)

Table 7.4 (*Continued*)   Avoiding Common Mistakes in Organizational Change

Organizational Mistake	Lean Transformation Roadmap Risk Mitigation Activities
Failing to Create Short-Term wins	Value stream rapid improvement plans with quick wins
	Kaizen rapid cycle improvement
	A-3 thinking
	Managing for daily improvement
	Measurement capture
Declaring victory too soon	True north measures
	Deep versus wide pace of change
	Visual management
	Managing for daily improvement
	Value stream mapping and analysis
Neglecting to anchor the changes firmly in the new corporate culture	Chapter 5: "Make organizational improvement the new culture" addresses how to prevent this common error

standard work, will actually address several of the common mistakes simultaneously, leveraging even further their effectiveness in developing a culture of continuous improvement. Take a moment to reflect on the list and think about a large change effort with which your organization has been involved. Has your organization been at risk from any of these possibilities?

There are many other risks associated with embracing a Lean enterprise transformation. The board could oppose the changes and a union could become active. Another key risk is that a key change agent will depart from your organization. Good change agents are in high demand and will be sought by many organizations and recruiters, particularly change agents with demonstrated Lean expertise. Another key risk to the change effort is that the CEO or another key member of the senior leadership team leaves or retires. I have seen many great initial transformation efforts get off track when an important leader departs the organization. This possibility exists until Lean is embedded into the DNA of the organization. However, if I listed all the potential reasons why organizations fail to create a Lean enterprise, I would need a much longer chapter. With respect to failing to transform, I also like to differentiate between reasons and excuses. Every organization has the *capability* of becoming a Lean enterprise, but not every organization has the *will* to succeed.

I have seen where organizations have followed the key steps in the transformation roadmap (having avoided skipping certain steps) and taken their organization to a place where everyone is engaged in seeing and eliminating waste to provide a healthcare system focused on the patient. They provide a system of care that is safe, outcome-focused, evidence-based, cost effective, and timely. Their healthcare system is not complacent with each improvement, and new opportunities are constantly being discovered. As these opportunities are addressed, these organizations continue to create a great future for their patients and families, for their support staff, medical staff, and volunteers, and for their suppliers and service partners. In a Lean environment in concert with the two pillars of Lean, continuous elimination of waste and respect for all people, everyone wins. Following the transformation roadmap will assist your organization in avoiding the common mistakes that organizations make and shorten the lead time for success while mitigating risk of failure.

Summary: Key Points from Chapter 7

- Most organizations fail to get to world-class status.
- Any organization embarking on a cultural transformation can get to "better" and many can get to "great." The reward for trying to transform exceeds the risk.
- Organizations make common mistakes when trying to deliver on a Lean enterprise transformation. These mistakes include
  - Wasting the first 6–9 months by skipping steps in the transformation roadmap
  - Failure to monitor the breadth and depth of change
  - Failure to get everyone involved
  - Failure to shut down the traditional healthcare system in favor of the new Lean healthcare system
- Tracking event participation is a proxy for engagement in the first few years of your journey.
- Following the transformation roadmap will help your organization avoid all of the common errors to organizational change efforts identified by John Kotter in his work *Leading Change*.
- Every organization has the ability to become a Lean enterprise, but not all organizations have the will to succeed.

Chapter 8

Closing Thoughts

It is impossible to attain perfection, but that should be the goal. Less than 100% of your effort toward objective is not success, regardless of how many games are won or lost.

Coach John Wooden

The book began with the age-old discussion of the differences between leadership and management. Management is a set of work processes that keeps an organization operating effectively. Leadership is the set of processes that create organizations then helps organizations change to meet ever-evolving business conditions. Lean transformation, creating a culture of continuous improvement leading to world-class rates of improvement in performance and culture, is a leadership process. The key aspects of leadership include creating and sharing the future vision of the organization, aligning the financial and human resources of the organization to achieve the vision, and then inspiring and engaging people to realize the new vision.

Transforming healthcare will require significant amounts of leadership. I envision creating an entire healthcare industry where world-class healthcare quality, patient safety, and customer service are the norm; a workplace that can be transformed to one where support staff and medical staff are engaged in their work and inspired to do better and be better every day. Using Lean approaches, you can help shape a healthcare system that delivers more "value" to patients, families, and their surrounding communities.

I offered a roadmap for transformation in this book. Unfortunately, there is no "how to" manual to transform. Each organization will have to find its own way. The key leadership and management practices described in the earlier chapters can serve as a reference for you to use on your journey. My one piece of advice is that, although the steps may vary in their timing, try not to skip steps in pursuit of "faster" or "easier" transformation. I can assure you there is no easy button to change an organization's culture.

The ingredients of true commitment to Lean—persistency, consistency, and tenacity—will all be needed to get your organization to escape the pull of your current culture. Carefully consider each of the activities contained in the roadmap and work them into your transformation plan toward becoming a world-class healthcare organization. I have found it easier to address and manage the activities proactively rather than reactively. Each of the tools, techniques, and approaches were added into the roadmap to avoid common mistakes organizations make when trying to change their culture. Learning from these valuable lessons will shorten your lead time for success and mitigate the risk of failure.

Lean healthcare is a system where

- Work is constantly scrutinized to eliminate waste and deliver more value to your patients.
- The support staff and medical staff continuously improve the quality and safety of care, approaching a defect-free system, reducing wasted time and freeing up capacity for other work, decreasing lead times for services, and lowering the cost of the delivery of these services.
- Healthcare is delivered with accurate and timely information shared seamlessly amongst the care team and patients.
- The medical staff and support staff collaborate to provide patient-focused, evidenced-based care with seamless transitions between specialties and subspecialties.
- A system where the patients, families, and communities participate in the design of the services leading to healthier communities with preventative strategies driving lower and lower costs.
- Care is delivered with outstanding customer service leading to an enhanced customer experience.
- A work environment where patients, support staff, medical staff, and management have high levels of satisfaction.

If you work in healthcare, then you or your organization are already aspiring to be in this place. Lean leadership will require you and your organization to establish and communicate your vision of becoming a Lean enterprise. The roadmap provided in the previous chapters offers leadership approaches on establishing the infrastructure and processes to align the resources to achieving the vision. Also, the roadmap offers leadership tools, techniques, and approaches to inspire the team by getting everyone involved to realize your vision.

I would like to close the book with exactly the same closing comments I used in my first book, because I believe this statement applies equally to Lean leadership.

> Fortunately, more and more healthcare organizations today are discovering the beauty of Lean: A management system of simple principles and methods that can be implemented in any organization to generate measurable, lasting results of improvement. You have taken the first step by simply reading this book. Now I encourage you to move forward with Lean in your organization. Inspire others and lead positive change. Watch how "Lean thinking" revitalizes your organization and sets the stage for great achievements ahead. So much is possible when you apply the Lean approach to everything you do.*

Believe this: You **can** make this happen.

---

* Bercaw, R. 2012. *Taking improvement from the assembly line to healthcare.* Boca Raton, FL: CRC Press, p. 147.

Glossary of Lean Terms

2P: This is the short form of the term Process Preparation. 2P is an approach used to develop a new process or product. 2P begins with a voice of the customer activity, develops seven ways to operationalize each key task in the process, analyzes the seven ways using a Pugh analysis, and ends with the seven flows to define the new process.

A-3: Both the process and thinking for problem solving based on the scientific method. The A-3 is frequently used to document, organizational strategy, problem-solving exercises, status reports, and business cases. Named the A-3 as the report is associated with the size of paper (11 × 17) the report is documented upon.

A4: Both the process and form for root cause analysis of a recurring problem. The A4 uses both the cause and effect diagram and five whys as part of its methodology. Named then A4 as the report is associated with the size of the paper (approximately 8.5 × 11).

Asaichi: Japanese word for "morning fish market." The process of reviewing defects from the previous day first thing in the morning while the defects are still "fresh." During the market, defects are touched, felt, and understood, and then team-based root cause analysis is assigned and problem solving occurs.

Andon: A visual or audible signal that identifies when an abnormal condition has occurred. Typically combined with a "stop the line" mentality where a process stops following an abnormality until its source can be detected to prevent recurrence of problems.

Antibody: A term used to define a person resistant to change.

Batch: An approach where large quantities of items (batches) are processed then moved to the next operation.

Cause and Effect Diagram: Also known as a fishbone diagram or an Ishakawa diagram. The cause and effect diagram is used to develop possible causes of a know effect (problem). Key areas for brainstorming are developed around a standard set of categories. Typically the 6Ms (manpower, measurement, methods, materials, mother nature, and machinery) and or the 4Ps (people, process, policy, place).

Communication Circle: A tool used to show the waste of transactions and handoffs of information.

Continuous Improvement: A mindset adopted by organizations to repeatedly identify and eliminate waste.

Control Plan: A set of activities developed and deployed to sustain improvement. These activities may include audit, inspection, standard work, and monitoring of visual management systems.

Current State: Workflow of the operation as it currently performs. Used as part of value stream mapping.

Cycle Time: The time it takes to complete a process, as observed through direct observation.

Cycle Time/Takt Time Bar Chart (Ct/Tt bar chart): Also known as a loading diagram. This tool visually displays how each staff person is loaded against the takt time. Shown on the tool are the process takt time, the manual cycle time of each person in the process, and the minimum staffing calculation. Minimum staffing is equal to the sum of the cycle times divided by the takt time. The Ct/Tt bar chart is used to highlight wasted manpower and bottlenecks, and is a key in improving productivity.

Defect: Work that needs to be redone or clarified. An error that finds its way to the customer.

Design of Experiments: The design of information gather experiments where variation is present. In statistical terms, the design of experiments is used for controlled experiments to assess the key sources of variation or interactions between sources of variation.

Direct Observation: The Lean approach used to best identify waste. Direct observation involves going to an area and observing the process to identify waste. Direct observation is often combined with capturing time elements of the process to "quantify" waste.

Failure Mode Effects Analysis: A quality tool used to identify key risk factors in a process and take action to mitigate the risk. Also known as an FMEA.

Fishbone Diagram: *See* Cause and Effect Diagram.

Five S: Five terms, beginning with the letter S that are used to develop a high performing work area. **(Sort) Seiri:** Remove unneeded or unwanted items from the workplace (equipment, tools, supplies, materials, information); **(Set in Order) Seiton:** Neatly arrange the remaining items. A place for everything and everything in its place; **(Scrub) Seiso:** Thoroughly clean the workplace and return the area to like new condition; **(Standardize) Seiketsu:** Create standard conditions to keep the workplace standardized and organized. Create work practices that enable standard work and proper work flow: **(Sustain) Shitsuke:** Personal discipline to main the first four Ss.

Five S Event: A team-based, rapid-cycle process used to implement 5S in a work area, while simultaneously training the staff.

Five Whys: An approached used to identify the root cause of a problem. Beginning with the problem you see (the direct cause), ask why the problem occurred and give an answer that directly addresses that question. Repeating the process five times will get you to the root cause of the problem. This approach is used to develop people.

Flow: Processing one unit of work through a series of steps in a continuous manner, at the rate of customer demand, in a standardized way. Ideally, only value-added tasks are linked together.

Flow Diagram: A Lean tool used to document a process. The flow diagram is used to show work flow and highlights process stops and starts, hand-offs, and disconnects.

Freeze Point: Term used to describe a point in time when a product or process specification is agreed upon and "frozen" for the balance of the project. Assigning freeze points eliminates delays and rework caused by changing specifications later on in a project.

Future State: Workflow created as a vision for what the new workflow will be. The future state is developed using the Lean design attributes of flow, pull, defect free, and visual management. Used as part of value stream mapping.

Gemba: Japanese term for "real place." Used to describe the place where work is done.

Gemba Walk: A management approach used to develop a subordinate. Following the master/apprentice model, the experienced leader walks through the work area with the subordinate to teach how to identify waste, and develop and evaluate plans for improvement. The mentor teaches the subordinate to practice kaizen (see and eliminate waste).

Genchi Genbutsu: Japanese term for "go and see." This philosophy to solving problems implies that, in order to truly understand a situation, one must go and see the situation at the place where work is done and value is created.

Heijunka: The leveling of volume and mix of work over a fixed period of time. A concept used to reduce batching while efficiently meeting customer demand.

Heijunka Box: A tool used to level the mix and volume of work.

Hoshin Kanri: Also known as hoshin planning or policy deployment. A management approach to identifying key strategic goals and developing plans to realize these goals. The process concludes with monthly review of both process and outcomes.

Huddle: The process of assembling the staff to briefly review the performance board. The huddle is part of the managing for daily improvement system.

Inventory: Materials and information that accumulate between process steps.

Ishikawa Diagram: *See* Cause and Effect Diagram.

Kaizen: A process used for continuous improvement to eliminate waste and create more value.

Kaizen Event: Team-based approach to rapid cycle improvement. Spanning two to five days depending on the scope of the activity, the scientific method is followed during this activity to deliver an improved process in a portion of a value stream ending with standard work, visual management, and process control.

Kamishibai: A management system of cascading peer audits used to maintain a standard. Kamishibai works under the premise that the auditor, when completing the audit, reinforces their understanding of the standard leading to better following of standard work.

Kanban: Japanese term loosely translated to mean "signboard." Kanban is a scheduling system based on the principle of pull used determine what to make, when to make, and how much.

Leadership: The activities used to create and organize and evolve the organization through an ever-evolving set of business changes.

Leadership Standard Work: This is the "standard work" for management and leadership. Leadership standard work (LSW) incorporates structured rounding on the visual controls established in the work area, conducting tiered huddles to resolve issues and assign ownership of problems and projects. The process requires a disciplined manager/leader to be successful and is an integral part of the individuals manager Lean self development. Oftentimes, LSW is the key ingredient in sustaining improvement.

Leveling: The process used to ensure an even flow of work to a downstream person or machine to eliminate peaks and valleys in activity. Leveling is used to smooth both mix and volume.

Line Balancing: A method used to even work between workstations after waste has been eliminated. Ideally, each staff member will be loaded equally with a work amount equal to or slightly less than the takt time.

Loading Diagram: *See* Cycle Time/Takt Time bar chart.

Managing for Daily Improvement: A technique that combines the use of performance boards with a short daily staff meeting to review yesterday's performance and to take corrective action to improve performance in an area every day.

Management: A set of management practices used to operate an organization efficiently and effectively. These practices include scheduling, payroll, attendance monitoring, etc.

Mistake Proofing: Work methods designed into the process that prevents the person doing the work from making an error. (Also known as error proofing.)

Motion: Operator movement in excess of that required to complete a task.

Nonvalue-added: An activity that takes time, space, or resources, but does not directly meet the need of the customer. (Also known as waste.)

Obeya: Loosely translated to mean "big room." The big room is used to support all of the work done in the creation of a new product or service.

Overprocessing: Doing work related tasks in excess of value as defined by the customer.

Overproduction: Producing/doing more, sooner, or faster than the next step in the process.

Performance Board: Tool used to show results from a process. The performance board differs from the process control board in that it details outcome results in lieu of process measures.

Plan, Do, Check, Act (PDCA): A cycle of improvement based on the scientific method. Used to propose a change in a process, implement the change, measure the result, and then take action to standardize or stabilize the change.

Policy Deployment: *See* Hoshin Kanri.

Poka Yoke: Japanese term for mistake proofing. Poka Yoke is a quality control method that designs the work in a way that makes it impossible to create a defect.

Process at a Glance: A visual depiction of the seven flows of process that define how work will be organized, completed, and improved before beginning work.

Process Control: A tool used as part of visual management to discern abnormal conditions in the output of a process. The common design shows both the plan and the actual output and sources of variation are documented in real time.

Process Control Board: A tool used to visually display process control. The board shows plan and actual performance of the process.

Production Control Board: Industrial term for a Process Control Board.

Pugh Analysis: A quantitative technique used to evaluate multiple options against a set of criteria.

Pull: A signal used to link areas of continuous flow together. A method to control work by having downstream activities signal their upstream requirements. Used to reduce/eliminate the waste of overproduction.

Quality Function Deployment: A Lean tool used to capture the voice of the customer, develop alternative solutions, evaluate those solutions, and assess project complexity. Also know as a QFD.

Sensei: In Lean circles, a sensei is an experienced person who has mastered the Lean approaches to both Lean improvement and Lean management.

Sequence of Operations: The recipe for a process. Step-by-step detail of the standard work. The sequence of operations makes up one third of the requirement of standard work.

Seven Flows: A description of the seven areas that allow value to flow or not to flow. In manufacturing these would include raw material, work in process, finished good, operators, machines, information, and engineering. In healthcare, the seven flows include the flow of staff, materials, equipment, information, methods, quality, and improvement. Analysis of the seven flows allows for a deep understanding of the process and delays associated within them.

Seven Quality Tools: A name given to seven common approaches to analysis often used in solving quality-related problems. The seven tools include: the cause and effect diagram, the flow chart, the check sheet, the control chart, the histogram, the scatter diagram, and the Pareto chart.

Seven Wastes: Forms of waste found in operations. These wastes include overproduction, overprocessing, waiting, motion, transportation, inventory, and defects.

Shewart Cycle: Named for Walter Shewart, who defined the four step process for improvement, we now call the PDCA cycle.

Skills/Competency Matrix: A visual management tool that shows which skills each staff member has, which ones they are training on, and which are absent. Used by the staff and management to promote skill building and cross training.

Spaghetti Map: A diagram used to show the path and distance of travel for a person, supply, or machinery. The map highlights the waste of motion and/or transportation.

Standard Work: Work procedures used to define how an operator will complete a task or process. Standard work is based on three elements: sequence of operations, takt time, and standard work in process.

Standard Work Combination Sheet: A worksheet used to document standard work. The sheet provides a format to document the sequence of operations and the takt time. The sheet also provides task times including manual task times, automatics task times, and walking.

Standard Work in Process: The amount of inventory needed between two processes necessary to maintain continuous flow.

Steering Committee: A body designated to govern Lean improvement. The steering committee can be at the value stream or the enterprise level of the organization.

Strategy Deployment: *See* Hoshin Kanri.

Takt Time: A theoretical calculation used to provide the rhythm of output for a process in time units. The calculation consists of taking the available time to do work divided by the volume of work to be done.

Time Observation: *See* Direct Observation.

Toll Gate Review: A meeting of necessary project stakeholders to ensure that all of the criteria to pass a project milestone have been met before starting on the next phase of a project. The review meeting is used to make sure waste doesn't escape from layer to layer in a project, and to capture lessons learned to be applied to future projects.

Toyota Production System: A management system for excellence based on providing customer's the highest possible quality, in the shortest time, at the lowest cost by removing wasted time and activity.

Transportation: Unnecessary movement of people, materials, equipment, etc. Transportation is also known as the waste of conveyance.

True North Measure: Operational excellence comes from five key areas: staff morale (human development), quality, delivery (lead time), cost, and growth. A high-level strategic measure of one of the five areas of operational excellence is known as a true north measure. These measures become the compass for the organization to align effort and direction.

Value-Added: An activity that directly meets the need of a customer.

Value-Added/Nonvalue-Added Analysis: A technique used to identify in each task step whether the step adds value or doesn't. Typically a value-added task is given a green dot and a nonvalue-added task is given a red dot. A typical process is no parts nonvalue-added to one part value-added.

Value Stream: The activities completed to deliver value to a customer.

Value Stream Mapping: A tool used to show waste in a value stream and develop a plan for improvement.

Variation Reduction Kaizen: A dedicated kaizen event used to understand process variation and use statistical tools and analysis to reduce process variation.

Vertical Gantt Chart: *See* Vertical Value Stream Map.

Vertical Value Stream Map: A planning approach for projects used to simultaneously deliver the correct value to the customer in the least waste way. The process begins by defining the milestones and then backward plans the tasks needed to meet the milestones, thus ensuring the majority of the project is value-added.

Visioning: The action of using a Pugh Analysis to prioritize key value streams or key core processes against a set of true north measures. This method is used to select the areas in an organization that best meet the strategic goals.

Visual Management: A management system that makes normal from abnormal conditions transparent to allow problems to be identified at a glance so they can immediately be corrected.

Voice of the Customer: The process of capturing the needs and wants of the customer when designing a new product or process.

Waiting: Customer delays caused by the absence of supplies, equipment, information, resources.

Waste: Any activity that consumes time, space, or resources, but fails to create any value for a customer.

Zero Defects: A mindset based on the premise that while humans are prone to errors, these errors need not make it the customer, thus becoming a defect. It is possible to achieve a zero defect system.

Index